I0825433

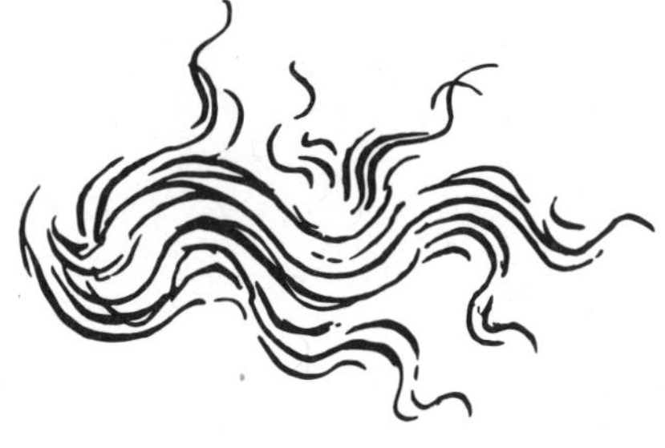

TABLE OF CONTENTS

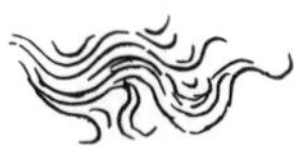

WINTER 2026
VOLUME VI, ISSUE 2

LIBERTIES: A JOURNAL OF CULTURE AND POLITICS is published quarterly in Fall, Winter, Spring, and Summer by the Liberties Journal Foundation.

LIBERTIES JOURNAL FOUNDATION is a nonpartisan 501(c)(3) organization based in Washington, D.C., devoted to educating the general public about the history, current trends, and possibilities of culture and politics. The Foundation seeks to inform today's cultural and political leaders, deepen the understanding of citizens, and inspire the next generation to participate in the democratic process and public service.

EDITORIAL OFFICES
1101 30th Street NW, Suite 310
Washington, DC 20007

ISBN 979-8-9922010-1-7
ISSN 2692-3904

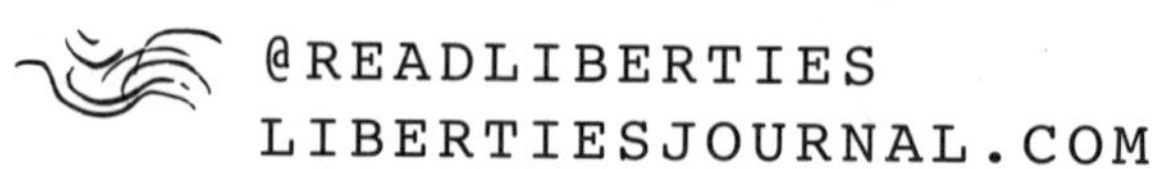

Liberties

WILLIAM BAUDE

Marbury *Now*

Consider a showdown between an institutionalist Chief Justice of the United States and an ambitious and opportunistic President of the United States — a showdown in which the Chief Justice wishes to both lay bare the president's violations of law and norms, and to bolster the Court's power and authority. And yet the president is a canny one, a powerful one, an intransigent one, who will not meekly accept what even the Chief Justice may dictate.

No, I am not talking about President Donald Trump or the Roberts Court — though I will return to them — but about the Founding era. This showdown took place between Chief Justice John Marshall, the last hope of the defeated Federalist Party, and President Thomas Jefferson, the leader of a new political coalition that had defeated them. Their showdown, more than two centuries ago, produced the Supreme Court's decision in *Marbury v. Madison*.

Marbury is part of the canon of constitutional law, known for establishing the principle of judicial review. Under canonical *Marbury*, federal courts are the guardians of the Constitution: they sit implacably to decide whether the actions of Congress or the president are constitutional. This is what *Marbury* stands for. This is constitutional bedrock.

But like so many canonical texts, the *Marbury* of legend is just a tale. *Marbury's* real lessons are more complicated, less triumphant, and yet even more urgently relevant. *Marbury* did render an important defense of judicial review under the Constitution. But *Marbury* also contains the seeds of executive power, and a logic that leads to the Supreme Court's recent decision in *Trump v. CASA*, in which the Court ruled that federal courts could not issue "universal" injunctions, and thus that executive officials could disregard judicial interpretations at least some of the time. *Marbury* also demonstrates — through sleight of hand and indirection, not plain statement — the ways in which practical judicial power may depend on political calculation.

First, the legend.

The central setup of *Marbury* was this. In 1801, John Adams lost the presidency to Thomas Jefferson, marking the first partisan transition in American history. As Adams' Federalist Party prepared to hand over power to Jefferson's Democratic-Republicans, they also rushed through a lot of business during the last few months before the inauguration — what we now call the "lame duck" period. This business included legislation expanding and restructuring the federal courts, and also creating offices for some relatively minor jurists — such as the "justices of the peace" in the District of Columbia.

One of these would-be jurists was a man named William Marbury. He was a local businessman and political climber who had become active in Federalist Party politics, trying to help Adams win reelection. Adams rewarded him with an appointment as a D.C. justice of the peace. Adams sent Marbury's name to the Senate as one of forty-some last-minute appointments, and the appointment was confirmed on the last full day of the Adams presidency. But something went awry.

The last step in appointment to constitutional office is a "commission" — a formal document, like a property deed, that authorizes the holder to exercise government power and proves that he is the one who got the job. Even today, many judges are known to hang their commissions framed on their office walls, as both mementos and proofs of authority. In the eighteenth century, with slower communications and no instant background checks, these commissions were even more important. In the haste of the last hours of the Adams administration, however, Marbury's commission was never delivered to him. The outgoing secretary of state botched the delivery, and when Jefferson swept into the White House he trashed the undelivered commissions and attempted to rescind all of the last-minute appointments.

This produced the famous precedent of *Marbury v. Madison:* Marbury sued for his commission, and the Supreme Court ruled that Marbury had a legal right to that commission in an opinion authored by Chief Justice John Marshall. Indeed, said Marshall, our government could not be "termed a government of laws . . . if the laws furnish no remedy for the violation of a vested legal right." Even more importantly, the Supreme Court also said that it had the power of constitutional interpretation and judicial review. As Marshall elegantly explained, what we now recognize as judicial review is a consequence of two elementary rules of constitutional law. One is that the written constitution is superior to ordinary laws. Congress and other government officials hold office only under the terms of the Constitution. The Constitution itself creates the institutions of American government. Moreover, it makes clear that the officials who govern us ultimately do so in our name, on behalf of "We the People." They, in constitutional terms, are the agents and we (collectively) are the boss.

Marshall explained that this ideology — a form of democratic originalism, if you will — was what led people to create written constitutions. They constitute "the fundamental and paramount law of the nation, and consequently the theory of every such government must be, that an act of the legislature, repugnant to the constitution, is void." The Constitution trumps ordinary law. That is the first rule.

The second rule is that judges are allowed — in fact, are obligated — to open their eyes and read the Constitution. Indeed, wrote Marshall, "it is emphatically the province and duty of the judicial department to say what the law is." What is the alternative, Marshall asked? Must judges "close their eyes on the constitution, and see only the law"? No, he answered. "This is too extravagant to be maintained."

To Marshall this second rule was obvious for practical reasons. Without judicial review, the legislature would have "a practical and real omnipotence" because it could ignore whatever the Constitution required. It was also required by individual honor. The Constitution requires judges to take an oath to support the Constitution — to govern their own official conduct by our founding document. How could they do this if they could not read it?

From these two rules, Chief Justice Marshall distilled one of the most recognizable (and widely exported) features of American constitutional law — the principle that courts will be guardians of the constitutional order. As the Supreme Court later glossed the case, during the dismantling of Jim Crow: *Marbury* "declared the basic principle that the federal judiciary is supreme in the exposition of the law of the Constitution, and that principle has ever since been respected by this Court and the Country as a permanent and indispensable feature of our constitutional system."

Now the real *Marbury*.

This story is not false. Everything I have just written is true. But it omits two startling things.

First, the idea of judicial review was not at all new when *Marbury* was decided. Alexander Hamilton had explicitly defended it in *The Federalist* before the Constitution was ratified, referring to "the rights of the courts to pronounce legislative acts void, because contrary to the Constitution"; legal precedents for it had already existed in the colonies; and the Supreme Court itself had been engaged in judicial review for over a decade between the creation of the Constitution and the decision in *Marbury*. And second, William Marbury never actually got his commission, and the Supreme Court did not order anybody to give it to him. Despite the Supreme Court's stern language about Marbury's rights, and despite its conclusion that it had the duty "to say what the law is," the Court nonetheless found a convoluted path to rule against Marbury, and in favor of President Jefferson, while simultaneously emphasizing the Court's power and independence.

This was, frankly, a difficult trick. To pull it off required some clever shenanigans from Chief Justice Marshall that at times veer into legal technicality. But these shenanigans were important to the making of *Marbury*, and important to thinking about the Supreme Court today, so please bear with me briefly as I unpack them.

Like a good magic trick, the Chief Justice's opinion in *Marbury* involves several moving parts. Indeed, the choreography was key to what Marshall accomplished. Marshall began by considering the abstract question of whether Marbury should have gotten his commission. Marshall answered "yes," partly for a series of technical reasons about the details of commissions, deeds, and so on. Only then did Marshall turn to the more dispositive legal question of what the Court could do about it. Here things got more complicated. Marshall concluded that a federal law, a part of the Judiciary Act of 1789, gave the Supreme Court the ability to hear Marbury's case. (Because the law said that "the supreme court . . . shall have power to issue . . . writs of mandamus" — a "writ of mandamus" being a court order to an official to do his duty). But Marshall then concluded that the federal Constitution did not allow the Supreme Court to hear the case. (Because the case had been brought in what is called the Supreme Court "original jurisdiction," meaning it had not been previously brought to another court.)

It was these technical interpretations, reached at this stage of the case, that finally set up the legal question for which *Marbury v. Madison* became famous — the question of judicial review. *Marbury* did not use the phrase "judicial review," which was not coined until the twentieth century. Marshall instead framed the issue as one of "repugnance" to the Constitution and of judicial "duty" to apply the law. In *Marbury's* terms, the question was whether "an act of the Legislature repugnant to the Constitution" could nonetheless, "notwithstanding its invalidity, bind the Courts and oblige them to give it effect? Or, in other words, though it be not law, does it constitute a rule as operative as if it was a law?" And the Court's answer to this was an emphatic *no*. Here is one of Marshall's crucial statements of what we now call judicial review:

> It is emphatically the province and duty of the Judicial Department to say what the law is. Those who apply the rule to particular cases must, of necessity, expound and interpret that rule. If two laws conflict with each other, the Courts must decide on the operation of each. So, if a law be in opposition to the Constitution, if both the law and the Constitution apply to a particular case, so that the Court must either decide that case conformably to the law, disregarding the Constitution, or conformably to the Constitution, disregarding the law, the Court must determine which of these conflicting rules governs the case. This is of the very essence of judicial duty.

Thus, the Court summarized in the last sentence of its ruling, "a law repugnant to the Constitution is void, and . . . courts, as well as other departments, are bound by that instrument."

Yet the upshot of all of *Marbury*'s discussion and exercise of judicial review was that William Marbury lost. He lost even though he had a right to his commission. He lost even though Congress had authorized the Supreme Court to hear the case. He lost because the Supreme Court exercised judicial review to refuse to hear the case. The main function of judicial review in *Marbury* was only to vindicate the Supreme Court's own authority.

Even this discussion does not fully capture the many maneuvers that produced *Marbury*. Briefly, there were four others:

John Marshall's conclusion that there was a conflict between the Judiciary Act of 1789 and the Constitution relied on a forced interpretation. Most scholars agree that the Judiciary Act did not actually authorize the case. The Court's conclusion that it did just gave it the excuse to hold the Act unconstitutional, arriving at the same place.

Given where the Court ended, the opinion was written in the wrong order. Once we know that the Court does not have the power to hear Marbury's case, there is no reason for it to opine at length about Marbury's right to his commission. Indeed, doing so is what is called "obiter dictum" — the expression of irrelevant opinion that is not necessary for the decision.

Moreover, it is not clear the opinion should have been written by Chief Justice Marshall at all. Another factual complication is that the Secretary of State who was in charge of issuing the last-minute commissions in the Adams administration was none other than John Marshall himself, who had delegated some of the deliveries to his younger brother James. (Even then, the Justices came to the Court from lively political backgrounds.) In adjudicating a case where he himself was a key player, Marshall was certainly pushing the bounds of propriety.

Finally, it is not clear an opinion about the principles of judicial review needed to be written at all. What Marshall wrote there about judicial review was all true, well and convincingly explained, and deserved to become canonical. But also, as noted above, the idea of judicial review was not novel. The Court had entertained serious constitutional challenges years earlier, in cases involving federal taxes, the adjudication of veterans' benefits, and other things. In these cases, judicial review was taken for granted.

In sum, *Marbury v. Madison* used a forced and questionable legal vehicle to navigate a series of technical obstacles so as to vindicate what should have been obvious principles of constitutional law, even though they were not really relevant to anybody but the Court.

Why? Why did Chief Justice Marshall, an able and wily man, spend so much energy pulling a rabbit out of a hat, only to stuff it back in again?

Scholars have concluded that Marshall was in fact executing a somewhat savvy political ploy. It is true that judicial review had been an assumption of constitutional law at the creation of the Constitution. The Constitution itself referred to "judicial power" in "all cases, in law and equity, arising under this Constitution." Alexander Hamilton, as mentioned above, had defended the Constitution's grant of judicial independence because of "the rights of the courts to pronounce legislative acts void, because contrary to the Constitution" which he argued would make the courts "bulwarks of a limited Constitution against legislative encroachments."

But it was not yet clear what judicial review would mean in practice. For in the same article of *The Federalist* Hamilton also downplayed the power of the judiciary, calling it "the least dangerous" branch because it had "no influence over either the sword or the purse," and had "neither FORCE nor WILL, but merely judgment." Would the Court really be willing to rule against the more dangerous branches, in a case of any consequence? And if it did it, would other branches of the government listen?

These questions were very much alive at the time of *Marbury*. And they put the Court in something of a bind. If it did not act to vindicate Marbury's rights, that might be a signal that the Court had no guts, no real power in the cases that mattered. The case was one of several test cases about the relationship between the old Adams administration and the new Jefferson administration, and the judiciary was close to the last hope the old Federalists had of retaining any check against the Jeffersonians. Yet if the Court did order Thomas Jefferson, or his Secretary of State James Madison (hence the *v. Madison*) to deliver Marbury's commission, could it make them do it? "You and what army?" is a playground retort, but it is unfortunately applicable to the courts of law.

Marshall's maneuvers allowed him to simultaneously do three things that might have seemed impossible together: to publicly proclaim that a loyal Federalist, Marbury, had been wronged by President Jefferson; to reaffirm and to defend the power of the federal courts to review the constitutionality of the acts of the other branches of government; and yet to do both of these things in a way that President Jefferson could not immediately defy. Avoiding immediate defiance was key for the first two proclamations to have power.

Marshall's decision to make sure that he ruled in favor of President Jefferson thus gave him freedom to make aggressive legal declarations against Jefferson's interest. Since they did not require anything of Jefferson in the immediate case, there was nothing for Jefferson to defy, and no way for him to demonstrate his power over the Court. Instead, Marshall effectively banked possible power for the future, establishing the Court's authority, even as Marbury himself twisted in the wind.

This may not be turning square corners, but this is judicial institutionalism. Marshall was less focused on doing justice, or being honest, in the particular case and more focused on what would be good for the judiciary in the long run. He took a long view, and a view that was aware of the moment in history. He faced the challenge of getting people to respect a new kind of authority — a Supreme Court for a new nation that would grow into an empire. To do this required not just legal skill but political skill. John Marshall, we might say, had to be shrewd — manipulative, even — so that his successors would have the freedom to be principled.

But what the courts can do, others can do too.

While *Marbury* put an exclamation mark on the power of judicial review, it also laid the groundwork for aggressive executive interpretation of the Constitution — a power that the

Trump administration has not been shy about invoking, and that came to a boil in the recent *CASA* decision.

Recall that Marshall's chief arguments were that the Constitution trumps ordinary statutes, and that judges are allowed to read it. Judges are allowed to read it because the Constitution requires them to decide cases according to law, and also requires them to take an oath to support the Constitution. These arguments are why judges can decide for themselves what the Constitution means, even if Congress and the president disagree. Yet an ingenious and ambitious president might ask, what about me? May the president also propound his own interpretations of the Constitution, even if Congress and the courts disagree? *Marbury's* own logic actually suggests that the answer is yes. Just like judges, the President is required to conduct his actions according to law — indeed, the Constitution says that "he shall take care that the laws be faithfully executed." And just like judges, the President takes an oath to support the Constitution. Indeed, the wording of his oath is (uniquely) spelled out in detail in the Constitution itself. If judges can and must open their eyes to the Constitution, then so must the president.

Judges are also lawyers, learned in the law and in the Constitution's precedents. (Though nothing in the Constitution says that judges must be lawyers, and some presidents, such as Barack Obama and Richard Nixon, have been lawyers too.) But the Constitution does not establish a monopoly of lawyers. Its very first words proclaim that it is the act of "We the People," not of "Our Learned Counsel." And as John Marshall wrote in a different famous case, the Constitution is not written in the form of a "legal code" precisely because if it were, "it would probably never be understood by the public." *Marbury* boldly established that judges could read the Constitution, even when popular politicians did not want them to do so. But it did not establish that only judges could read the Constitution.

A century and a half after *Marbury*, the judges-only position did gain steam. Some politicians found interpreting the Constitution tiresome and needlessly controversial. (Constitutional interpretation is, and should be, intellectually taxing.) It was easier to defer constitutional questions to the courts, and sometimes easier to sell controversial interpretations of the public if they seemed to come from outside of politics. Some began to regloss *Marbury*, as if it had said that it was "exclusively" the province of the judiciary to say what the law was.

Indeed, the Supreme Court itself did this in the Little Rock case in 1958. In response to a campaign of interposition and massive resistance to the desegregation ordered by *Brown v. Board of Education*, the Court wrote an opinion condemning state officials for disagreeing with the Court's interpretations. (Even though state officials, too, take an oath to support the Constitution, just as judges do.) Purporting to describe "settled doctrine," the Little Rock Court parsed *Marbury* for "the basic principle that the federal judiciary is supreme in the exposition of the law of the Constitution, and that principle has ever since been respected by this Court and the Country as a permanent and indispensable feature of our constitutional system."

"It follows," wrote the Court, "that the interpretation of the Fourteenth Amendment enunciated by this Court in the *Brown* case is the supreme law of the land, and Art. VI of the Constitution makes it of binding effect on the States 'any Thing in the Constitution or Laws of any State to the Contrary notwithstanding.'" But it does not follow. Article VI makes the *Constitution* binding and supreme law — but it does not follow that every interpretation of the Constitution, even the Court's interpretations, are the same thing as the Constitution itself.

As Justice Frankfurter once put it, more accurately, "the ultimate touchstone of constitutionality is the Constitution itself and not what we have said about it." This aphorism emphasizes that an interpretation is only as enduring as it is accurate. Moreover, the difference between "the Constitution itself" and the courts' interpretations also shows how phrases like "settled doctrine" can mislead. What the Supreme Court settles it can also decide to unsettle, as sometimes it has and must. The term "settled doctrine" arises precisely when the doctrine is under attack —

like a lazy rhetorician who starts his most controversial claim with "obviously" to try to mask its nonobviousness. Similarly, the theater of judicial confirmation hearings called for nominees to describe cases like *Roe v. Wade* as "settled" precedent because *Roe* was under threat. To call *Roe* settled law was technically true, but the real question was whether the Justices would choose to unsettle and overrule the precedent, as they did in *Dobbs*. The invocation of "settled precedent" was a ritual that could misleadingly reassure the laity even though all lawyers understood how little it promised.

To return to Little Rock: not only did it extrapolate too wildly from the Constitution, it also overread *Marbury*. It is not really true that *Marbury* contained a principle of judicial supremacy, nor that such a principle was "ever since ... respected." This is the dirty secret in the history of judicial review. President Jefferson, President Jackson, President Lincoln, and many others questioned and even refused to subordinate their own views to Supreme Court interpretations. Many Presidents have exercised independent judgment rather than closing their eyes to the Constitution and seeing only the judicial decisions. The interpretation of the Constitution by judges is not the same thing as the Constitution itself. Judicial review does not make puppets or robots out of the executive and legislative branches.

Moreover, after Little Rock, even as the Court insisted on its judicial supremacy against the states, it did not insist as forcefully against the president and Congress. Indeed, as documented by Gerald Rosenberg in *The Hollow Hope: Can Courts Bring About Social Change?*, the Court's desegregation program only became real because it was enforced by legislation and executive action.

Now, Donald Trump is no Abraham Lincoln. Neither is Joe Biden. But both presidencies put further pressure on these assertions of judicial supremacy. In case after case, partisan enemies of the administrations challenged the administration's initiatives in front of sympathetic trial courts, which awarded "universal injunctions" — injunctions that controlled executive conduct everywhere, even if it had nothing to do with those who had sued. The premise of the universal injunction is judicial supremacy — and not only of the Supreme Court either. Once "the federal judiciary" has concluded that the administration is wrong about the law, the universal injunction holds, the administration has to agree. It is not entitled to have a contrary interpretation of the Constitution, even in other cases involving other people.

In *Trump v. CASA*, decided at the end of the Supreme Court term last June, the Supreme Court rejected the universal injunction. In rejecting the universal injunction, it vindicated the idea that the president may make his own determinations about the Constitution, at least until specific and nonuniversal relief is ordered by the courts. Indeed, under *CASA* injunctions by lower courts are not even comprehensively binding within an individual district or circuit; relief is about the parties, not the court. A consequence of limiting judicial relief to the parties before the court is to free up the executive branch to take its own view of the law as to every party not before the court. And the current administration has not been shy about asserting the president's own constitutional determinations or preferences — of broad executive power, limited protection for dissent, against reprisal, and so on. These determinations have now been coming furiously across the dockets of the federal courts.

This leads us back to *Marbury* now. Obviously, *Marbury* reminds us that the Supreme Court can and should be able to review the constitutionality of laws and executive actions today. The Justices are not supposed to take President Trump's actions on faith. If his actions are unlawful or unconstitutional — and many of them are — *Marbury* seems to call the courts to arms.

And yet the Supreme Court has not been ruling against the Trump administration, for the most part. In two dozen cases, involving the dismantling of federal agencies, the impounding of federal funds, the cancellation of grants, the detention and summary deportation of immigrants, the revocation of birthright citizenship, and more, the administration has prevailed in case after case. These cases have mostly been on the Supreme Court's shadow docket (though this term stings so much that the politically correct term is now "emergency docket," or perhaps "interim docket"). In these cases, the Court has been exercising its discretion to allow the administration to come forward, outside the normal appeals process, to pause many of the rulings against it. It might seem to many observers as if the Supreme Court and the Trump administration are close institutional partners, working hand in glove. Do these decisions reflect a Court in complete agreement with the Trump administration agenda, or a forfeiture of the lessons of *Marbury*? Perhaps they reflect neither.

Remember that William Marbury never did receive his commission, and John Marshall worked very hard to make sure that he never told President Jefferson to issue it. Just as Marshall was not at all sure where the Court stood against President Jefferson, what if the current Justices are not at all sure where they stand against President Trump? What would Chief Justice Marshall do?

We do not yet know whether the Supreme Court is ready to confront the Trump administration, but what it has done so far is surprisingly consistent with Marshall's *Marbury* strategy. Its shadow docket rulings have almost entirely been procedural victories for the Trump administration. The Court has said almost nothing about whether the actual decisions made by the administration are lawful. In some cases, it has made this proceduralism explicit. In others, in an inversion of *Marbury*, it has not been "saying what the law is" at all. (This is a lamentable fact of life on the shadow docket.) And yet most intriguingly, some of the decisions contain important material that might later support ruling against the executive, wrapped tightly into decisions that the executive cannot so easily defy.

Consider three examples, all drawn from the authoritarian abuses of the government's immigration power.

First, there was the Alien Enemies Act. A statute enacted

back in the Adams administration gives the President the power to expel immigrants who are part of an invasion or a "predatory incursion" by a foreign government. In American history it was used only in major wars (1812, World War I, World War II) until the Trump administration decided to use it to deport immigrants without judicial review or due process. Since the United States is not in fact being invaded by South American countries, this use of the law is illegal. But if the deportations could be done swiftly enough, or the courts could be convinced to look away (by the incantation of "national security"), perhaps the administration could get away with it.

The courts did not look away, not all of them. One particularly dramatic showdown occurred in front of Chief Judge James Boasberg of the District of Columbia, who acted quickly to stop the summary deportations. The Trump administration went to the Supreme Court, arguing that the case should be taken away from Boasberg for procedural reasons — the reasons being that the aliens should be made to file individual cases through the ancient writ of habeas corpus in the districts of Texas, where they were being detained before removal.

The Supreme Court cannot have missed the broader context of the case. While these arguments were drying on the page, supporters of the administration were calling for Judge Boasberg's impeachment as a traitor. Administration officials had already come close to defying Judge Boasberg's authority, shipping detainees out of the country as he prepared to order them not to do so. It was not entirely clear whether the administration would obey a Supreme Court decision affirming Judge Boasberg.

The Supreme Court reversed Judge Boasberg in *Marbury*-esque fashion. The Court agreed with the administration on the procedural issue. Judge Boasberg should not have heard the case, and future cases would be filed more locally, in front of federal judges scattered across the vast state of Texas. But this Trump administration victory was bundled with a rebuke. The same opinion also stressed that those subject to the order were entitled to prompt and meaningful judicial review, including the "interpretation and constitutionality" of the law. This was a significant holding because the point of the Alien Enemies Act gambit was to shortcut extensive judicial review. Despite ruling for the administration, the Court sideswiped the administration and enabled further challenges in federal courts throughout the country (which continue, somewhat successfully, to this day). Moreover, as in *Marbury*, the administration could not directly confront the ruling because they were disarmed by their own victory on the procedural issues.

Then there is the case of Kilmar Abrego Garcia. As part of their roundup, the Trump administration accidentally deported a Maryland man whose deportation had been paused by an immigration judge several years earlier. Shocking to say, these kinds of mistakes have happened before, and the routine practice has been for the government to facilitate the alien's return to the United States. But the Trump administration refused, choosing instead to turn its mistaken treatment of Abrego Garcia into a national spectacle.

As the administration tried to resist lower court orders to make it right, it once again went to the Supreme Court for vindication. Once again it got a *Marbury*-esque ruling in return. The Supreme Court agreed with the Trump administration that the lower courts might have "exceed[ed]" their "authority" by demanding that the government "effectuate" Abrego Garcia's return to the United States, and this portion of the decision led members of the White House to claim that their intransigence had been vindicated by the Court. But in the very same decision the Court also held that the government *did* have an obligation to "'facilitate' Abrego Garcia's release from custody in El Salvador and to ensure that his case is handled as it would have been had he not been improperly sent to El Salvador." This lingering admonition shadowed the administration for months as the litigation continued, and it has since felt compelled to return Abrego Garcia to the country to face criminal charges — hardly a reassuring outcome at a human level, but in some sense an important victory for due process.

And then, at the end of the summer, there were the Los Angeles raids. Roving patrols of federal agents throughout Southern California began stopping, harassing, and detaining Latinos throughout the Los Angeles metropolitan area, demanding immigration or citizenship papers. Again, lower court judges ordered the Trump administration to stop part of this practice as unconstitutional, and again the administration went to the Supreme Court for vindication. In *Noem v. Vasquez Perdomo*, the Supreme Court allowed the patrols to go forward, this time without deigning to offer an opinion. But Justice Kavanaugh rushed into the breach, offering his own account of the Court's need to greenlight the Trump administration's raids. Putting aside the various legal arguments, one especially notable feature of his opinion was how much it seemed to contradict reality. In Justice Kavanaugh's telling, the government could only "briefly stop" people to ask about their immigration status, and it must quickly let them go if their status was lawful. It was not supposed to use excessive force. And so on.

As the dissenting Justices, the lower court record, and plenty of news reports all showed, this is not actually what was happening. Masked agents were creating panic and fear across the city by terrorizing Latino citizens at gunpoint, refusing to accept their answers, and sometimes worse. Justice Kavanaugh surely knew all of this. But perhaps his opinion was written the way it was precisely to nudge the administration into line. As Richard Re has written, Kavanaugh's opinion "can be viewed as engaging in constraint by affirmation" — like a parent or teacher who pretends to believe the best of their charge — "Oh, I know you would *never* put chewing gum on another student's seat," he might say, knowing all too well that is what has happened, to send the message that it cannot happen again.

To be sure, not every recent decision has been like this. In many others the Court has simply ruled, silently or with minimal explanation, in favor of the Trump administration. Even as the Justices publicly reassure the country that they are there to exercise the judicial review that *Marbury* promised, it might seem as if that review will never be applied with any real scrutiny to the Trump administration.

Yet we are less than a year into the second Trump administration, and perhaps a *Marbury*-esque pattern will also emerge on an even broader level. It is no secret that the administration resists legal constraint, is ready to demonize any judge who rules against it, and that some members of the administration may be ready, even eager, to directly defy a court order. The Court knows this, as we all do. And yet the outcome of an open constitutional war between the judiciary and the executive is hard to predict.

Faced with this, we might consider a strategy that we might call "give and take." Considering not just individual cases but a broad range of cases over two or even four years, the Court might let the executive branch win some close calls, in part to build up institutional capital for the cases where it loses. As in *Marbury* itself, there is potential injustice in this, depending on the magnitude of what is taken and what is given. But to understand the Court as an institution we must think of the big picture.

There is a logic to this strategy. Every time the executive branch wins in the Supreme Court it celebrates and publicly strengthens the Court's legitimacy. These rulings can also affect the game of thrones played by different lords of the Trump administration. When the administration's lawyers score victories in court by making legalistic arguments, their standing in the administration increases. They have more authority to press legalistic arguments in the future. By contrast, if the Court had started out ruling against the administration in every case, Stephen Miller might have convinced the President to sideline the lawyers and ignore the legal process. So perhaps, by giving the administration a long leash, the Court gives itself time to get a firm grip on the handle.

There are dangers to this strategy too, to be sure. For one thing, legalistic arguments can be used to paper over bad faith. Leah Litman and Dan Deacon describe the administration's current strategy as one of "legalistic noncompliance." Demanding only these legalisms can be a path to a mere semblance of due process, not the real thing. And perhaps courts should not be strategic at all — instead just calling balls and strikes and hoping that the players listen.

But in any event this strategy finds a strong echo in *Marbury*. Facing an intransigent president popular with his own party, Chief Justice Marshall gave the Jefferson administration a victory in the case before him, as part of a broader strategy to build the institutional strength of the Court. It is possible that we will come to see that today's Court has been doing something similar. It may be that today's Trump administration victories will be matched or outweighed by some future losses. It may be that soon enough the Court will rebuke the administration's birthright citizenship order, its abuse of the Alien Enemies Act, its selective targeting of the regime's enemies, or even the tariffs.

If this happens, the effectiveness of the Court's ruling will partly be a function of its institutional position. It is uncertain how the administration would take a significant loss in Court. No amount of "give and take" can necessarily avert a war between the Court and the White House. But it can help to ensure that the war takes place on the Court's strongest ground, with many members of the administration already well invested in the Court's power and legitimacy.

But be careful. There is a coda to the *Marbury* story, one that reads as a warning today. In its time *Marbury v. Madison* was not perceived as the only test case about the ability of the judiciary to check the ascendant Jeffersonians. There loomed another, bigger dispute than the commission of William Marbury. That bigger dispute was the constitutionality of Jeffersonian legislation that had restructured the judiciary, repealing Federalist judgeships and imposing additional duties on Supreme Court Justices. This dispute was more explosive; John Marshall had already written privately to his colleagues about the legislation's unconstitutionality, and yet Jeffersonians were pressuring the Court to uphold it. If *Marbury* was hoarding judicial capital for a bigger fight, *Stuart v. Laird* would seem to be the bigger fight.

And yet the week after deciding *Marbury*, the Supreme Court also ruled for the Jeffersonians in *Stuart v. Laird,* a case which involved the judgment of a circuit judge whose position had been abolished by the repeal of the Judiciary Act of 1801. The Court upheld the Jeffersonian legislation, which had been on the books for a couple of years by that time. The Court did not even defend the legislation on first principles, drily calling it "sufficient to observe that practice and acquiescence . . . afford an irresistible answer" and that this "practical exposition is too strong and obstinate to be shaken or controlled." In other words, whatever the Justices might argue about how the Constitution *should* be interpreted, the facts on the ground had proven "too strong." The capital that Marshall had theoretically earned by the *Marbury* maneuver proved insufficient.

The lesson of *Stuart* amends the lesson of *Marbury*. Sometimes a planned strategy of "give and take" can turn out to become one of "give and give and give." That sobering lesson will haunt the Supreme Court in the coming years. If the Court is not in complete agreement with the lawfulness of the Trump agenda, will it do anything about it? Does the Roberts Court have the will and the power to do what the Marshall Court could not?

ABBAS MILANI

Ali Khamenei: A Profile in Dogma

Ali Khamenei is a man of obdurate dogmas and dogged animosities. Since becoming the "Supreme Leader" of Iran some thirty-six years ago, he has played a pivotal role in the Islamic Republic's every strategic decision. He has rarely missed an opportunity to choose a pathway detrimental to Iran's national interests, or even to the survival of his own regime. He is tactically nimble, strategically numb, or in the words of the old English proverb, penny wise, pound foolish. The Iranian theocracy finds itself at the weakest moment in its history, and yet Khamenei has been unwilling to admit any error of judgment, any failure or defeat of his policies. Even when he wants to repivot the foundational ideas undergirding his claim to power, he not only does not admit error, he goes on the offensive. His discourse is invariably peppered with attacks on real or imagined "enemies" — from the defiant women of Iran who have been unwilling to accept misogynist laws to America and Israel, which he has labeled respectively "Great Satan" and "Little Satan." In his regime, financial corruption is the norm and has become the scourge of genuine development. He has absolute control of assets estimated to be more than a hundred billion dollars; and no one, not even his hand-picked parliament, has any oversight over this fortune.

The regime's explanation for its claim to power has been that the Constitutional Revolution of 1907 was a wrong turn in Iranian history, and that the man who had it right was a mullah named Sheikh Fazlollah. He was against constitutional government (*Mashruteh*) and advocated a government based on Sharia (*Mashroue*.) So reactionary was his idea that even then the highest Shiite clergy of the time not only admonished him but also issued a fatwa for his death. Now, as Khamenei's house of cards crumbles, he claims that his despotic regime is actually the embodiment of the ideals of the Constitutional Revolution! He also adds, with no hint of cognitive dissonance, that the Constitutional Revolution itself was a conspiracy of the British.

In a move that puts Orwellian doublespeak to shame, Khamenei and his vast ideological apparatus have consistently claimed that his regime defeated "Israeli Zionism" and "American imperialism" in what has come to be called the Twelve Day War. This declaration of victory is of course delusional: it utterly denies the debilitating attacks by Israel on the regime's proxies and allies in the region, as well as the undeniable structural setbacks to the regime's military, nuclear, intelligence, and authoritarian apparatus. Understanding why Iran is in its current state requires understanding the vision of Seyyed Ali Khamenei. One must consider his intellectual development and political ascent if we hope to unravel the paradoxes of his person, his persona, and his politics, and the current situation in Iran.

Khamenei's strategic decisions are based on his vision of an ultimate and imminent victory for Islam, and on his hope that the world is near a "historic turn," one that will herald a global victory of Islam. His aversion to facts and his incurable addiction to dogma and apocalyptic dreams are rooted in this belief, and its accompanying idea that modernity, materialism, Western hegemony, capitalism, socialism, and Zionism have all failed. As the victory of Islam grows near, Khamenei — the self-declared "representative" of the Twelfth Imam, Shiism's anticipated messiah — conceives of himself as the midwife to this divine fate. Yet beneath this grandiose persona there also lurks an insecure character, ill-at-ease with the position that he has "usurped."

The current regime in Iran came to power in the Revolution of 1979. Like other revolutions, the most ruthless and radical organized group — invariably representing a minority of those who rebel — managed to seize power. In the case of the Iranian revolution, the usurpation of the democratic aspirations of the revolution against the Shah was sinister but subtle. That legerdemain culminated in the anointment of Ayatollah Khomeini as the Supreme Leader. Khamenei's ascent has been a far more brazen usurpation.

The first Supreme Leader of Iran, Ayatollah Ruhollah Khomeini came to power after he — by his own admission — engaged in *Tagiyeh*. This is a peculiar Shiite precept that allows, indeed requires, the faithful to lie to promote the faith and preserve the faithful. *Tagiyeh* is sometimes translated as "righteous dissimulation." In the months before coming to power, from his headquarters in France, Khomeini repeatedly promised democracy in a form inspired by the Fifth Republic. Many Westerners, as well as many of Iran's dissidents, fell for this cunning performance. Once in power, however, Khomeini created a form of clerical despotism which treated the people of Iran like sheep, bereft of the capacity for governance, stipulating that they required the clergy as their shepherds, or "Guardians." The policy was particularly brazen because almost a century earlier, during the Constitutional Revolution of 1907-1909, Iranians had won the right to democratic governance and to the constitutional axiom that sovereignty belonged to the people of Iran.

The tragedy was that when Khomeini deceptively replaced popular sovereignty with divine ordination, he enjoyed a great measure of popular support. That support — along with his own charisma, the euphoria often accompanying an unfolding revolution, and his promise that only a limited number of top posts would be awarded to the clerics — somehow distracted from the audacity of his power grab. As soon as the romance of revolution wilted and the public (particularly women, whose rights were immediately trampled on by the new regime) realized the calamity that had befallen the country, they began to fight for their lost sovereignty. In the end, Khomeini ruled over the regime he had created for less than a decade.

Seyyed Ali Khamenei succeeded him in 1989. *His* rise to power was even more flagrant. For all his destructive despotism, Ayatollah Khomeini's rise to the top was the result of the unanimous support of the clerical body of eighty-six men who were empowered by the new constitution to elect the Supreme Leader. Not so for Ayatollah Khameini: there are leaked tapes of the meeting at which Khamenei was chosen as Khomeini's successor, and they record that the meeting was not a genuine election but a well-choreographed play, or an "electoral coup." Hashemi Rafsanjani, a Shia who was then a close ally of Khamenei and had been, next to Khomeini, the second most powerful man in Iran, claimed to have heard Khomeini say that Ali Khamenei was his worthy successor. After that declaration, few dared to challenge this choice. It is important to recall that the most divisive split in the history of Islam happened at the time of Mohammad's death, when most Muslims claimed that they should, according to tradition (*Sunna*) elect a successor, but a small minority were partisans (*Shia*) of the claim that the prophet had designated his son-in-law, Ali, as his successor. Rafsanjani was tapping into that cultural memory when he announced Khamenei as the designated successor; and in recent years Khamenei, too, had been trying to tap into that same history by letting his associates hint that his chosen successor was his son Mojtaba — a figure who has lurked in the shadows ever since his father became the leader and is known to have close ties to the intelligence apparatus of the Islamic Revolutionary Guard Corps (IRGC).

The reality is that Khamanei lacks the gravitas and the popular respect that Khomeini had when he anointed his own successor. And at the same time contemporary Iranian society — markedly more secular and disgruntled with the status quo than it was in 1989 — does not seem willing to accept another "anointed" leader. In 1989, with echoes of Shakespeare's Richard III, Khamenei "reluctantly" accepted a post that he and Rafsanjani had conspired to usurp. And yet in a moment of rare candor and self-doubt Khamenei, on the way to accepting the role of the leader, declared that we should weep for a nation that has him as its leader.

The "humility" passed quickly. Once in power, Khamenei not only stubbornly clung to his position but expanded its reach. A few years ago, the same Rafsanjani who facilitated Khamenei's rise to the pinnacle of power hinted at trying to limit the power of the Supreme Leader. Khamenei aggressively rejected the idea. His supporters claimed that Khamenei was not "elected" but "discovered," and thus only Allah can take his power away. In fact, the Constitution allows the Assembly of Experts to impeach a Supreme Leader when he is no longer deemed competent to fulfill his duties.

Wielding such absolute power requires both determination and self-confidence. Khomeini had both; Khamenei has too much of the first and too little of the second. His combination of dogmatic arrogance and personal paranoia explains how Khamenei has ruled Iran for the last thirty-six years and why he is in his current limbo. With an iron fist he increasingly tried to make the country and its policies congruent with his often-quixotic vision of enemies, allies, divine interventions, and even the interference of jinn (supernatural beings who apparently sometime work for Islam and intervene in human affairs on its behalf), and of course the demonic Zionists. Khamenei and his propaganda machine invoke medieval antisemitic tropes to fan the flames of antisemitism. In fact, in the aftermath of the Twelve Day War, some in the Khamenei regime claimed that papers with

Hebrew curses against the state printed upon them were discovered in the streets of Tehran.

Khamenei was born in a milieu where such drivel was ubiquitous. He was born on April 19, 1939 to a lower middle-class family steeped in Islamic pieties and superstitions. Mashhad, the city of his birth, has been for more than millennium a destination for Shiite pilgrims wishing to visit the shrine of Imam Reza, the eighth Imam of Shiism. For virtually its entire long history, the city has been a city at least partially dominated by religious zealots, inclined to preserve what they claim to be the city's singular and sacred place in the pantheon of holy cities. Khamenei's mother was a pious woman who also loved poetry and apparently shielded her children against their father's cruelest demands. His father was a harsh and stern self-appointed twentieth-century guardian of the divinity of the city and the puritan pieties of his family. In an ironic but revealing twist of fate, under his son's tenure Mashhad has become the subject of some derision for the fact that hotels owned by the city's religious endowment, itself controlled by Khamenei, offer two rates, one for just a room, the other for a room with a *Sigheh*, or "temporary wife" — a peculiar law specific to Shiites that allow a man and woman to legally "wed" for as short a time as they desire, and for as much remuneration as they mutually accept. Some scholars condemn the practice as legalized prostitution, particularly in light of the limits placed on women for their choices; others praise it as a sign of Shiism's acceptance of human carnal desire.

Ali Khamenei was the second of five children. In his own words, at the time of his birth the family lived in a small house of "one room and a dark claustrophobic basement." When the father had a visitor, which was often, the rest of the family was forced to retreat to the basement. In a practice that was not uncommon in the days before 1979, some of the more affluent devotees of Khamenei's father eventually bought the adjoining land and built the family a three-room home. Khamenei's father was so religious and suspicious of modernity that long after electricity had come to the city he refused to use it in the house. Radio, television, and gramophones, too, were banned by him, lest the family be tempted by the seductions of music and the frivolities of secular programs found on radio and television at the time. After the revolution, most of the families of the clergy chose lives of luxury in fancy houses confiscated from members of the Shah's regime, but Khamenei's father remained in his humble abode even after his son's rise to power.

Khamenei's supporters consider his father's asceticism and the Supreme Leader's own "simple life" as bona fides that he is a man of the people. All evidence indicates that Khamenei does in fact live a simple life and avoids the kind of luxury enjoyed by erstwhile pious revolutionaries. Khamenei's detractors, on the other hand, point to the endemic corruption in the system that he has created—and to the immense fortune that he and his office control. There are hundreds of corporations owned by Khamenei's office — *Beyt*, in the parlance of the time — and religious endowments that he controls; no less economically significant are the many companies run by the IRGC that Khamenei at least nominally controls as the commander-in-chief. The role of his office and its myriad companies involved in everything from the production of COVID vaccines to construction and telecommunication companies is considered emblematic of the crony statist capitalism of his tenure. And the businesses owned and operated by the children of clergy and top IRGC commanders constitute another layer of parasitic companies that dominate the collapsing Iranian economy. In contemporary Iran the word *agazadeh* — its closest English equivalent is perhaps "nepo baby" — refers to the corruption passed on to the next generations, rather like the "princelings" in China and the *nomenklatura* in the Soviet Union. Only one of Khamenei's sons — that same shady Mojtaba — is reported to be a silent partner in some of these parasitical companies. Khamenei's own greed is not for wealth and its luxuries, but for power and its perks.

Inside Iran, the enormous unsupervised wealth at Khamenei's disposal has allowed him to create a patronage system more powerful than any Tammany Hall could have imagined. With a snap of his fingers, Khamenei can almost immediately make allies wealthy beyond their wildest dreams. Almost as easily, he can deprive his critics of their fortune, even of their liberty. Indeed, for virtually the entirety of the Islamic regime, the ruling class in Iran has been an interlocking elite of clerical sons and daughters who often intermarry to keep power and privilege in a close circle of the ostensibly pious. According to one study, led by Mehrzad Boroujerdi, it is only about 2,300 men (and a handful of women) who make up Iran's post-revolutionary political elite. For this reason (except for a few defiant figures such as the former prime minister Hossein Mousavi and the academician Zahra Rahnavard, both now in their twelfth year of house arrest, and Mostafa Tajzadeh, once a deputy minister and for the past ten years in prison) even the "reformist" critics of the regime have been reluctant to criticize Khamenei's leadership or challenge his despotism.

In the aftermath of the Twelve Day War they have lined up even more openly behind the Supreme Leader. In the months before Israel's bombings of Iran, every indication predicted a perfect storm of domestic disarray, regional isolation, and a new assertiveness by Netanyahu that would result in an attack. Khamenei, caught in the cocoon of his dogmas, refused to heed any advice or warning, insisting instead on forging ahead with his policy of getting closer to Russia and China, demanding the destruction of Israel, even prognosticating its imminent collapse, and refusing to allow any direct negotiations with the United States. Some of his sillier sycophantic allies even suggested that direct negotiations with the United States is forbidden in the Qur'an.

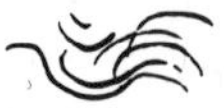

What secures Khamenei's obstinacy even in the face of realities that may lead to the failure of his regime? His predecessor might seem one obvious source: Khamenei often pays profuse homage to Khomeini. But in fact most of Khameini's ideas and actions have been influenced by two other Islamists. The first is a rabble-rousing Iranian Shiite cleric-*cum*-terrorist, the other an Egyptian Sunni intellectual and the spiritual father of Egypt's Muslim Brotherhood.

As Khamenei has said himself, the person who first inspired him to enter the world of political Islam was Navvab Safavi, a young Shiite seminarian who returned from his unfinished religious studies in Iraq in 1944 determined to assassinate Ahmad Kasravi, a distinguished Iranian historian and secularist who had dared to publish what is still the most radical critique of Shiism. Kasravi was particularly critical of what he called Shiism's superstitions and irrational ideas, and its cult of melancholy and martyrdom. The impetus for Navvab's plans to murder Kasravi was a book published by Ruhollah Khomeini in 1942 denouncing the work of Kasravi and two Shiite clerics who advocated a kind of Reformation in Shiism. In retrospect, despite the many "progressives" and Islamic reformists who have supported Khomeini, he was a pillar of Shiism's Counter-Reformation, a figure reminiscent of the eighteenth-century German "magus" J.G. Hamman as he was brilliantly depicted by Isaiah Berlin. In Khomeini's book, his first published work and an early harbinger of his future practices, he called Kasravi "a corrupter of the earth." This was then a novel concept, wrought from Shiite theology; but after 1979 the appellation "corrupter of the earth" would increasingly be used in kangaroo courts that killed or imprisoned thousands of members of the old regime, along with critics of the new regime, dissident intellectuals, and religious minorities — particularly the Bahais, whom the regime refuses to accept as a religion and persecutes as a "Zionist" and "colonial" concoction. In recent years the Ayatollah Hussain Ali Montazèri, once designated as Khomeini's successor, tried to soften Shiism's stance on the Bahais, but Khamenei has continued to persecute them with a relentless zeal reminiscent of Javert in *Les Misérables*.

In his book Khomeini had asked why no Shiite had been "man enough" to use an iron fist to "cleanse" the world of "shameless... dimwits" like Kasravi. (Much of the language used by Khomeini about Kasravi he would adopt again, in February 1989, in his fatwa against Salman Rushdie.) The extremist Navvab Safavi decided to take up the challenge. While his own attempt to assassinate Kasravi failed in 1945, the historian and his assistant were brutally murdered by followers of Safavi while he was on trial for "slander against Islam" in Tehran in 1946.

In the aftermath of Kasravi's murder, Safavi issued a defiant proclamation called *Religion and Retribution*, threatening the life of anyone who dared to criticize his version of Islam. He also announced the establishment of an organization called *Fada'ian-e Islam*, or Devotee Martyrs of Islam, that became the most lethal and influential terrorist organization of modern Iran. In 1945, the highest Shiite cleric in Iran, Ayatollah Hussein Ali Boroujerdi, banned the incendiary Safavi from all seminaries. Two clerics dared to defy that ban, albeit quietly: a teacher at the seminary in Qom and a novice seminarian in Mashhad. The first was named Khomeini and the second was named Khamenei. In the years of the latter's rule, the Devotees gained more political power than ever before.

When Navvab Safavi was first building his network, he visited Mashhad to deliver sermons. Khamenei was then a fourteen-year-old seminarian. He was so taken by Safavi's first sermon that, as a gesture of deference, he went out to greet the terrorist and his entourage in the street as they arrived for his second sermon. The tiny-looking cleric arrived surrounded by a group of tough-looking supporters and guards. This was no coincidence. Safavi was an early champion of an idea that would later become a key strategy of the IRGC. As he explained, Islamists must use "individuals who, up to now have disturbed the peace in neighborhood, like hoodlums, roughnecks, thugs and neighborhood bullies." To Khamenei's delight, the radical preacher noisily walked the streets gesticulating with his arms, shouting slogans, declaiming that "Islam must rule." When the surly sermonizer ran across innocent bystanders wearing a tie, he accosted them, claiming that a tie was a vestige of colonialism and even a hidden Christian sign — of the cross, or of a priest's vestments.

More than once during Khamenei's tenure, commanders of the IRGC have openly confessed to deputizing thousands of criminals serving time in prison, arming them with a gun and a motorcycle and using them against demonstrators. At the height of the massive civil disobedience movement of Women, Life, Freedom in 2022, Khamenei met with a group of his street-louts-*cum*-militias and told them that when fighting deviants from Islam, they should take the law into their own hand and if necessary "fire at will." Navvab Safavi was the early theorist of this kind of neo-fascist vigilantism and it was Khamenei who put it into practice, particularly against Iran's defiant women.

Navvab Safavi's political program vociferously promulgated the repression and control of women, and stipulated that any woman who does not wear her *hijab* must be banned from the streets. Under Khamenei, a whole infrastructure for "Advocating the Good and Prohibiting the Forbidden" has been created precisely for this purpose. Again, the first bureaucratic design for such a center was outlined by Navvab Safavi in 1946. In the last decade, as Iranian women have valiantly fought for their right to appear in public without the hijab, more clerics and religious scholars have argued that there is no compulsion for women to wear a veil, and advocated tolerance on this draconian dictate. Yet Khamenei has been the most unbending and powerful advocate of the theory that mandatory veiling is nothing less than Allah's writ and the regime should never give up on this policy. Even in the aftermath of the Twelve Day War, Alam-al Hoda, one of Khamenei's closest allies and the de facto "viceroy" in Mashhad, declared that mandatory veil is an existential line of defense for the regime, and that the "enemies" are using the women question in their sinister design to defeat Islam.

Some of Safavi's strangest ideas concern economics — and they have become a backbone of the economic theory with which Khamenei is most identified. It is known as the Economy of Resistance and it is the pillar of his prescription for how to fight globalism and dependency and create a just and viable "Islamic economy." Khamenei's model in essence is like Navvab's teaching, who claimed that reliance on trained economists is hubris, and another example of the arrogance that begot the expulsion of humanity from the primordial paradise — or "the fall" in the parlance of theology. Humans "fell"— in Islam it is called *Hobut* — because they forfeited Allah's prescriptions and preferred human reason. The best way to run the economy, Safavi instructed, was similarly antirational: put it into the hands of the pious local grocer whose ultimate guide is Allah's words in the Qur'an. Indeed, in Iran over the last forty-four years, there has been a running debate between different factions in the regime about whether appointments should be made based on expertise or piety. Khamenei has consistently put not just piety, but also sycophantic fidelity to his leadership, as the most important qualification for his appointments. In the economy, no less than in politics and culture, he advocates a jihadi disposition. On rare occasions he has instrumentally valued someone's expertise—as, for example, the case of Iran's one-time foreign minister Mohammad Javad Zarif. When Khamenei thought there was no choice for his regime but to negotiate with the Americans, he approved Zarif's appointment as foreign minister. Yet he refused to accept responsibility for the nuclear deal that Zarif negotiated at the behest of his master.

The same lack of courage to accept responsibility is evident, incidentally, in the events leading to the recent ceasefire with Israel and the United States. By law, Khamenei has the sole authority to declare war or accept a ceasefire. He has yet to indicate even his approval of the Islamic regime's decision to agree to a ceasefire. The contrast with Khomeini is rather telling. Khomeini had the courage of his convictions and when he was forced to accept an end to the eight-year war with Iraq, he declared that he reluctantly drank the hemlock of peace. Khamenei has all too many convictions, invariably based on dogma, yet he lacks the courage to accept responsibility for any of them. Many of these convictions come from Navvab Safavi.

Not long after the slaying of Kasravi, Safavi published a book that set out, in surprising detail, his plans for the creation of an Islamic State. It is founded on the idea that only Allah's divine laws can deliver solace in this world and salvation in the next. The book's title captures the essence of his vision: *Guide to Truth: A Small Representation of the World's Luminous Truths*. It is a bombastic manifesto that declares on its cover page, "Study carefully, since with the help of the powerful God, [the book] will be effective in the ways of the world and will change the path of humankind ... and it will allow all children of men to be definitely saved from ignorance." It certainly has not changed the world, but virtually every one of its zany ideas have been put in practice during Khamenei's years in power. And while his devotees murdered Kasravi more than eighty years ago, in today's Iran Kasravi's ideas and writings are more in vogue than ever before.

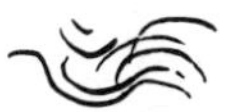

In addition to Navvab Safavi, another crucial source for Khamenei's ideology was a Sunni Egyptian radical. If Khamenei's affinities with Navvab Safavi were the result of a chance meeting, his inclination toward Sayyid Qutb was a premeditated selection. This is particularly surprising given that Khamenei is often regarded as the main architect of the effort to create a "Shiite Crescent" in the region. In fact, despite a long history of animosities between Shiites and Sunnis in the Middle East, there is, except for the likes of ISIS, a political convergence between the radical political Islams of Shia and Sunni, and the Supreme Leader in Iran is the embodiment of this convergence. Hints of that convergence were evident even in his youth in the 1940s. During his trip to Egypt in 1954, Khamenei met with Qutb and was impressed by his radicalism.

In the years before the revolution of 1979, Khamenei, still a little-known cleric in the city of Mashhad, undertook the unusual task of translating three of the books written by Sayyid Qutb. He was in the process of translating a fourth when he was arrested for his antigovernment activities and sent to internal exile by the Shah's security forces. Khamenei did not give up the project, entrusting the task of completing Qutb's fourth book to one of his brothers, a fellow cleric.

Khamenei's choice among Qutb's more than twenty-four books reveals much about his intellectual and theological anxieties and visions, his method of tackling intellectual problems, and his eschatology. Clearly the most dominant motif in Khamenei's published writings, sermons, and translations is the future of Shiism, the question of modernity, and its secularism, rationalism, nationalism, artistic freedom, the woman question, capitalism, colonialism, and the place of Jews in history. For Khamenei, as for Qutb, the political question of Zionism is inseparable from the contested theological debate about Islam's views on Jews and even from the debate about modernity itself. Like Qutb, Khamenei had an early interest in literature and dabbled in poetry and criticism. In his early days at the apex of power, he still took pride in the fact that in his youth he had been friend and disciple of some of Iran's prominent artists and intellectuals — Akhavan Sales, a great modernist poet, and Saidi Sirjani, a daring scholar and essayist who was killed while in prison during Khamanei's tenure.

Maybe it is owing to those early affinities that a consistent part of the persona that he has tried to cultivate, and a constant theme of the hagiographies written about him, is that he is not just a mullah but also an intellectual. Yet despite these early affinities and his choreographed meetings with "poets and artists," even in his youth Khamenei's driving intellectual force was some version of political Islam. It began with his affinity for Navvab Safavi; it morphed into his tutelage as an occasional student of Khomeini; and then his most sustained theoretical engagement was with the writings of Sayyid Qutb. In Qutb's ideas, he found a rich reservoir of arguments, jeremiads, and animosities which were, in a cruder form, already percolating in the writings of Safavi and Khomeini. In the strange welter of these sometimes discordant ideas, mixed with his own anxieties and aspirations, prejudices and prognostications, he forged his own vision and strategy. In the Twelve Day War, and in the events leading to it, those ideas and his incumbent strategy crashed on the hard rock of reality.

Khamenei had a four-pronged plan — three kinetic and the fourth cultural. To export his revolution and its doctrines, and to establish "strategic depth" for his regime, he set out to create armed proxies and allies, Hezbollah in Lebanon, the Houthis in Yemen, Hamas in Gaza, and the Assad regime in Syria foremost among them. He sent thousands of Afghanis, Iraqis, Lebanese, and Iranian citizens to their deaths, and at the cost of tens of billion dollars he propped up the Assad regime in Syria — all to create his wonted "Shiite Crescent" and to increase what he presumed would be a deterrent pressure on Israel and the United States. He rejected, ignored, or silenced any critic within the regime who questioned the wisdom of such policies. (His disdainful dismissal of Rafsanjani in the last years of the latter's life is a prime example of such behavior.) Secondly, Khamenei doggedly pursued a nuclear program that was ostensibly for peaceful purposes but could be leveraged as both a deterrent and a bargaining chip in the regime's negotiations with the West. He tried desperately to keep the military component of the program hidden from the West and from Israel's constantly watchful eyes. Finally, he jettisoned the early mantra of the revolution's foreign policy — "Neither East nor West" — and turned Eastward, seeking to sign long-term security agreements with China and Russia and entice the former to invest in Iran to help solve the dire economic situation.

Even before the recent Twelve Day War, China, and to a lesser degree Russia, had shown little eagerness to make any serious commitment to Khamenei's strategic vision. During the war, too, neither side offered anything other than perfunctory diplomatic declarations. In the months before the war, the regime's proxies in Lebanon and Gaza were debilitated, Assad was overthrown, and the regime's allies or proxies were in no mood to offer practical support. Even domestically the regime was under siege by strikes, civil disobedience by women, and a near total rejection of the regime's ideology by Iran's youth. Yet Khamenei, nestled in the isolation of sycophants and his own towering certitude, ignored all these signs and forged ahead with his disastrous strategy. His ongoing fight with cancer must have exacerbated his isolation and his delusion, which bring to mind Garcia Marquez's words about despots and patriarchs who in their autumn are "lost in the solitude" of their immense power.

Of the four pillars of Khamenei's strategy, the only one that has not yet proven a total disaster is his effort to create a sophisticated multi-layered infrastructure to fight what he has repeatedly called a "culture war" against "Cultural NATO." Imperialism and Zionism, he believed, had lost the kinetic war against his regime and were resorting to what Joseph Nye called "soft power." The same emphasis on the cultural domain also played a key part in what was hailed as Khamenei's Manifesto, issued on the fortieth anniversary of the Revolution in 2019. Central to the Supreme Leader's Manifesto was the idea that the culture war must be a key component in any security strategy for the regime. In his view, not only is modernity a curse, but Judeo-Christian hegemony and Western imperialism have all failed. The world is looking for a new source of salvation, and Islam, or more specifically his iteration of it, is that solution. Khamenei's endless enmity toward the United States as "imperialist" is inseparable from his view of America as a champion of modernity and secularism, and a country whose politics and culture are "controlled by Zionists."

Khamenei's "culture war" has a domestic component as well as an international one. Inside Iran, it has included a tightly controlled social media, ideological commissars in every educational institution, censorship of all books, cinema, theater, and banning of most kinds of music, banning women vocalists, and promoting "Islamic values." Khamenei's project has utterly failed at home. Iranian society has become more secular, more impatient for modernity (at once Iranian and global), and more averse to dogmatic Shiism than ever before. Khamenei has been a vocal critic of Iranian nationalism as a form of heresy, and a Judeo-Christian trope against Islam; he has advocated the "religious community" (*ummah*) in place of the nation (*melat*) — yet in his first public appearance after the Twelve Day War he asked for the performance of a nationalist song in praise of Iran, with a few awkward incongruent interlaced words about Islam. A more poignant image of the failure of his domestic "culture wars" is hard to imagine.

The international front of his culture war has consisted of the creation of a major international university — modeled on the Soviet Union's Patrice Lumumba University — that educates thousands of students in Iran and in campuses around the world according to Khamenei's anti-modern, anti-democratic, anti-American, and anti-Israeli worldview. Another part of this apparatus is cultivating, coordinating, and empowering intellectual proxies in Western academia and cultural domains. The nature of the regime's work in this domain is similar to what China has accomplished. While China's soft power has received much attention, the Iranian regime's similar effort has received less scrutiny. In his discourses, and in the regime's work, Khamenei carefully cultivates the overlapping anxieties and concerns of "progressive" forces around the world with Iran's own ends and interests. The silence of many Western progressives about the Iranian women's movements, or about some of the regime's most egregious behavior, is indicative of the regime's relative success. And even in this domain, when all else fails, the clerical regime has used terror to kill or abduct its most radical critics. More than a hundred twenty such cases have been identified in Europe; in a few of these cases, Khamenei has been directly named as the person who ordered the attacks. Arguably the most obvious example of Khamenei's success in co-opting fellow travelers has been his ability to launder his ideas against Israel as simply anti-Zionist and hiding some of its antisemitic roots. In offering support for radical Islamist Palestinian groups, he has camouflaged his profound enmity to the two-state solution and to most Palestinians who live under the Palestinian Authority and have grudgingly come to accept the idea of an Israeli state alongside a Palestinian one.

Khamenei constantly blames Israel, and more specifically Jews, for much of what ails the world, the region, and Iran. Here again he resembles Qutb. One of Qutb's most important books is a multi-volume foray into the field of Qur'anic exegesis, or *Tafsir*. He wrote *In the Shade of the Qur'an* while serving a long prison sentence in Egypt late 1950s and early 1960s. Even those such as

Paul Berman who criticize Qutb as the "philosopher of Islamic terror" praise *In the Shade of Qur'an* as "one of the most remarkable works of prison literature..." and a "vast vividly written, wise, broad, indignant, sometimes demented, bristly with hatred, medieval, modern, tolerant, intolerant, paranoid, cruel, urgent, cranky, tranquil, grave, poetic, learned and analytic" manifesto. The narrative, written after the establishment of the state of Israel, is riddled with anti-Semitic ideas and ideologies. Khamenei chose to translate the first book of Qutb's exegesis covering the interpretations of the first chapter of the Qur'an.

The subject of the chapter is the tensions that existed between the prophet and the Jews of Arabia at the time of Islam's inception. Instead of treating these verses as historic references to events of the past, Qutb construes them mostly as suggestions that Jews in general, and not just Jews at the time of Muhammad, are Allah's most accursed creatures and the most persistent foes of Islam. He writes of the "enmity towards Islam, which filled and continues to fill the hearts of Jews, has always been the real force that motivates their plotting and scheming. The Qur'an makes this very clear as it describes the relentless Jewish efforts to shake the foundations of Islam." Muslims, in response, are "urged to pursue the faith of God," and be watchful of Jews. He refers to Jews as people whose soul and spirit are "cold and barren," and whose hearts are as hard as "a rock." In another passage, he writes that "Jews in their mendacity and trickery are still trying to turn the *ummah* away from its religion and the Qur'an," and continues, "anyone who turns the *ummah* away from Islam and Qur'an is knowingly or unknowingly, wittingly or unwittingly, a lackey and agent of the Jews." These are the texts that Khamenei was moved to translate. Khamenei's footnotes as a translator to the text not only do not soften the tone, they usually add more venom to the already bitter narrative.

Iran's three-thousand-year peaceful history with its substantial Jewish population is a repudiation of Khamenei's violent and bigoted worldview. For thirty-six years his regime has disfigured Iran. The citizens of Iran dream of a different tomorrow.

But Ali Khamenei, ensconced in the palace of his supposedly divine dogmas, has cruelly aborted the chance for Iran to realize the possibilities that its unique combination of human, natural, historical, cultural and geostrategic capital affords it. Only on the ruins of his palace can Iran emerge from its benighted days.

SUSIE LINFIELD

The Politics of the Hardened Heart: The Left Since October 7

Cataclysmic world events — the fall of the Soviet Union, the Iranian Revolution, September 11, Donald Trump's ascendancy — should cause cataclysmic, or at least fundamental, changes in thought. To be an intellectual, or a citizen, means to respond to history, to think anew, rather than be beholden to one's oldest, fondest, but no longer useful ideas. The Hamas attack of October 7, 2023 was surely one of those history-altering events; so is the war in Gaza. But rather than inspire honest reassessments and new modes of thought, they have birthed, instead, dangerously Manichean analyses among a coterie of leftist intellectuals. For too many writers, it has evidently become impossible to keep two — much less several — thoughts in one's head simultaneously.

Though some try to simplify, which is to say, falsify, the Israeli-Palestinian conflict, it is one of the most convoluted problems of the past one hundred years. That is a very long time, and rather than abating it has become increasingly, terrifyingly inflamed. Here are two peoples, each with a deeply ingrained sense of persecution and loss, fighting over a tiny land. Here are two national liberation movements — and, increasingly, religious messianic movements — whose members have killed each others' children. After such sorrow, what forgiveness? Any account of the conflict, and any proposals for its resolution (however dim that now seems) must reckon with all this — not occasionally, but consistently and steadily.

This is a difficult task, at which we all fail at times; the cruelty of the Hamas attacks, and of Israel's war in Gaza, have made it immeasurably harder. I sometimes think that too much death and too much hatred have driven us all slightly insane; it sometimes seems that one must choose which one — but only one — of these cruelties to abhor. As if surrendering, in defeat, to the complexity this conflict demands, too many intellectuals have retreated into almost ludicrously reductive modes of thought — what Zadie Smith described, in an essay on the campus protests, as "the atavistic pleasure of violent simplicity"— along with nostalgic reveries, inapt historic analogies, nonsensical proposals, and patently dishonest historic accounts that occlude any possible understanding of the volatile times we are living through. And crucially, they seem to lack the tragic sense of history that this conflict demands. But if intellectuals fail to reveal knowledge and enable critical thinking, it is not clear what value they have.

The tumult and the savagery of the last two years — the October 7 attacks, the Gaza war with its horrific death toll, the abandonment of the hostages, the demonstrations on college campuses and elsewhere against Israel, as well as those in Israel against the government, the vilification of "Zionists," the charges of genocide, the weakening of the "Axis of Resistance," the Twelve Day War between Iran and Israel and America — require a wide-angle lens that can take in many contradictory factors at once. Instead, too many writers have grown more rigid and fastened their blinkers ever more tightly. I will be writing here about the failures of the left — like Albert Memmi, I feel, despite everything, that they are my people — but the right, too, has responded to the atrocities with derangements of its own. The Lilliputian revolutionaries at Columbia and elsewhere who distribute Hamas leaflets and revere Hassan Nasrallah have inspired a kind of moral panic about higher education and the place of Jews within it. For some conservatives, the people of the book have, for perhaps the first time in our history, become enemies of the book. *"Hit Harvard with everything you've got,"* Abe Greenwald, the executive editor of *Commentary*, wrote in May. "The current enemies of the Jews must be taken down. . . . In the present, my thinking is binary. There are the Jews, and there are those who are trying to wipe us out. . . . As far as I'm concerned, Donald Trump can't lean too heavily on Harvard." In a subsequent column, Greenwald decried the "illegal immigrants [who] have spurred on or joined in the Jew-hunt." When it comes to Israel and Palestine, historical complexity, political complexity, and moral complexity are all of a piece. Lose one and you lose them all.

It is possible to find glimmers of alternative ways of thinking on the left — to find, that is, intellectuals who have not betrayed their calling. "I support its genesis unequivocally and loathe its prosecution vehemently," Jack Omer-Jackaman wrote in the left-Zionist magazine *Fathom*, referring to the war against Hamas. But writers who resist the lure of absolutism and who insist on nuanced analyses find themselves accused of spinelessness, cowardice, and moral evasion. To think precisely yet capaciously, and to extend empathy beyond the constricted confines of "our side," is now regarded as a moral and intellectual failure.

Several recent books addressing the war in Gaza, written not by ignorant students shouting "globalize the intifada!" but by public intellectuals and seasoned academics, exemplify the trend toward Manichean thinking: Pankaj Mishra's *The World After Gaza: A History*, Enzo Traverso's *Gaza Faces History*, and Peter *Beinart's*

Being Jewish After the Destruction of Gaza: A Reckoning. Mishra is the author of books on Buddhism and Kashmir, and a contributor to publications such as the *Guardian*, the *New Yorker*, and the *New York Review of Books*. Enzo Traverso, an award-winning Italian historian who currently teaches at Cornell , works in the tradition of critical theory and has been influenced by neo-Marxists. (Though he is not Jewish, so far as I know, he is very interested in Jews; he once wrote a good book called *The Marxists and the Jewish Question*, which analyzed why the former had misunderstood the latter.) Peter Beinart is an editor at large of the anti-Zionist magazine *Jewish Currents*, a contributing Opinion writer to the *New York Times*, and a professor of journalism at the City University of New York.

These books illustrate how anti-Zionism has become not only the central preoccupation of the contemporary left but also the essence of its moral self-affirmation. They share similar strategies of misrepresentation and avoidance. These include rickety — and morally indefensible — comparisons between Nazi Germany and the State of Israel; cherry-picking quotations; lack of context; mischaracterizing the work of other authors; and deceitful, or at best radically incomplete, historical narratives that paint the Israeli-Palestinian conflict as one between mighty imperialists and helpless natives.

The problem with bad history is not just that it is, well, untrustworthy, though certainly that offends anyone who wants that increasingly maligned discipline to flourish. The problem is also practical. We look to history to understand how the perplexities and crises in which we find ourselves came to be. Historians cannot — or at least should not try to — predict the future. Yet it is impossible to think rationally about what might come next and, hopefully, begin to find our way out of the current nightmare of mutual Israeli-Palestinian destruction, without a thorough and honest grounding in the past. The Marxist historian Eric Hobsbawm once wrote that while political passions may influence the questions a historian asks, they should never determine the answers that he finds. This is a lesson the writers under consideration here have not learned, which is why their accounts are closer to ideology than to any commonly recognized intellectual discipline.

"Israel was created by displacing roughly 750,000 Palestinians in 1948, and it displaced several hundred thousand more in 1967," Beinart neatly explains. True, but hardly the whole causal picture: he largely neglects the Arab nations' rejection of partition, which would have created the state of Palestine in 1948, and their invasion of Israel — the original cause of the "displacing." (The origins of the Nakba are now widely obscured; even the *New York Times* uses evasive phrases such as "the conflict that set the boundaries of the Israeli state in 1949," as if no one actually started the 1948 war.) Beinart evades, too, the precipitating events of the 1967 war — which began as a war of existential self-defense — and, therefore, of the occupation of the Palestinian territories. Mishra briefly mentions the Second Intifada but says nothing about the suicide bombings in Israeli cities that were its essence, thereby rendering the demise of the Israeli left unintelligible, and he implies that Israelis had nothing to fear in the lead-up to the 1967 war. (Egypt's expulsion of the UN peacekeepers, its military pact with Jordan and Syria, the buildup of troops on the border, and the bloodthirsty annihilationist promises of Arab leaders, the Palestinian Liberation Organization, and the Arab street are all omitted.) Traverso sums up the mid-century Zionist movement by writing, "Whereas anti-fascists tried to create a mass movement against Nazism, Zionists made an agreement with Hitler"; in doing so he displays not just his own animosities but, more important, an alarming lack of basic historic knowledge. When he asserts that Hamas has "condemned... antisemitism," that its fight is "not against the Jews," that has accepted a Palestinian state within the 1967 borders, and that it is "defending" besieged Gazans, he has entered a world of delusion. "I am not a specialist on the Middle East, nor on the Arab-Israeli conflict, nor on Palestine," he pleads. Clearly this is true. He evinces as little understanding of jihadist Islamism as he does of Zionism.

By consistently denying the Israeli history of vulnerability, these writers make Israeli politics seem unaccountably malicious and the Israeli psyche inexplicable, even delusional. They also make it seem as though the current decimation of Gaza is just another iteration of Israel's conventional policy toward the Palestinians; in fact, both the October 7 massacres and the destruction of Gaza are precipitous and despicable deviations from the past. Presenting such drastically simplified — and even worse, patently false — accounts of an infernally complex conflict makes productive thinking, which is to say politically useful thinking, impossible. By doing so, these writers condemn Israelis — and, even more so, Palestinians — to continued suffering. This is a betrayal of the very people they profess to defend.

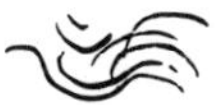

But each of these books also accomplishes an exigent task: they insist that we confront the destruction of Gaza, a destruction that, long before the ceasefire and hostage release were arranged in October, no longer had any conceivable military rationale and continued to shred Israel's moral standing. Yet it is a fantasy that the war in Gaza could ever have been either simple or morally clean. I do not mean to suggest only that innocents die in all wars. Any war against Hamas, hidden in underground tunnels and among civilians, would have led to high civilian deaths — something that Yahya Sinwar certainly figured into his strategic-apocalyptic calculations and in fact sought for propaganda purposes. Even a liberal Israeli government would have waged a justifiably fierce war after the murders, rapes, and kidnappings of October 7. Nor could the hostages have been saved by commando raids; this was not Entebbe. And yet it is now inescapable that, long before I wrote this in the late summer of 2025, the death raining down on Palestinians each day had no purpose *other* than death. Gazans were (and as of this writing still are) starving, Gazans were (and still are) sick, Gazans are orphans. Gazans are homeless, bereaved, and shell-shocked. The cruelty of the Hamas atrocities has been met by the cruelty of the Israeli response.

This catastrophe for Palestinians is also a catastrophe for

Israelis, though they may not know it yet; with some exceptions, the Israeli media has shielded its audience from the reality in Gaza. In doing so, they have failed their population and their increasingly tattered democracy. (The country is now ruled by a rogue government that is crushing democratic norms as much as it can.) Far from protecting Israelis, this ignorance has endangered them — though they could of course discover the truth if they wished. Three fears now haunt me. First, that Palestinian society will never be able to reconstitute itself. The demolition — of people, families, clans, social relations, homes, schools, universities, hospitals, shops, restaurants, businesses, and everything else that constitutes a world — may be too complete. What is there to return to? Second, that when the war does end, Israel will be unable — and unwilling — to begin the excruciating process of confronting its failures and crimes, including its abandonment of the hostages. Third, that the state of the Jewish people will remain an international pariah for the rest of my life.

But Beinart's book also points to the ways that left-wing thinking after October 7 has calcified. He views any version of political Zionism as a form of Jewish "supremacy," and he has long advocated a single "democratic binational state" in what had been Mandatory Palestine. Presumably, the lions and the lambs — or rather, the lions of Israel's messianic right and those of Hamas and Islamic Jihad — will lie down together and nuzzle each other toward democracy and mutual acceptance. Always a fantasy, this vision has become ever more imaginary since October 7. "I'm not going to be fellow citizens with any of Gaza's Nukhba Forces terrorists or their hundreds of thousands of supporters," the historian Fania Oz-Salzberger, a longtime member of the peace camp, recently told *Haaretz*. "There will be no one state, Israel-Palestine, in our lifetimes, and probably not our children's lifetimes, because the next generation are victims of October 7 too — on both sides." Yet the Hamas attacks have done nothing to shake Beinart's beliefs: a sure sign that he is responding not to events on the ground — not to the history that men and women actually make — but to the ideological chorus in his head which insists, against all evidence, that he must be right.

A tragically confounding repercussion of the October 7 massacres is that they made the need for a Palestinian state alongside (not instead of) Israel both more pressing and less possible; a substantive majority of Jewish Israelis now oppose it. (The journalist Akiva Eldar bitterly describes this as Hamas' victory.) But Beinart has long held, and still maintains, that Israelis' fear of a Palestinian state has little to do with current or even recent events. It is, rather, an anachronistic holdover of "Jewish trauma" rooted in the Holocaust — a view that is one of the oldest and cheapest debating points in this controversy. He explicated this view in *Jewish Currents* in 2020: "Ever since the Holocaust, Jews have retroactively projected Nazism's exterminationist program on Palestinian opposition to pre state Zionism. But this Holocaust lens distorts how Palestinians actually behaved: not like genocidal Jew-haters, but rather like other peoples seeking national rights."

The distortion, however, is Beinart's. To support this thesis in his new book, he must, of necessity, erase more than seventy-five years of history. He largely ignores the decades of irredentist terror attacks that aimed to destroy the Jewish state and created the Israeli sense of precarity. That sense is *empirical*: it is based in Israel's history, not neurosis, and it was, inevitably, radically exacerbated by the massacres of October 7. When Oz-Sulzberger recently observed that "there's not a single person [in Israel] who cannot be described as 'post-traumatic,'" she was referring to the Hamas attacks and the subsequent war — definitely not to the Holocaust. And in fact, much, though not all, of the Palestinian movement, from the pre Oslo PLO to today's Hamas and Islamic Jihad, has been openly exterminationist, as are Hezbollah and Iran; this is hardly a paranoid Jewish fantasy. The cause of justice will not be furthered by such willful misinterpretations. Beinart would do well to look more to the full inventory of facts — to the suicide bombings and the burning of the kibbutzim — and less to Hitler. Instead he, like Mishra and Traverso, leaves readers with the impression that Israelis have lived in relative peace and security for the past seventy-five years and are simply relentless, irrational warmongers who love sending their children into battle. Judging from my own experience of teaching in an American university, this is the only "history" that many students know. But surely it is the job of any responsible intellectual to offer far more than highly selective historic accounts that evade inconvenient, yet absolutely salient, facts.

Pankaj Mishra was born in India in 1969 and raised in a Brahmin family of Hindu nationalists, and his book is in part a *Bildungsroman* that traces his trajectory from a naïve philo-Zionist to a sectarian anti-Zionist. Growing up in the 1970s, he had never met a Jew, but he was an ardent admirer of what he regarded as Zionism's muscular nationalism and its ethos of self-reliance and self-respect. A photograph of Moshe Dayan adorned his bedroom wall.

Mishra takes pains to express his admiration for the Jewish people, and especially for those (dead) twentieth-century Jewish intellectuals who did so much to create the modern world. His book opens with quotations from Primo Levi, Hannah Arendt, and Sigmund Freud; he also likes Marx, Luxemburg, Trotsky, Einstein, Kafka, and Proust. He exhibits a welcome sensitivity to the Jewish history of exclusion, pariahdom, and persecution, although he seems to think that such adversity began in the nineteenth century. "At different times in my life, and in diverse ways, I had been aware of the uniqueness of the Jewish fate, and felt an affinity to it," he writes.

But there is one kind of Jew that, today, Mishra does not like: the Zionist who is very much alive. Perhaps inevitably, his adolescent love affair with the Jewish national movement — his "wistful historical romance" — could not last. In 2008 he traveled to the West Bank, where he witnessed Palestinian oppression firsthand. He also discovered — and here he falls into one of the most hollow cliches of our time — "people who looked like me." (A quick Google Images search reveals this to be true only if one subscribes to the racist notion that all nonCaucasians look alike.) Unfortunately, Mishra's fixation on the "color line," and his insistence on viewing global conflicts as a manifestation of it, lead him to radically misunderstand the intensely national-religious essence of the Israeli-Palestinian conflict. And, I would argue, others: terrible conflagrations — think of Ukraine and Sudan — that have nothing to do with race. In those places, the killers look just like the killed, as they often do in Israel and Palestine. Compare the photographs of fallen IDF soldiers with those of Hamas and Hezbollah fighters on their "martyrdom" posters: you will find two groups of young men who look like (but are not) brothers.

I have neither the desire nor the ability to defend the Israel of Benjamin Netanyahu and his Kahanist confreres. Still, it is hard to accept Mishra's view that contemporary Israel is the most immoral place on Earth, bar none. In his telling, every aspect of its culture, including its literature, exploits the Holocaust. (Has he read any Israeli novelists lately?) Its Arab citizens and its Mizrahi ones, in his account, are objects of unrelenting humiliation and racist repression. Its "national ethos" is "pitiless." It is a "laboratory . . . used by other ethnonationalists to repress their peoples." In sum, the country is a "calamitous failure" and "the portent of the future of a bankrupt and exhausted world."

It is obviously true that, after the trauma of October 7, Israel is suffering from the "pathologies of survivalist nationalism," as Mishra charges. But he doesn't pay October 7 much mind. *The World After Gaza* is littered with detailed descriptions of Israeli atrocities, including "snipers shooting children in the head, often twice" and "metal sticks inserted into the rectum of naked prisoners." Such horrors must be written about until they stop; no amount of outrage is too much — though here, as throughout his book, Mishra unaccountably provides no source notes. Yet how is it possible that the atrocities of Hamas — who, after all, instigated the war — are of so little concern? Mishra is too delicate, or dogmatic, to mention the Hamas rapes and mutilations, the families burned alive, the terrified children and old people kidnapped and then murdered. And he entirely ignores the jihadists' glee. Is he embarrassed by the sadism of these so-called anticolonialists? Or is it simply that, in his view, Jewish lives don't matter?

Enzo Traverso also makes light of October 7. Like too many others on the left — Judith Butler, for example, and the editors of the *Intercept* — he insists that there is "no proof" of Hamas rapes, and he derides the "inventions" and "fantastical rumors" of Hamas atrocities propagated by the Israelis and the perfidious Western media, strangely unaware that Hamas itself proudly disseminated its abominations. In Traverso's world, as in Mishra's, cruelty, and what the latter calls the "orgy of bestial violence," has only one address. Here is the Manichean mind at work: in this view, one can oppose Israeli crimes in Gaza only by ignoring the barbaric (a word Traverso puts in sarcastic quotation marks) Hamas attacks. The dialectical imagination seems to have failed at precisely the moment it is required.

Aside from being repulsive, the denial of Hamas' barbarism (no quotation marks) is confusing, for it makes everything that has happened since October 7 difficult to understand. Mishra does, however, have a theory about the Gazan war and its ferocity — and it is here that his fundamentalist obsession with race leads to his most foolish, indeed absurd, pronouncements. For Mishra, the massacres of October 7 were a blow against the "fierce fortress mentalities" of "white supremacism." He writes, "The surprise assault . . . represents, after 9/11, the twenty-first century's second Pearl Harbor to many shocked and horrified white majoritarians. And, as before, the perception among them that white power had been publicly violated has 'triggered . . . a rage bordering on the genocidal.'"

Are only "white majoritarians," whomever they are, shocked and horrified by the deliberate murder of children? Is Zionism synonymous with "white power"? Is Netanyahu's pitilessness toward Gazans best understood as that of a white supremacist, rather than of a cynical opponent, even a hater, of Palestinians and Palestinian sovereignty in any form? Mishra's racialist analysis, which is shared by writers such as Ta-Nehisi Coates, makes neither moral nor political sense. This is the dead end to which racial reductionism leads.

Mishra and Traverso argue mightily against Israel's exploitation of the Holocaust to further its political aims. And they are right: think, for instance, of the Israeli delegation to the United Nations wearing yellow stars after October 7. But, just like the Israelis whom they condemn, these writers are imprisoned in a repetition compulsion and prone to the very pathology they decry.

Traverso never actually claims that Israelis are Nazis, but his steady barrage of Nazi-Israeli analogies could well lead readers to believe that they are. He compares the assertion that Hamas' attacks precipitated the war in Gaza, which is obviously true, to the fallacious claims of the right-wing German historian Ernst Nolte, who notoriously attempted to rationalize Nazi crimes as a reaction to the rise of Bolshevism. Palestinians rejoicing over the Hamas massacres are likened to "the wan smile[s] on the faces of Auschwitz inmates when they heard the news of the bombing of German cities." These analogies move from the perverse to the obscene when he writes that Hamas fighters "inevitably suggest" the partisans of the Warsaw Ghetto. As we shall see, Traverso is hardly alone in twisting the most noble moments of the anti-Nazi resistance into support for the anti-Zionist cause. This is a desecration of the dead.

Mishra argues, rightly, against conflating Palestinians and Nazis, as Netanyahu and members of his far-right government have. But like Traverso, he has no compunctions about conflating Israelis and Nazis. He opens his book with an account of the screams emanating from the Warsaw Ghetto and segues, two quick pages later, to the screams of a Gazan mother. From a humanitarian perspective, this makes sense: suffering is suffering and all screams are alike. This is the basis upon which NGOs such as Doctors Without Borders operate. But Mishra is a political critic, not an aid worker, which means that his job is to make distinctions. His analogy here omits so much as to be morally specious. The Jewish leadership of the Warsaw Ghetto had not launched a murderous attack against German civilians, much less promised to do so again, nor was it dedicated to eradicating the German state and its citizens. The Nazi assault on the Jewish people, in the Warsaw Ghetto as elsewhere, was entirely gratuitous; the Israeli war against Hamas, though indefensibly brutal, is not.

Still, the Nazi analogies pour forth in successive waves. Mishra compares the Israeli victory in the Six-Day War to the Nazi Blitzkrieg, thereby ignoring the difference between self-defense and murderous aggression. He writes that "both Nazi Germany and Israel seemed determined to cleanse their states of alien and potentially disloyal elements" — a claim he supports in the latter case with zero facts. He quotes Victor Klemperer, who called the Zionists "just as offensive as the Nazis." (Klemperer, a proud German patriot, was the rare Jew who remained in Germany during the war and survived.) Mishra can find no real distinction between what he calls Israel's "legacy of the Shoah" and the German project of *Lebensraum*.

This Pavlovian invocation of the Holocaust is not a nervous tic. It has a clear, though never quite admitted, political purpose. Its aim is not to stop the ongoing destruction of Gaza, to undermine Netanyahu's crazy government, or to support the democratic forces in Israel. All these are worthy, indeed necessary goals; none requires use of the term "Nazi." The purpose is, rather, to delegitimize the Zionist movement: past, present, and most of all, future. In this view, Zionism was not a response to genocide; it is synonymous *with* genocide, and has been at least since the state was founded. (In fact, the Zionist movement was born decades *before* the genocide against the Jews, as a response to antisemitism and persecution, and the *yishuv* was developed before Hitler came to power.) Mishra and Traverso accuse Israelis of weaponizing the Holocaust in support of their political project, but they are themselves guilty of this: they hijack the Holocaust to delegitimize Zionism in any iteration.

This is not a theoretical issue. The equation of Zionism and Nazism became a trope of the global protests that exploded immediately after October 7, as the plethora of protest banners with swastikas and Stars of David attest. The presumed similarities, albeit imaginary, between the two movements have seeped into other aspects of political life and will, I am certain, continue to do so, though sometimes in reverse ways. In June, Zohran Mamdani, then a Democratic candidate for mayor in New York City, tried to justify the slogan "Globalize the intifada" by likening it (shades of Traverso) to the Warsaw Ghetto Uprising. (The U.S. Holocaust Memorial Museum, which Mamdani cited as support for his comments, quickly rejected them as "outrageous.") I have no reason to believe that Mamdani is an antisemite, yet in some sense I think that is irrelevant. I do know that while in college he founded a chapter of the stridently anti-Zionist group Students for Justice in Palestine, supports the anti-Israel boycott campaign and its "right of return," is a member of the Democratic Socialists of America ("for a free Palestine from the river to the sea"), and criticized Israel, not Hamas, directly after October 7. These are his instincts, his innate political ideas. But as with the issue of campus antisemitism, his electoral victory has inspired a moral panic among some Jews. *The New York Times* reported that Jill Kargman, a Jewish writer, likened Mamdani's primary electoral victory to "a spiritual Kristallnacht." This perverse desire to appropriate the suffering of others is as ugly as any other usurpation of the Holocaust. (Mamdani, a gifted politician, has since tried to modify his intifada remarks, though he has twisted himself into a pretzel in doing so.)

The most bizarre example of the Zionist-Nazi conflation and of Holocaust appropriation occurred this past June at the meeting of the First Jewish Anti-Zionist Congress (yes, that's a thing), which convened in Vienna. The city was chosen, a speaker named Dalia Sarig explained, because Austria was "the very country where Herzl launched Zionism as a racist colonist ideology"; she added that contemporary Austria, which is supposedly in a "deliberate alliance with Zionism," remains "on the wrong side of history." (Austria was Hitler's birthplace and home to a rabidly antisemitic fascist movement, which might also place it on the wrong side of history.) "We are following in their footsteps," an anti-Zionist Israeli named Ronnie Barkan proclaimed, referring to the Warsaw Ghetto's fighters. (Yes, yet again.) The dead could not rest in peace: in an astonishing statement, Barkan avowed that most of "the six million Jews who died in the Holocaust . . . were anti-Zionist." Turning from the past to the future, Haim Bresheeth, a professor at London's prestigious School of Oriental and African Studies, helpfully explained that "like de-Nazification in 1945, there has to be a de-Zionization of every single institution, every single group" in Israel in order to transform the Zionist hellhole into the Palestinian heaven. Conference participants chanted "Neither Herzl nor Hitler!" in unison. By coincidence, the convention was held as Israel was bombing Iran's nuclear facilities, assassinating its scientists and military leaders, and controlling the country's airspace. This did not prevent an Egyptian journalist named Rahma Zein from confidently predicting "the beginning of the end of Zionism."

It is easy to dismiss the Vienna conference as a form of lunacy divorced from history, morality, and the reality principle. But its essential ideas are easy to find in more sober and intellectually respected venues. In a recent issue of *New Left Review Sidecar*, the French philosopher Frederic Lordon argued that "anti-Zionism, far from being equivalent to antisemitism, is a bulwark against it." He added, "Here then, the fundamental features of Zionism are exposed in full light: it is colonial, racist — that much was already clear — and, when necessary, genocidal. . . And this, after all, is logical: there is no Zionism with a human face."

Needless to say, or maybe now it is necessary to say, such a mentality precludes empathy, which depends, precisely, on the recognition of a human face. Since October 7, we have witnessed the stark division of the world into victims and perpetrators; in this telling, Israel could not have been the former on October 7 because it is the latter in Gaza and the West Bank. (Though it should not be forgotten even for a moment that Hamas, too, is a perpetrator in Gaza: against Israeli hostages, Israeli troops, and Palestinian civilians.) Traverso complains that "while Israel destroys Gaza under a hail of bombs, Israel is presented as the victim of 'the greatest pogrom in history after the Holocaust'." Yet both parts of that sentence are true; one does not negate the other. Indeed, to understand anything that has happened in the past two years, and that might happen in the future, one is required to understand that both parts of that sentence are true. In Traverso's view, October 7 was a project of Israel rather than of Hamas, for the attacks were "methodically prepared by those who would now like to be seen as victims." By insisting that "victim" and "Israeli" are antonyms—even when the latter are murdered—Traverso expels Israelis, which is to say Jews, from the family of man. This is hardly a new phenomenon.

Jews in the twentieth century became prime symbols of modernity and, therefore, of the revolt against it. Jews were viewed as the messengers of capitalism and communism, of psychoanalysis and the revolution in physics, of the cosmopolitan, the universal, and the secular. Jews were regarded as the agents of social and economic transformation and of educational achievement rather than inherited privilege, which means they were also identified as the culprits of instability and anxiety, and bitterly resented as such.

Against all this, the Zionists aimed to create a normal state — which, they believed, would dispel the Jews' punishing symbolic centrality and be the solvent for antisemitism. And which, they hoped, would be accepted by the world community of nations. But despite this desire for normalcy, the new Jewish state inherited the symbolic burdens that the Jewish people had carried for so long. Israel, Mishra writes, "was always going to have greater significance than the creation of any other new state. . . Jews in Israel and the diaspora would remain as both objects and agents at the very heart of the modern world's vast and fateful confrontations." This has proved to be true, but Mishra never questions *why* this obsession with the Jew — an obsession that he fully shares — has persisted. And crucially, he fails to understand how this worldwide fixation on the Jew explains, at least in part, why Gaza has captured the imagination of the global left in ways that nothing else has — or could — and why it has assumed such a central place in the culture wars. Last June at the Glastonbury music festival in

Britain, the punk rap duo Bob Vylan led an enthusiastic crowd in screaming "Death, death to the I.D.F!" Israelis are, so far as I know, the only national group that is boycotted by the cultural elite of writers, artists, and academics in the West.

Palestine, too, is fetishized — though in the opposite way. If the Jewish state represents the malicious and the powerful, Palestine represents the good and the powerless. The Egyptian-American writer Hussein Aboubakr Mansour has observed that by the end of World War II many Arab intellectuals, both secular and Islamist, viewed Palestine as "the crucible of sacred history, the test of moral truth, and the goal of redemptive war." This attitude permeates today's global left, which regards the Gazan war, and by extension Israel, as uniquely criminal. "Much has happened in the world in recent years," Mishra writes, and then adds, astonishingly, "Yet no disaster compares to Gaza." In what must be a conscious echo of the ways in which many historians and philosophers have regarded the Holocaust — think of Adorno's proscription against writing poetry after Auschwitz — Mishra writes that the Gaza war "has ruptured time" and is "the defining event" of our century.

I bristled when I read these words. Other recent disasters — Rwanda, Bosnia, Darfur, Congo, Ethiopia, Sudan, Syria — have had higher casualties than those of the Gazan war, and the cruelties to which their victims were subjected, including torture and mass rape, were no less severe. Apparently, however, they did not rupture time (except, perhaps, for their victims). Yet at the same time, I — and, I believe, many others — expect more, much more, of Israel than I do of Rwandan or Serbian death squads. And although Israel prohibits journalists from entering Gaza, the entire world (other than Israelis) has witnessed its razing — now it looks like a moonscape — and the subjection of its inhabitants to two years of carnage, fear, hunger, expulsion, and deprivation of humanitarian aid. One can debate the term "genocide" — though I doubt that Palestinians under bombardment care too much about nomenclature — but there is no way to normalize this. There is no doubt that the Gazan war, and the world's inability to stop it, has outraged, electrified, and radicalized a generation. In his book *One Day, Everyone Will Have Always Been Against This*, the Egyptian-American author Omar El Akkad writes of how Gaza bred his disillusionment with the West's human rights commitments: "And yet I believed the cracks could be fixed, that the thing at the core, whatever it was, was salvageable. Until the fall of 2023. Until the slaughter." He predicts that Gaza will "be remembered as the moment millions of people looked at the west, the rules-based order, the shell of modern liberalism. . . and said: I want nothing to do with this." That may be true, and yet I can't help but wonder: having rejected the modern liberalism of the West, where will El Akkad look to create a world of justice, the rule of law, and diminished violence?

Throughout his book, El Akkad scorns the concept of complexity, which he associates with moral evasion. But complexity is unavoidable. It is true that Israel is guilty of war crimes, and of indefensible brutality, in Gaza. It is equally true that in Gaza Jews are the ones dropping the bombs and sending in the soldiers, which to much of the world makes those bombs and those soldiers immediately suspect. Syria, too, looks like a moonscape; I doubt that Bob Vylan ever voiced a whisper of protest against the bombs that Bashar al-Assad dropped for thirteen years, not to mention his torture gulag. Mishra can claim that "no disaster compares to Gaza" because for him Israel is not a complicated country embroiled in a multi-faceted conflict and a messy war but, rather, a symbolic Rorschach test: "Simply by existing, Israel holds up a mirror, impelling other peoples and societies to identify themselves and their moral consciousness," he writes. This is precisely the role to which the Jewish people — *simply by existing* — have been assigned for thousands of years. And this is why Mishra's account of Israel, the Israeli-Palestinian conflict, and even the Gazan war are, of necessity, so tendentious. Jews are the eternal Other, a "mirror" for the world to use. As such they, and the state they built, are expected to be better than others but always turn out to be worse than others. They cannot be morally complex, which means they cannot be fully human.

A common strategy of manipulative polemicists is the misuse of quotations, either by omitting their larger context or distorting their original meaning. This device is a key technique of Mishra's book: a veritable tsunami of quotations pours down on the eventually exhausted reader. He especially likes to cite Jewish thinkers, such as George Steiner (twice), who called Israel "a bitter relic, an absurdity." The aim is clear: everybody — even Woody Allen! — dislikes Zionism and the country it created. Mishra claims to be writing a history, but intellectual honesty demands that even the most partisan accounts be accurate and provide the necessary background. And there is something cowardly about the way he hides behind the words of others, using them to say what he doesn't quite want to articulate outright.

Mishra addresses a famous debate when he quotes Hannah Arendt's oft-cited letter to Gershom Scholem in 1946, in which she argued against Jewish sovereignty as "stupid and dangerous." Yet Scholem's response is mysteriously absent: "You denounce Jews in Palestine for maintaining an otherworldly separation from the rest of mankind, but when these same Jews make efforts to fend for themselves. . . you react with . . . derision." But it is Scholem's criticism of Arendt's arrogant purism which speaks to our post-October 7 moment. He noted that Zionism "has created a situation of despair, doubt, and compromise — precisely because it takes place on earth, not on the moon. . . The Zionist movement shares this dialectical experience of the Real (and all its catastrophic possibilities) with all other movements that have taken it upon themselves to change something in the real world."

Mishra also makes the common mistake of confusing criticism, however harsh, of Israeli policies with anti-Zionism. The reader who approaches this book with scant historical knowledge will leave with the false impression that writers such as Primo Levi, Pierre Vidal-Naquet, and I.B. Singer were anti-Zionists. Levi's voice weaves throughout the book as one of its most prominent; Mishra has the chutzpah to imply that Levi's reflections on the

Nazi genocide suggest that he would have agreed with Mishra's own views on Gaza. In short, Mishra uses Jewish writers as objects of his own projections, just as he uses the Jewish people.

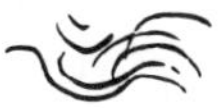

Yet his book's most egregious misrepresentations concern the work of the critic Jean Amery, whose austere, unforgiving writings have had a profound influence on my own thoughts and emotions. Mishra's exploitation of Amery feels like a wound, because Pankaj Mishra is exactly the kind of leftist thinker that Amery feared and reviled.

Amery was born as Hans Mayer in Vienna in 1912, the son of a Catholic mother and a Jewish father who was killed fighting for the Kaiser in World War I. Growing up, he had no connection to Jews or Judaism. Amery had never read the Bible or attended a shul; he knew nothing of Jewish history or rituals, and he remained staunchly anti-religious throughout his life. But with the promulgation of the Nuremberg Laws in 1935, he realized that he had become "a dead man on leave." In 1943 he was arrested in Belgium for distributing anti-Nazi leaflets and was tortured by the Gestapo which, upon discovering his Jewish identity, sent him to Auschwitz. After the war he moved to Brussels and took his new nonGerman name (an anagram of Mayer). In 1964 — the time of Germany's Auschwitz trials, which would shake the younger generation — he began addressing a German audience in a series of severe, implacable radio lectures, including "Resentments" and "The Intellectual in Auschwitz." Amery described himself as a "catastrophe Jew": it was Hitler who made him a Jew and a Zionist. He always rejected the soothing designation "survivor." In 1978, at the age of sixty-five — in ill health, depressed, and embroiled in an unhappy love triangle — he killed himself.

Mishra, too, has been influenced by Amery, and his account of the writer is, as far as it goes, highly sympathetic. He is especially taken by Amery's insistence that torture — including that of Palestinian prisoners by Israelis — is a red line that can never be crossed. But Mishra never reflects upon the gist of Amery's later political writings: the series of essays about — and addressed to — the European New Left, which he wrote in the 1960s and 1970s. This was the era of PLO terrorism; of the Syrian-Egyptian war against Israel; of the Arab states' unyielding, violent opposition to Israel's existence. Amery castigated the young revolutionaries' idealization of Palestinian terrorism as a betrayal of the humanist values to which the left has, in its best moments, subscribed. Moreover, he argued that the left's relentless delegitimization of Israel could, in league with its armed enemies, lead to the state's destruction — and he regarded that state as the sole guarantor of Jewish survival.

Reading Amery's essays today, in our desolate post-October 7 world, is a spooky experience. Written over fifty years ago, they make me wonder if the bleakest histories and the most dangerous intellectual delusions will simply continue to repeat themselves. Amery always considered himself a man of the left, and he described a political landscape much like our own, in which "those of us who have been compelled to recognize that we bear the Jewish lot have been expelled from the community of which we were a part only yesterday." Expelled, that is, unless, like Naomi Klein and M. Gessen, one abjures Zionism. They are the left's definition of the Good Jew.

Amery elaborated several key ideas in these essays that are as true today as when he wrote them. First, that anti-Zionism would inevitably inspire antisemitism: "This much is for sure: antisemitism resides in anti-Israelism and anti-Zionism as the thunderstorm does in the cloud." Protesting that one doesn't hate Jews — that one even likes them! — is of no account; what matters is one's political stance. He bemoaned the "terrifyingly simplistic" analyses of the Palestinian refugee problem, which are still in full bloom today. He critiqued the aggrandizement of the conflict — evident in the books under consideration here — which had transformed it from a "normal" territorial dispute into a metaphysical battle between good and evil. He noted that the "Middle Eastern question" — in today's parlance, the war in Gaza and, more recently, between Iran and Israel — is in fact the Jewish Question.

Most of all, Amery noted a tendency that is glaringly evident in the works of Beinart, Traverso, and Mishra. Anti-Zionism has become, to some on the pro-Palestinian left, a way station on the road to utopia. "Antisemitism in the guise of anti-Zionism has come to be seen to be virtuous," Amery charged. Cleansing the world of Israel will also cleanse it of colonialism, imperialism, racism, inequality, and war. It is, you might say, the ultimate mitzvah.

Here is the twisted mutation of our — and Amery's — time. Ordinarily, the project of eradicating a nation is considered a fascist one: think of Hitler with Poland, Pakistan with Bangladesh, Nigeria with Biafra, Russia with Ukraine. When it comes to the one country in the world that represents the Jewish people, however, annihilation — or, in more polite parlance, Zionism's "dismantling" or "undoing" — becomes a purportedly progressive demand. Amery charged that this eliminationist anti-Zionism represented a "total conceptual confusion and the ultimate loss of moral and political standards." He was right.

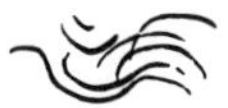

There are some writers on the left who have resisted the temptations of simplicity, which is to say that they have continued to think. Last year, Raphaël Glucksmann and Daniel Cohn-Bendit wrote in *Le Monde*: "We mourned with the Israelis on October 7, 2023. . . We are deeply attached to the existence of Israel, and we are well aware of the extent to which Hamas, Hezbollah, and the Iranian theocracy . . . aim to destroy it." Perhaps thinking of the likes of Traverso and Mishra, they condemned those in the international left whose refusal of empathy for the murdered Israelis was "tinged with antisemitism and remains repugnant." But, they continued,

> We cannot bear the unbearable. The total destruction of Gaza is unbearable... How can we fail to see the piling up of corpses

> in Gaza and the methodical annihilation of any possibility of a Palestinian state with the colonization of the West Bank? . . . Are we going to close our eyes to the suffering of the Palestinian and Lebanese people because others have refused to open theirs to Israeli suffering?

Why is it so hard to say both these things — all these things — at the same time, in the same breath? And doesn't the inability to do so render any individual sentence morally bankrupt? Glucksmann and Cohn-Bendit are, I believe, the true sons of Amery, for like him they insist that the offenses committed against us must not be elided — and must, simultaneously, open us up to the wounds for which we are ourselves responsible.

I have no solution to the Israeli-Palestinian conflict, or even to the modes of thought that I have criticized here. Frankly, I have given up on solutions for the moment, though not on a cessation of the killing. When I seek glimpses of light in the darkness, I usually find them among left-wing Israelis, who of necessity are more realistic, and more ethically acute, than "progressives" in the West. Those I look to are a small and beleaguered minority, but not, I would argue, an irrelevant one. The group Standing Together, which is neither an NGO nor a political party, consists of (mainly young) Jewish and Arab Israelis working to organize a mass movement in support of peace and equality for all Israelis; its bold and beautiful aim is to build "a shared home for all of us." Its fifth annual conference, held in July in the Galilee (one month after the Jewish Anti-Zionist Conference in Vienna!), drew hundreds of people under the slogan "Building Power, Making Peace." These brave activists, who refuse cynicism and despair, are fighting against the headwinds of an increasingly racist, ultra-nationalist society marked by escalating settler terrorism — and impunity — in the West Bank. But perhaps strong trees will grow from the seeds they are planting.

Far more courageous, by necessity, are the members of the Gaza Youth Committee, a tiny NGO based in the decimated territory and directed by Rami Aman, who lives in exile in Egypt.

(In 2020, after participating in a Zoom meeting with Israeli peace activists, he was arrested and tortured by Hamas.) Echoing small groups of Israelis who attend demonstrations while silently holding photographs of Gazan children killed in Israeli airstrikes, members of the Youth Committee recently posted pictures of themselves displaying photos of the Bibas children who, along with their mother, were kidnapped and murdered in captivity by Hamas. In Israel, the Gaza Youth Committee's postings went viral. Despite Palestinians' anguish, Aman told *Haaretz*, "[we] still recognize the humanity of 'the 'other'." The organization recently launched a video campaign, aimed at Israelis, called "We Live Together, We Die Together."

It may be that amid the carnage, fear, distrust and hatred, there are few people in Israel or Palestine who want to hear this or would believe it if they did. Yet that message, that value, of solidarity is the one that must be listened to if the ruin of two peoples is to be avoided — or, rather, stopped. (I hope it is not too late.) Once again, Amery's words should be heeded. Even in the midst of Palestinian terrorism and despite his genuine fears of another Holocaust, he insisted to Israelis, "Acknowledge that your freedom can be achieved only with your Palestinian cousin, not against him."

JAMES WOLCOTT

Gloire Days

Though democracy is ostensibly the opposite of monarchy, the mass culture that is American democracy has betrayed in every age a deep atavistic yearning for royalty. From the days of "King" Andrew Jackson to those of the "Kingfish," Huey Long; from the era of the Robber Barons to the age of the movie "kings" and "queens"; from the first black demagogues, Marcus Garvey and Father Divine, to the "Prophet," Elijah Muhammed; from the earliest Mafia chieftains to the bowing, kneeling, and hand-kissing of The Godfather*; from the regal F.D.R. to the "Imperial Presidency" of President John F. Kennedy to the Great Pretender, Richard Nixon (who ordered the White House police costumed in the Graustarkian uniforms of European palace guards), Americans have fulfilled their craving for royalty and the trappings of royalty in so many ways that the impulse to set up kings and worship them must be reckoned one of the basic features of the national character.*

—FROM ALBERT GOLDMAN'S *PROLOGUE TO ELVIS*, 1981

Every king, no matter how humble or dubious his origins, requires a palace, a lavish sanctuary where he can hold court and hang with the homies, sign documents with a flourish, consign enemies to shackles, and seek comfort in the soft recesses of a favored mistress when the missus is in one of her "moods." A noble pile where he can privately indulge his appetites for feasting, elaborate theatricals, and ample helpings of flattery, gossip, and groveling. Elvis Presley, the King of Rock and Roll, whose incarnation as Sun King was proclaimed by the gold lame suit worn with a swagger on the album cover of *50,000,000 Elvis Fans Can't Be Wrong: Elvis's Gold Records, Vol 2*, escaped the squealing throngs behind the gates of Graceland, where he relaxed and roistered until pudge and pharmaceuticals took over. Hugh Hefner's Playboy Mansion West, described as "Versailles in miniature," offered a distinctly American pairing of pagan hedonism and the Protestant work ethic. Michael Jackson, the diamond-gloved King of Pop, took his leave at the Neverland Ranch compound, about which the less said the better.

They were all descendants of the original Sun King, Louis XIV of France, whose reign spanned a staggering seventy-two years, 1643 to 1715. He reigned over, and from, the clockwork operetta stage of Versailles, the star of this story. In South Florida, where dreams go to glisten, the incorporated vision of Versailles as palace, command center, and clubhouse for the elite resides at Mar-a-Lago, the Palm Beach enclave that functions as a personal estate, membership club, feeding trough for donors and dealmakers, and a theme park with a singular, irregular attraction: its owner President Donald J. Trump, the man who would be Sun King.

For aspiring world conquerors and other overachievers, for supercity planners from Dubai to Abu Dhabi, Versailles remains the gold standard of grandeur — literally, symbolically, aesthetically. Other palaces may possess a touristy charm, museum-quality artifacts, a storied past, crenelations, buttresses, and whatnot, but when it comes to historical resonance, architectural beauty, stately grounds (gardens, fountains, topiary, statuary, the orangery, the Great Lawn), scientific advancement, political intrigue, legendary dalliances, epigrammatic witticisms, piercing repartee, sumptuous banqueting, and voluminous anecdotal lore, nothing surpasses Versailles for enduring transplendence. It was the birthplace of ballet and for that alone we should bend the knee and try not to creak.

At its peak of importance, Versailles was immensely full of itself, chin high with hauteur and pinched in every orifice. And why not? Once Louis XIV relocated the royal court and government to Versailles in 1682, it supplanted Paris as the capital of France and considered itself a society apart ("*ce pays-ci,*" as it was known to its residents, "this country"), outfitted with its own distinctive mores, etiquette, protocols, code phrases, pecking order, and personal locomotion: the "Versailles glide," in which women, encased in *grand panniers* covered in layers of rich, adorned fabric, slid across the floor as if on rollers. Since no one in court was permitted to turn their back to the king, the assembled would form ranks, bow, and back out of the room like little choo-choo trains. This reverse exit is one of the entertaining tidbits in the film *Jeanne du Barry*, starring Maiwen as Louis XV's mistress and a rouged Johnny Depp drolly pursing his lips as the king. At one point in the film Marie Antoinette chucks a fit over being denied entry to the royal chamber, exclaiming, "This is ridiculous!," only to be coolly corrected, "No. It's Versailles."

The flipside of Versailles' decorum, refinement, and strict politesse was a latrine funk swamping the air until it almost approached sentience. The shortage of bathrooms, urinals, bidets, and sanitation infrastructure resulted in a tidal buildup that turned parts of the palace into an indoor outhouse. The king had his own official Bearer of the Royal Chamberpot (it appears in the Versailles segment of Mel Brooks' *History of the World, Part One*), but nearly everybody else had to make do, relieving themselves against walls or wherever was handy. The royal dogs, unhouse-trained, left their own deposits. Nimble reflexes were necessary when the contents of chamberpots were pitched out of a window — *look out below!* Snuff, spritzes of cologne, and scented handkerchiefs were liberally applied to ward off olfactory intruders, while others found unique approaches to personal plumbing. From the devourable memoirs of the Duc de Saint-Simon, the recording-avenging angel of Versailles, we learn of a duchess who merrily chatted away while, crouched behind her and, hidden under the voluminous skirts, a maid engineered an enema, establishing a new frontier in multi-tasking. The *panniers* and tight bodices thwarted some women at royal receptions from being able to relieve themselves in time, and carriage rides could be a bladder-straining ordeal. Men were free to get out and pee; *les femmes*, not.

Over time, hygienic improvements were introduced, and the collective body odor became less of a biohazard. Yet such is the grip of nostalgia that some former denizens of Versailles would remember its signature stench with fond regard, an *eau de 1759*, much as aging punk veterans recall with a tender shudder the stark bare throne of CBGB's graffiti'd bathroom jutting like a rotten tooth. For foreign visitors and other unprepared notables, however, Versailles could be a rude awakening, an olfactory shock to the system that revised their perception of the French. So much finery, such deplorable untidiness. "I shall never get over the dirt of this country," rued Horace Walpole, the greatest English letter writer of the age, who couldn't wait to get back to the tonic fragrance of his Gothic folly at Strawberry Hill.

No matter how often the opulent heyday of Versailles is unfolded for rapt inspection in illustrated coffee table books and meticulous historical studies, biographical portraits, film documentaries, lavish period productions (Roberto Rossellini's *The Taking of Power by Louis XIV*, Sofia Coppola's confectionary *Marie Antoinette,* Albert Serra's *The Death of Louis XIV*, *Marquise*, *Ridicule*, *A Little Chaos*, *The King's Daughter*, *Jeanne du Barry*), television series (*Versailles*, Masterpiece Theatre's *Marie Antoinette*, the dashing *Nicolas le Floch*, adapted from a series of period detective novels by Jean-Francois Parot, and Apple TV's *Careme*, loosely based on the exploits of Talleyrand's versatile chef, spy, and rake Marie-Antoine Careme), Versailles replenishes and replicates itself, a multiverse. Spattered with grime and glorious excess, teeming with an unmatched array of archetypal manipulators and eminences, haunted by the specter of pox, poison, and sinister plots, Versailles' vainglory is transportable to any stage set, strategic chessboard, or moody theater of the mind, its wardrobe department open to every possibility. It is especially transportable to Hollywood, with its own helium intake of grandiosity.

The press lord Charles Foster Kane's Xanadu estate in *Citizen Kane* (1941) is Versailles for a king without a court, a storage hangar for broken, discarded illusions and shaken pride. Norman Mailer's novel *The Deer Park* uprooted Versailles' "Parc-aux-Cerfs" to Palm Springs, California, renamed Desert D'Or, where a colony of Hollywood exiles engages in a rondelay of the damned, which sounds more fun than it reads on the page. Mailer prefaced the novel with a quotation from Bartelemy Mouffle D'Angerville's multi-volume chronicle of *la vie privee* of Louis XV, condemning Parc-aux-Cerfs for its immoral abominations and debauchery, not to mention its drain on the national coffers. Nancy Mitford, in her biography of Madame de Pompadour, tamps down the notion that the original Deer Park was quite all that. "It was said to have been a harem fit for a sultan, the scene of orgies without name, and to have cost the country millions. In fact, it was a modest little private brothel, run on humane and practical lines." (Mailer, exiting the time machine, would have found it utterly bourgeois.) Tony Montana's mansion in Brian de Palma's *Scarface* is a Miami mirage of Versailles conjured from snow mounds of cocaine.

The annual Costume Institute Benefit, more familiar to us wee folk as the Met Gala, changes themes from year to year but never deviates in its service to the wishes and commands of her supreme highness Anna Wintour, Global Chief Content Officer at Condé Nast and Queen of the Big Top. The most explicit nod to Versailles was made at the party in 2024 by Sarah Jessica Parker, who wore "a Richard Quinn appliquéd hand-cut lace dress, dripping with crystals," reported Stephanie Sporn for *Architectural Digest*. "A grand yet timeless classic, much like Versailles, Parker's French connection was solidified by her chandelier-esque handbag, designed by Benedetta Bruzziches, evoking the palace's own light fixtures in the Hall of Mirrors."

It is the Valhalla Viagra effect of Versailles — the heightening boost of boundless sanctifying reflections in the Hall of Mirrors — that has most endurably captivated the show-off dreams of the self-made American aristocracy and lesser fireflies. "Versailles was one of the models that Gilded Age American tycoons used in designing their residences," Colin Jones writes in *Versailles: Landscape of Power and Pleasure*. "The Vanderbilt Marble House constructed between 1888 and 1892 in Rhode Island, for example, a pastiche of the Trianon, is but a single example of a whole wave of similar acts of architectural homage." Alva Vanderbilt's bedroom at the Marble House was originally modeled after an eighteenth-century bedroom suite à la Pompadour. Rosecliff, built in 1902 for the silver heiress Theresa Fair Oelrichs, was modeled after the Grand Trianon of Versailles by the architect Stanford White, its ballroom the largest in Newport, Rhode Island. Marble House and Rosecliff did double duty as Jay Gatsby's mansion in the 1974 adaptation of *The Great Gatsby*, where it was Robert Redford with the closetful of heavenly shirts. 1895 saw the completion of the Biltmore House in North Carolina's Blue Ridge Mountains, a two-hundred-and-fifty room French Renaissance Revival chateau built by George Vanderbilt, its gardens designed by Frederick Law Olmstead and a scenic tourist spot today for Gilded Age aficionados. Culturally, socially, and influentially, Versailles persists as one of the chief donors to the upper crust division of the American Dream, where rooms open upon endless corridors and ancient disputes are resolved by dueling croquet mallets at dawn.

Something about the pomp and ceremony of early-modern royal France acts as an aphrodisiac on its American counterparts, arousing them to break out the ruffles, bustles, and white stockings, dab on a beauty mark or two, and get wiggy with it. Versailles furnished the theme of the grandest fete in the previous century: James Hazen Hyde's costume ball of January 31, 1905 in New York, where six hundred guests in period clothes paid homage to the *ancien regime* through dance, drama, poetry reciting, and group portraits. (Over two hundred photographs of the guests were taken in a special gallery, an invaluable documentation of the evening.) A senior officer in the Equitable Life Assurance Company, which he inherited from his father, this young blade orchestrated the evening with the ringmaster élan of a Diaghilev: male dancers dressed as Pierrot, debutantes swinging baskets of roses. The dining room was converted into a Versailles garden beneath a canopy through which electric lights winked like sylvan fairies. Dinner was served by waiters in white wigs and white stockings, and one of the offerings on the menu was *Salade Madame de Pompadour*. (The soup was called *Consomme Voltaire*.) The ball was a triumph, the guests did not want to leave, but the subsequent uproar and backlash from the press and public led to a cataclysmic financial scandal at Equitable Life Assurance that revealed millions of dollars missing from the company books, including seven million for unspecified disbursements, which to the uninitiated suggested a personal slush fund. Hyde absconded to Europe, leaving others to deal with the aftershocks. (He died in 1959. For a complete rundown, retrieve a copy of Patricia Beard's *After the Ball: Gilded Age Secrets, Boardroom Betrayals, and the Party That Ignited the Great Wall Street Scandal of 1905*.)

In our Gilded Age II, when bubbly champagne has been supplanted by ketamine and human growth hormone and mere multi-millionaires have given way to billionaires making early bookings to Mars, the production and premium values of Versailles emulation have gone likewise berserk. On the cliffs of California's La Jolla Bay reclines The Sandcastle, a mansion with marble floors, opera house chandeliers, a private beach composed of imported white sand, and a guest house inspired by Versailles' Le Petit Trianon, the chateau occupied by Madame du Barry, then Marie Antoinette. If heavy rains ever send The Sandcastle sliding into the bay, it will be quite a sight. Then there is designer Phillip Plein's Chateau Falcon View in Bel Air, with a guest house modeled on Le Petit Trianon, neoclassical columns, gold lamination galore, Swarovski-crystal chandeliers, a staircase inspired not by the Sun King's architect but by Disney's *Beauty and the Beast*, and cathedral ceilings. Chateau Falcon View has its own Instagram account with over seventy-five thousand followers, proof that the attention economy is a bottomless void.

Even more of a roller coaster ride is the cautionary tale of the "Queen of Versailles," Jackie Siegel, who with her billionaire husband David A. Siegel set out to build a super chateau of their own only to get blindside tackled by the financial crisis in 2008. Lauren Greenfield's well-received documentary *The Queen of Versailles* four years later managed to squeeze some poignancy out of their predicament and turn it into a parable about the American yearning for sandcastles in the sky and the dust storms of capitalism. The Jackie Siegel saga has been staged as a Broadway musical starring that mighty pair of lungs, Kristin Chenoweth, who, posed on a throne in the promotion photos, appears begoldened. The fine actor F. Murray Abraham plays her moneybags husband because a job's a job, and historical parallels are supplied by actors playing the ghosts of Louis XIV and Marie Antoinette. The show may be closed by the time you read this or valiantly hanging in there.

The vanity of invoking Versailles can invite a severe comeuppance for the likes of a Jackie Siegel, not that that's proven to be any deterrence. The conspicuously swank always think it will never happen to them, oblivious to the ominous mutterings outside the gates. When the self-inflated newspaper tycoon Conrad Black — once upon a time Canada's answer to Charles Foster Kane — and his scathing columnist wife Barbara Amiel attended an Eighteenth Century Ball at Kensington Palace in 2000, Black arrived robed in red as Cardinal Richelieu, a beaming Amiel at his side looking more *Naughty Marietta* than Marie Antoinette. After Black fell into financial and criminal disgrace, found guilty of fraud and obstruction of justice in 2007, the photo was gleefully reprinted again and again as confirmation of the couple's hubris. (A year after publishing an unctuous ode to Trump in 2018, *Donald J. Trump: A President Like No Other*, Black was granted a full pardon by the president. As Johnny Carson was fond of saying, "Sucking up *does* work.") Although not formally Versailles-themed, the all-star, estimated fifty-million-dollar June nuptials of Jeff Bezos and Laura Sanchez in Venice excited a rash of "let them eat (wedding) cake" hashtags and captions. Poor misquoted Marie Antoinette, the poster child for callow privilege whenever the ultra-rich insist on rubbing it in.

One onlooker described the Bezos-Sanchez wedding-palooza as "more Vegas than Versailles," but that's a narrowing distinction, a parsing of glitz. In the twentieth century, the allure of Versailles was commodified for the masses to give them a buffet sample of the good life. What is Las Vegas, after all, but Versailles supersized with pulp-fiction neon, silicone implants, Cirque de Soleil spectaculars, and obscene parking fees? The mesmerizing musical waters of the Bellagio Hotel pay daily homage to the fountains of Versailles and the Paris Las Vegas Hotel and Casino, complete with its own replica of the Eiffel Tower, offers a Versailles Executive Suite for courtiers carrying briefcases. Lodged within Vegas is the micro-Versailles of The Liberace Museum Collection, enshrined in Michael Jackson's former home at, no joke, Thriller Villa. Liberace's fealty to the style of Louis XIV was expressed not only in his stage costumes — such as his King Neptune outfit, a tribute to the Neptune Fountain of Versailles, whose twenty-six-foot cape was illustrated like a sea epic with fish, coral, and undulating waves — but everyday accessories, such as his Louis XIV golden sunburst tie-pin.

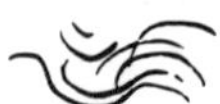

A cash-machine vision of Versailles fueled the industrial hum behind the high-rise ambitions of the Queens developer and future casino owner Donald J. Trump. "Except brilliant campaigns, there is nothing that signals the grandeur and intelligence of princes more than buildings," Jean-Baptiste Colbert, Comptroller General of Finances, told Louis XIV, a lesson the monarch took to heart. Trump didn't need such counsel. In the building of buildings, he got off to an early start, following in his father's footsteps and a publicity hound from his first haircomb. When it came to construction, Trump didn't go in for any of that minimalist

Bauhaus jazz or Philip Johnson hoity-toity. Trump was besotted with Louis XIV style (his favorite, he said) and he pimped out most of his properties in raptures of gold, the *pièce de résistance* being his three-floor penthouse at Trump Tower overlooking Central Park, a shelter-magazine extravaganza of gold, marble, mirrors, massive chandeliers, and gilded furniture suitable for a sultan. The glass cladding of the sixty-four-story Trump International Hotel in Las Vegas was infused with twenty-four-carat gold to reflect light and project luxury, gleaming like a solid gold bar on the skyline.

In the *New York Times* on March 15, 2016, Jason Horowitz reported this:

> "You can always tell when the king is here," Mr. Trump's longtime butler, Anthony Senecal, said of the master of the house and Republican presidential candidate.
>
> The king was returning that day to his Versailles, a 118-room snowbird's paradise that will become a winter White House if he is elected president. Mar-a-Lago is where Mr. Trump comes to escape, entertain and luxuriate in a Mediterranean-style manse, built 90 years ago by the cereal heiress Marjorie Merriweather Post.

The awe element of Versailles was introduced at Mar-a-Lago long before Trump got his mitts on it. For decades, Mar-a-Lago, whose name in Spanish means "sea to lake," was the estate of Marjorie Merriweather Post, the daughter of C.W. Post, the founder of General Foods Corporation. Writing for *Smithsonian* magazine, Michael Luongo provides the relevant stats: "Even by Palm Beach standards, Mar-a-Lago was grandiose: fifty-eight bedrooms, thirty-three bathrooms with gold-plated fixtures (easier to clean, Post believed), an eighteen-hundred-square-foot living room with forty-two-foot ceilings. Its one-hundred-and-ten-thousand square feet glinted with gold leaf, Spanish tiles, Italian marble and Venetian silks." (Gold leaf and gold-plated fixtures, music to Trump's eyes.) Its novelty touches had a storybook *jouissance*: frescoes galore, cherubs carved into the recessed panels of arched doors, and a child's room for his daughter, the future actress Dina Merrill, fitted with squirrel-shaped door handles; a homey palace, as palaces go. And with thirty-three bathrooms, there was little need of guests having to duck behind the bushes for quick relief in the *ancién regime* way. If they ducked behind the bushes, it was for other reasons. Mar-a-Lago's inspirational debt to Versailles was acknowledged at the outset. In March 1927, the year that building was completed at Mar-a-Lago, "Post and her second husband, Edward F. Hutton [co-founder of the brokerage firm bearing his name], had a few score guests over for dinner before the annual Everglades Costume Ball. The hosts wore costumes evoking the reign of Louis XVI." Not the happiest reign, but still.

For decades, Post presided over Mar-a-Lago like a beneficent, genteel queen, cognizant of her social responsibilities and custodianship. A successful businesswoman as well, lauded as the richest woman in the country, Post embodied the old matriarchal order of Palm Beach, an ideal of society based on manners, breeding, and philanthropy that attended to the niceties of hospitality and outreach while the men checked their bond portfolios and made sure their tuxedos were always pressed. (Preston Sturges made brilliant fun of all this in *The Palm Beach Story*.) During World War II, Post offered Mar-a-Lago as a training center for returning servicemen seeking to learn new skills, and the annual fundraising ball for the Red Cross was a social must-attend. Rather than Mar-a-Lago remaining a private Shangri-La, Post proposed it as a possible winter presidential retreat. It would become so with a vengeance.

Trump, seeing the opportunity to grab a hunk of paradise far from the cement mixers and porta potties of Manhattan construction sites, elbowed his way into control of Mar-a-Lago when it was languishing on the market after Post's death in 1973 and lacking a real estate *raison d'être*. Trump understood the potential of the property and shrewd, persistent gamesmanship drove the acquisition downfield. Laurence Leamer, who retailed the serpentine negotiations that led to Trump's acquisition of the property in *Mar-a-Lago: Inside the Gates of Power at Trump's Presidential Palace,* calls it the best investment Trump ever made with minimum outlay. "Today, Mar-a-Lago is worth as much as half a billion dollars, making Trump's initial purchase one of the greatest residential real estate deals in American history. And he did it with less than three thousand dollars of his own money." (That half a billion has ballooned since.) To mark the changing of the guard, Post's portrait was replaced with one lionizing Trump's lustrous younger self, painted with no discernible shame by Ralph Wolfe Cowan and titled *The Visionary*. It depicts a suave, cocky Trump in a white tennis sweater and slacks, looking like a Ralph Lauren creamsicle or Troy Donahue in his tawny prime — a gigolo on spring break.

Despite Trump's Gatsbyesque aspirations, or what the press inferred as his Gatsbyesque aspirations, his tenure at Mar-a-Lago got off to a tacky start. *Noblesse oblige* was never going to be one of his qualities, not when bluster and bumptiousness came so naturally. He threw a tantrum at his first gala when questioned about his then-rocky finances. He feuded with local columnists, berating one as fat, giving her the Rosie O'Donnell treatment. The footage of Trump and Epstein chumming it up at Mar-a-Lago in 1992, scoping out the dance floor like a couple of aging cool cats checking out the chicks, is so frequently replayed that it's almost an installation piece, a continuous loop of smarm. In 1995, Mar-a-Lago was transitioned into a high-fee private club for a new in crowd previously excluded, welcoming Jews and other minorities who had been denied membership at Palm Beach's restricted clubs. (All money is created equal.) The place began to bop. After Dina Merrill complained about her mother's estate being ramped up into an electric boogaloo, Trump retorted that Merrill was "born with her mother's beauty but not her brains," always having to have the insulting last word.

After Trump and his second wife Marla Maples separated, he hosted a "Freedom Party" where a couple of hundred leggy models were bussed in from Miami to spice up the scene. They had very little to do except mill around until it was time to reboard the buses. Trump's date that evening was *Playboy's* newly crowned

Playmate of the Year, whom he shoved into the pool, as if to cut her down to size, the usual overgrown frat boy stuff. Unlike Merriweather Post's charity fundraisers, Trump's were braggadocious affairs where, characteristically, he took credit for donations made with other people's money. Flouting Palm Beach ordinances, he installed an eighty-foot flagpole to fly a giant American flag, instigating a ruckus out of a big nothing, a preview of things to come. Trump claimed to the press that the size of the flag represented the magnitude of his patriotism and anything smaller restricted his freedom of expression. It was the sort of gloriosky stunt that appealed to talk radio; and, not incidentally, one of Palm Beach's most prominent residents was Rush Limbaugh, the mellifluous reactionary ruler of the AM airwaves and Trump's occasional golf buddy. (Limbaugh's compound, razed after his death, featured a salon intended to evoke Versailles.)

Palm Beach's old guard proved no match for the gorilla strength of Trump's money, brash tactics, and tireless conniving. Trump's superpower has always been the ability to wait everyone out with interminable litigation, wearing opponents down until they concede or quit the field. To lift Mar-a-Lago to the next tier of grandiosity and prominence, Trump unleashed the last garters on his inner Louis XIV and went the complete Liberace. "In 2005, a new $40 million, 20,000-square-foot ballroom for the Mar-a-Lago Club was unveiled, designed in the style of Louis XIV and modeled after the Hall of Mirrors at Versailles," Madoline Markham Koonce wrote in *Veranda* magazine. "He spent $7 million alone on 24-karat gold sheets that adorn the ceiling, along with 17 crystal chandeliers. The inaugural event for the Donald J. Trump Ballroom, which seats 700, was his wedding to Melania Knauss." It was a celebrity-filled affair, a gratifying kickoff for phase two of Trump's baronial aspirations. Oprah Winfrey would later throw an eightieth birthday party for the progressive Maya Angelou in the Mar-a-Lago ballroom. So taken was Oprah with the turkey burger on the menu that Trump and his executive chef presented her with the secret recipe on her show. This was before Trump did the heel turn that has defined him ever since.

Versailles: The best I can set down is to say that the whole seemed, almost, to flow in its wondrous horizontal order, and its colours of pink brick and cream stone to rise up in one harmonious chord, as though it had been conjured there, not be any architect but by a composer of Music.

—ROSE TREMAIN

Welcome to Mar-a-Lago, a magnificent place. It sure ain't no shithole!

—JEANINE PIRRO

With a spectacular ballroom and a noisy influx of flatterers, flunkies, and show ponies at the Mar-a-Lago Club, former naysayers and hecklers were left stranded at the curb. Trump was able to crow to the journalist Timothy O'Brien that "I'm the king of Palm Beach. They all eat here, they all love me, they all kiss my ass." (Then go home and bad-mouth me, he couldn't help adding.) Calling yourself the king of Palm Beach is in itself a paltry boast, a provincial rooster crow. Compared to the desert locale and fun architecture of Palm Springs, Palm Beach is a charmless sandbox for the super-spoiled — Rodeo Drive with a better view. Devoid of cultural vitality, money is its sole lubricant. Not for nothing did the Palm Beach Country Club become the happy hunting grounds for the fraudster Bernie Madoff, avid investors beseeching him to take their money. He took it, all right.

Were the ghost of Bernie Madoff to pad around the playing fields of Palm Beach today, he would feel right at home, eager for a bite of the action. Mar-a-Lago has become a global magnet for everyone on the make. Versailles under the kings was also a center of patronage, but the health of the state was central to its purpose and it served as a cathedral of soft power. In *False Dawn: Women in the Age of the Sun King*, Louis Auchincloss writes that history has tended to minimize the "bloody, useless wars" and religious persecution waged by Louis XIV to emphasize the plus side of the ledger, his repatriation of "the ancient concept of *gloire*." The king's "unification and restructuring of France, his conversion of the kingdom, so to speak, into a kind of vast formal garden with great alleys leading directly to the glittering palace of Versailles, produced a simultaneous explosion in art, architecture, and literature that made France seem a new Greece, to be emulated by all her neighbors."

Emulation isn't in the cards for America's neighbors and nearest trading partners, who either have been gravely disrespected (Canada as the fifty-first state) or threatened with invasion (Mexico), and tariffed sadistically. This is the dark side of *gloire*, as Auchincloss pointed out, using your hegemony to trample upon other countries' sovereignty and identity. Hubristic to the max, the Mar-a-Lago of Trump's second presidential term is a much meaner proposition than it was in the first, a reptile pavilion of personal and political influence-peddling, deal-making, and other colorful varieties of chicanery. Raking it in hand over fist is the order of the day and the Emoluments Clause is but a will-o'-the-wisp to the new buccaneers. "Business leaders can secure a one-on-one meeting with the president at Mar-a-Lago for $5 million, according to sources with direct knowledge of the meetings," reported Leah Feiger, Louise Matsakis, and Jake Lahut in *WIRED* magazine. "At a so-called candlelight dinner held as recently as this past Saturday, prospective Mar-a-Lago guests were asked to spend $1 million to reserve a seat, according to an invitation obtained by *WIRED*."

Even Trump's favorite leisure activity is a mode of extraction. What stag hunting was for Louis XIV and Louis XV, and go-kart races were for Elvis and the "Memphis Mafia," and amusement park rides were for Michael Jackson and guests, and grotto orgies were for Hef and his fellow libertines, the call of the fairway is for the president, a recreational activity that he carries to a sullen extreme, resenting any intrusion on his tee-time at the Trump International Golf Club, West Palm Beach or any of the other courses where he squanders taxpayers' time and money. Taxpayers! Such a quaint constituency in these days of plunder.

Due to nondisclosure agreements, a Bada Bing code of *omertà,* and the threat of retribution that pulsates from Trump Inc., Mar-a-Lago is reluctant to part with its secrets, even if spilling those secrets is in the national interest. Why was Trump sloppily stashing away those boxes of classified documents? There is so much we may never know, and probably precious little in the pipeline unless there's a double agent pushing the dessert cart and caddying for the undead. Our era of information overload doesn't extend to presidential secrets or intramural skullduggery. The infinite beehive of Versailles had the mighty Saint-Simon and the letters and memoirs of Francois de La Rochefoucauld, Madame de Sevigne, Madame de la Lafayette, Madame du Hausset, the Duchess d'Orleans, la Marquise de Montespan, and a caravan of others. The salons hosted by *salonnières* such as Marquise de Lambert, Marquise de Tencin, Julie de Lespinasse, Marie Thérèse Geoffrin (whose visitors included Diderot, Montesquieu, and Voltaire —Voltaire really got around) were private oases elevating the art of conversation into formation clouds of opinion that migrated across Europe, often unsettling and bedeviling the state and the clergy. However rarefied the discourse, however arch the locutions, the human particularities of the political actors and the supporting cast were rendered with precise strokes and impasto paragraphs in these letters and journals, even the dimmest of them still vivid on the page centuries later.

Mar-a-Lago, by comparison, is a dry gulch, an intellectual sandtrap. It's high-end nothingsville as far as evolving narratives are concerned. In lieu of the Versailles era's articulate and elegant prose, historical grounding, and backstage insights, what do we postmodern primitives get for our pains from Mar-a-Lago? Thunder bursts of social media blather, cable news commentary from the same wizened crocks ("Joining us today is the Ragin' Cajun James Carville..."), or numbers-spitting pollsters, professional YouTubers breathlessly posting five or six times a day, go-to Trump-explainer Michael Wolff expending gusts of inside hearsay and speculation — a mountain avalanche of wordage adding up to not much. As we saw with Trump's first term, later, buoyed with big advances, out roll the "inside" books by teams of *New York Times* or *Washington Post* reporters that are big on testy volleys between major players in the administration, deficient in observational acumen and irony, with a weak, indifferent grasp of policy impact and almost no grasp at all of literary craft — the Bob Woodward Beltway syndrome. Where's the color commentary? The cold roving eye? The Trollopean set piece? The New Journalism had its overexuberant faults but it was vital in cracking open the social dynamics of status chasing, the many guises of vanity and deception. Mortality has wiped the board clean. There's no longer a Tom Wolfe to cruise a Trump gala and deliver a rococo dispatch, a Norman Mailer to apply his swami gifts to perform deep readings of the darker energies at work beneath the pageantry and applause lines, a Joan Didion spreading a more solemn sobriety. Such parched journalism we are served these days, adding to the general dispiritedness.

Don't look to the performing arts for sustenance relief. Where Versailles presented *comédie-ballets, ballet de cour*, multi-day festivals, and plays and performances by Molière, the recorded music at Mar-a-Lago is personally controlled by Trump from his iPad, exerting top-down control over the Elton John set-list. At one holiday party, unattended by the president, the live performers included Vanilla Ice and a couple of Beach Boys released from Jurassic Park. In its ruthless pursuit of perfect deportment, Versailles was the original house of vogueing and remains a hallowed venue for fashion and film shoots, hosting epochal events such as *Le Grand Divertissement à Versailles*, better known as "The Battle of Versailles," which in 1973 pitted five renowned French designers against five insurgent Americans. Andy Warhol was in attendance, of course. Andy Warhol was always in attendance. The American team were the unlikely victors, skyrocketing the career of one of its designers, Halston. A large portion of success was credited to the American team's use of black models whose beauty and dynamism rocked the house.

If there were ever a "Battle of Mar-a-Lago," it wouldn't resemble a fashion showdown but a Halloween contest where the masks are stuck and askew, a pale zombie parade of distorted unblinking eyes, lipsticked clown mouths, and blinding veneers. *Mother Jones* magazine reminds us that Trump's Atlantic City Taj Mahal casino hotel "once offered a winner $25,000 worth of plastic surgery," and Trumpworld has never wavered in its devotion to the miracle scalpel and necessary filler. The hottest plastic surgery craze of 2025 is the "Mar-a-Lago face," a fembot construction of pillowed lips, etched cheekbones, smooth foreheads, spray tans, and glazed makeup. Even straight-on, Mar-a-Lagettes look as if shot through a fish-eyed lens. The leading ambassadors of this look include Kristi Noem, Ivanka Trump, Lara Trump, Hope Hicks, Alina Habba, and Kimberly Guilfoyle, who has gone full Vampirella. Wardrobe choices range from retro to bizarro to yikes. Party pics from Mar-a-Lago reveal a flotilla of mermaid gowns from some long-ago cotillion, or skintight outfits with plunging displays of V-shaped frontage a la the Real Housewives vipers. As for the men, a few seem to be aping the Jeff Bezos buff-up regimen but most seem content to be able to tuck their shirts into their pants, letting their wives and girlfriends do the presentational heavy-frontage. The exception in MAGA land would be the mercifully disgraced former congressman Matt Gaetz, whose makeover — slat brow, buttonhole eyes, terra cotta tan — lacked only astonished exclamation marks springing from his head, Spider-Man style.

Nearly everybody in the Mar-a-Lago party photos looks immensely pleased with themselves, and why not? They see themselves as winners in the lottery of life, where the weather's fine and the gloating is good. In Palm Beach, the triumphalism of Trump's ascension has lifted all yachts, to borrow a phrase, and jacked up already high property values. David Segal reported in *The New York Times* that "after the election in November, there was a 'Trump bump,' with $100 million worth of property in Palm Beach going under contract in the span of a week. Late last year, the Fox News host Sean Hannity purchased a $23.5 million mansion in nearby Manalapan, then spent $14.9 million on an oceanfront townhouse in Palm Beach in January." No price is too steep if it brings a communicant closer to daddy. The greatest vibe shift has come with "a noisy influx of young Republican partyers, favor-seekers and pols" on perpetual spring break. "The newcomers regard Mr. Trump as a living tourist attraction and Palm Beach as his buzzy natural habitat. They are now wedged into booths at recently opened private clubs and joyfully cannonballing into the island's once-placid infinity pool." Membership to one of these private clubs is quoted at $400,000, such exclusivity enhancing Palm Beach's allure as a watering hole for future red-pill overlords and ladies.

Once Trump won a second term, it became too much to hope that Mar-a-Lago and the White House would maintain proper separate identities. Trump's need for eye candy and personal imprint sweep precedent and propriety to the wayside. If Mar-a-Lago is the president's owner-operated Southern White House, the White House itself is being remodeled into Mar-a-Lago North, a tacky sister shrine. From the *Wall Street Journal*: "Administration officials said Trump personally oversaw the installation of the gold carvings on the mantel in the Oval Office. He also brought gold cherubs from Mar-a-Lago to be installed in the White House." The chairs in the Oval Office are now canary yellow, practically chirping, as if part of a pocket staging of *La Cage Aux Folles*. Trump has had numerous likenesses of himself hung around the White House, one of them displacing Barack Obama's presidential portrait. After scratching his creative itch as an interior decorator, the president branched out into landscaping, reprising his high-flying stars and stripes at Mar-a-Lago with a pair of one-hundred-foot flagpoles flanking the White House. Truly disfiguring was digging up the lawn of the Rose Garden — hallowed ground — for a Mar-a-Lago-like patio that looks, from photographs, like a suburban backyard for summer cocktail parties that nobody has anymore. (It's a blessing they didn't install a barbeque pit.) The capper will be the construction of a 90,000-square-foot White House ballroom, "a beautiful, beautiful ballroom like I have at Mar-a-Lago." White House tours were suspended indefinitely in

September as work commenced. The ballroom will be predominantly gold, of course; a golden womb like his sainted mother's.

Horning in on Trump's act is the Milken Center for Advancing the American Dream, an architectural aria to investment banking and corporate finance situated in a grandiose old bank building across the street from the White House, its kissing cousin. The Milken Center is the creation of Michael Milken, the disgraced former junk bond king who has been on an extended redemption quest ever since pleading guilty to securities violations and being released from prison after two years behind bars. Pardoned by Trump, he has erected a gilded tabernacle to crony capitalism: "Mr. Milken and [his] friends-slash-donors' beaming faces dangle off a faux gold 'Tree of Generations' that looms over the center's atrium...," Rob Copeland reported in the *New York Times*. Music and movie mogul David Geffen is the inspiration for the Geffen Hall of Dreams. "This gallery," states the official website, "showcases perspectives on the American Dream through visual data, polls, poetry and personal storytelling." And "overhead hangs the Esrailian Family Word Cloud—a serpentine chandelier composed of 64 'fins' with 128 LED screens, filled with ever-evolving definitions of the American Dream added by visitors." Sounds like the perfect place to drop acid and freak out.

The Mar-a-Lago-ization of the White House isn't a beautification upgrade for future (p)residents, or a gift to the American people. It is closer to the curse of the mummy. It's about extending the brand into perpetuity, stamping the TRUMP logo on every once-respected institution and leaving it warped and lopsided, as witness the petty dictator-ish takeover and possible renaming of the John F. Kennedy Center for the Performing Arts and reducing the Kennedy Center Honors to a loyalty rewards program. Remaking the White House in Trump's image also stokes the apprehension that he might be considering taking up permanent residency, canceling elections and establishing his own bloodline of succession. No longer content to be mere King of Palm Beach, Trump assumes the title of King of America, if not the whole wide world. "LONG LIVE THE KING!" he tooted on his own behalf on

Truth Social, upon issuing a royal proclamation announcing the end of congestion traffic pricing in midtown Manhattan. Congestion carriage parking is probably something Louis XIV would have left to one of his ministers, but our busybody-in-chief prefers to be more hands-on, especially when applying a choke hold. The White House boosted the meme with social media posts picturing Trump in a crown on the cover of a *Time*-like magazine.

"It's good to be the king," the much-quoted line from Mel Brooks reminds us. Along with the perks of throne life and the gratifying task of waving to your loyal subjects from the balcony, giving their humdrum lives a little thrill, kings — like popes, Supreme Court justices, and *New York Times* columnists — aren't subject to term limits. Royal imperiums are interrupted only by exile, abdication, natural death, or, in the case of French nobles, cranial removal (*plop*). Even allowing for violent upheavals and unforeseen crises that strain alliances, it's a sweet gig with a lot of leeway. Everything about it appeals to Trump's louche presumptions and dynastic cravings. His adult children, crypto- and Saudi-money enriched and blessed with Trump DNA, may already be plotting to find an abandoned mineshaft to drop JD Vance into to keep the line of succession in-house.

If in the past Americans harbored an infatuation with the kings and queens of entertainment and commerce, it may have been because this sort of super fandom was largely pillowy make-believe, a cosplay of the imagination, requiring no painful investment or sacrifice from the devoted and devoid of real-world consequences. Elvis Presley may have spread his cape as an Aztec-Egyptian high priest on the Vegas stage, but he wasn't whipping off Executive Orders about travel bans from his desk back home at Graceland, and Hugh Hefner wasn't cutting off health benefits between centerfold shoots, and Michael Jackson didn't trifle with foreign policy. As the nationwide turnout for the "No Kings" protests in June revealed, the country has become aware and alarmed about the permanent scars and fractures that a runamuck monarch can inflict on a democracy. A terrible president, Trump is an even worse wannabe king, too sulky and froggy to get the optics right. Decrepitude has crept in. What Auchincloss wrote of Louis XIV — "he was like a king in a legend: majestic, awesome, lofty" — will never serve as Donald the First's epitaph.

But what does he care? Trump has taken damaging hits, many of them self-inflicted, that could have (should have) ended most presidencies, but with a Republican majority and a Supreme Court he can call his own, he can plod on regardless. To judge from some of his public babblings, he is more concerned about the waiting line into Heaven than about his presidential legacy, which will be low on achievements but thick with personality-cult highlights. Unless death does us all a solid and intervenes, the ultimate four-bagger for Trump will be rounding the bases from president to king to Napoleonic emperor to American god, his radiant abundance immortalized across the ceiling of the Trump Ballroom in gash gold vermilion, long-tressed Melania soaring at his side. Even Louis XIV might have considered that a bit too-too. Once completed, the Trump Ballroom may not prove to be a baroque enshrinement of Versailles style but its last-gasp entombment.

A PALESTINIAN'S PLEA FOR ZIONISM

HAMZE AWADE

I was born in Dura, in the hills of Hebron southwest of Jerusalem, into a family that carries love for the land and the memory of loss with quiet dignity. My grandfather was a Palestinian *fida'i* (a martyr or "sacrifice") who was killed by the Israeli security forces in 1978. I was taught the details of his death, but they did not teach me to seek revenge; they taught me that courage must serve life. Since I was seventeen years old, I have labored to create spaces in which enemies could encounter one another as human beings. This has not been easy. Over the last two years, even in this fresh hell, notwithstanding the unprecedented bitterness between the two communities, I have worked to help young Palestinians and Israelis speak to one another as human beings. I studied at Birzeit University and at the Hebrew University of Jerusalem, and I try to let dignity lead toward repair.

People often ask me: if I am so critical of Zionism, why do I still believe that peace is the only way forward between Jews and Palestinians?

My answer, my creed, is simple and stubborn: because through the years I have met so many Jews, those who have caused harm, those who have healed, and everyone in between. Beneath every belief, every behavior, and every political attitude or orientation, I have always seen the same thing: a precious, vulnerable human being who longs to feel safe and free to be themselves. Even those capable of evil are also capable of love. This is true of Palestinians, too, just as it is true of all human beings.

My son looks an awful lot like the children who spoke Hebrew near where I was born – on both sides of the green line. When I look at a child, any child, I do not see ideologies. I see a longing for life, a longing to laugh without fear, to run without looking over his shoulder, to grow into a man or a woman unhindered by walls, checkpoints, accusations, or revenge. I see the same pure longing in Palestinian children and in Jewish children alike. Children should not be fed on revenge, it is a poison. I believe that if we choose to nurture our children's childhood rather than erase it, we can build a future where our safety is no longer bought at the expense of other people's dignity.

Ramallah, October 5, 2023. I was driving with my son in the car, turned a corner, and met rifles. Soldiers in the headlights, voices sharp, the air suddenly thin. We both recognized the IDF uniforms. His small fingers tightened on the seat. I spoke in Hebrew and English with my hands open on the wheel, each word chosen to lower the temperature of the moment. One soldier eased his weapon and said that it was a surprise, a lucky break, we were not killed, as if being alive was a reprieve for which we should be grateful. We were the exception. The instant we were clear, my son, six and a half years old, reached for his phone and played Bob Marley singing "Three Little Birds." Music filled the car. "Don't worry 'bout a thing./ Every little thing gonna be alright." We did not speak. In that quiet I understood something that years of dialogue had only suggested. Dialogue can open hearts, but it cannot build a safe reality — not by itself. Dialogue is too easily thwarted by power. Two days later, as the world woke to October 7, I fled the West Bank with my son. We will go back one day, when it is safe.

Criticizing political movements, including destructive policies carried out in the name of Zionism, is not remotely the same as harboring hatred toward Jewish people. I have loved and learned from Jews who challenged the very injustices I raised my voice against, and some of them raised their voices with mine. (I have also been hurt by actions taken in the name of other causes — Zionism is hardly the only political movement that has been scarred by cruelty). All of these experiences have taught me an essential wisdom: politics is often vicious and inhuman, but people are far more complex than the causes they champion. No nation or people should be reduced to the worst acts done in its name, and no good deed should be blotted out because of a crime committed by the person responsible for the goodness, or by the group of which he is a member.

My faith in the possibility of peace is not naïve. It is deliberate and it is open-eyed and it is stubborn. It has to be. I have cultivated it with intelligent intention. It is built on countless encounters: conversations that began with suspicion but ended in recognition, in acts of kindness that broke through long-calcified mistrust, moments when I sat beside strangers in discomfort and refused to let that discomfort harden into hatred. These experiences — some of which I happened upon by chance but many of which I sought out — proved to me that human beings can be shockingly altered by direct encounters with people we had mistaken for caricatures of themselves.

I must not erase you and you must not erase me. I must accept the legitimacy of your self-definition and you must accept the legitimacy of my self-definition. I must learn to speak without contempt about Israel and you must learn to speak without contempt about Palestine. I do not demand of others that they accept my politics. I demand only that they accept something simpler and more fundamental: that any system that denies one group's safety or dignity diminishes everyone's humanity. You cannot dehumanize others without disfiguring yourself. A permanent security must be built upon a foundation of justice and shared rights, not of humiliation and domination. Any other "plan" will be brittle and break. Is this really so hard to understand?

Imagine a homeland where streets are shared by people who observe different holidays, speak different languages, and vote for different leaders, yet live under laws which were written and are enforced to protect them equally. Imagine institutions that celebrate the richness of our faiths and identities instead of using them as bludgeons. These are not fantasies; they should be plans. Pluralistic societies exist elsewhere and they are built and inhabited by creatures no more or less human than us. Pluralism requires political courage, yes, and primarily the political courage to treat one another as equal and equally worthy. But there are times when courage is not too much to ask.

Why do I still believe in peace? Today, after all this hell? It is because I have seen your humanity, just as you have seen mine. It is because I believe in planting seeds for a future in which our children, Jewish, Palestinian, and others, can live without trading their dignity for someone else's safety. I hold this truth as clearly as I see the sun rising over Jerusalem: there can be no lasting peace without justice, and no justice without recognizing each other as fully human.

If anything in these words stings, let it be the sting of honesty, not hostility. My hand is extended not for victory, but for repair. Let us begin there.

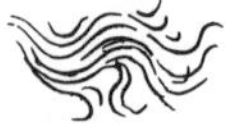

THE TACTILE SPIRITUAL

SHEILA O'MALLEY

My father was a librarian, an archivist, and a rare books collector. I grew up surrounded by books which were a hundred years older than I was nestled beside stacks of long-defunct short-lived Irish literary magazines, many of which were never digitized. My father would open his latest find to the copyright page, explaining why this particular object had value (not of the fiscal variety). The book was a link in a chain, a talisman of a continuum. Within the crush of shelved books he always knew where to find the one he wanted. In the middle of a discussion he would slowly get up, walk to a shelf, pull out a book, and read the relevant passage.

An example. In the late 1990s, my sister Jean and I went to Ireland to visit my younger sister Siobhan in studies overseas. While Siobhan was in class, Jean and I drove west and stopped at Clonmacnoise, an old monastery complex in ruins on the banks of the Shannon River in County Offaly. We had been there as kids but this trip was in November, off-season, and the expanse was deserted. We wandered along the sloping hills, weaving through the tilting lichen-encrusted Celtic crosses and slabs of ancient graves. The river snaked by below us, green grasses pushed up on the sides, melting into the water, no visible shoreline. Something about the river's surface and the flatness in which it rests is oddly dizzying. On a clear day the sky is perfectly reflected in the water and the world seems upside down. I got vertigo.

Once home, I told my father about the strange Clonmacnoise-illusion. He stood up, crossed to his bookshelves, scanned the titles briefly and then pulled out a volume. It was Seamus Heaney's recently published *Opened Ground: Selected Poems, 1966-1996*. He flipped the pages briskly then read aloud in the gravelly voice now faded to an echo in my brain:

The annals say: when the monks of Clonmacnoise
Were all at prayers inside the oratory
A ship appeared above them in the air.

The anchor dragged along behind so deep
It hooked itself into the altar rails
And then, as the big hull rocked to a standstill,

A crewman shinned and grappled down the rope
And struggled to release it. But in vain.
'This man can't bear our life here and will drown,'

The abbot said, 'unless we help him.' So
They did, the freed ship sailed, and the man climbed back
Out of the marvelous as he had known it.

My father gave me his copy of *Opened Ground* and I still have it. I also have little trinkets clustered on the windowsills — an angel made of twisted metal, a broken music box, a tiny piece of clear beach glass — all given to me by people I love. Remembering is a tactile experience.

In Joachim Trier's film *The Worst Person in the World*, in 2021, Aksel (Anders Danielsen Lie), a man dying of cancer, struggles to explain himself to his ex-girlfriend Julie (Renate Reinsve). "I grew up in an age without Internet and mobile phones," he tells her. Julie gives him a look that I, a Gen-Xer, know well. She is sympathetic, but there's a little bit of something else there, almost embarrassment at his nostalgia. Aksel sees the look on Julie's face and his smile is sad. He continues:

I sound like an old fart. But I think about it a lot. The world that I knew has disappeared. For me it was all about going to stores. Record stores. I'd take the tram to Voices in Grünerløkka. Leaf through used comics at Pretty Price. I can close my eyes and see the aisles at Video Nova in Majorstua. I grew up in a time when culture was passed along through objects. They were interesting because we could live among them. We could pick them up. Hold them in our hands. Compare them...I spent my life doing that. Collecting all that stuff, comics, books. And I just continued, even when it stopped giving me the powerful emotions I felt in my early 20s. I continued anyway. And now it's all I have left. Knowledge and memories of stupid, futile things nobody cares about...

I, too, think about it a lot. Before the internet, you had to collect things, especially if you were interested in movies, books, and music.

The concept of ownership has been transformed. We no longer expect ownership to be permanent. You can purchase a movie on a streaming platform, but you are beholden to the platform's landlords. If they want to dump the movie it's gone for you, too. If a movie is not streaming, good luck finding it. (Same goes for my father's undigitized Irish literary magazines: what treasures were in those pages, lost to us forever?) And so I evangelize for owning stuff. Do not trust a corporation with anything that matters to you. With every advance in technology, things are lost. They (there's always a "they") want us to believe that everything is now available with the internet. It's a lie.

The feudal system survives and not only in memory. Much of human history was lived by people who did not own the land they worked. They were enslaved, or in perpetual crushing debt. Today's overlords do not see the value in regular people being able to make a living, having a place to live, or even enjoying some leisure time.

Nostalgia was once considered a clinical disease, listed and discussed in medical journals in the eighteenth and nineteenth centuries. A combination of the Greek *nostos* (home) and *algos* (pain, distress), it spices up a lot of great art. James Joyce's nostalgia is different from F. Scott Fitzgerald's. L.M. Montgomery wrote twenty novels, starting with *Anne of Green Gables* in 1908, and all of them granted her return to Prince Edward Island where she spent her childhood.

Turning back the clock is impossible, but technological advancement forces erasure. You — if you were around — gave up your collection of vinyl and CDs and transferred everything to iTunes, not realizing that in so doing you were giving up your ownership. You scanned and uploaded your decades of photos to one of the storage platforms, perhaps not realizing at the time that when, say, Flickr tanked, your entire archive vanished into the maw of defunct technology.

In 2024, Apple launched a new ad for the iPad Pro in which a giant press crushed a number of objects: a piano, children's toys, a statue from antiquity. The most sinister aspect of that ad release was Apple's shock at the public's universal rejection of it. People recoiled. Apple believes that the human population is on board with an iPad Pro replacing Michelangelo's *David*. They think we don't value *pianos*. The ad was helpful intel. It showed us how they really think.

Near the end of his life, my father was so ill he stopped being able to speak. Those dark days are a blur. I can't say for certain the following anecdote was our last conversation but I know by the date it was close to the end. My mother and I sat up with him all night. His pain was excruciating. At around 5:30 in the morning my father spoke. He told me to get a book from the top shelf. "It's all Shane Leslie books up there," he managed to say. I reached up and pulled down book after book. He had me open each book to the copyright page. "No, that's not it." "That's not it." Finally: "That's the one."

It was a hardcover copy of Shane Leslie's book *The Passing Chapter*, from 1934, a biting attack on the collapse of English culture following World War I. My father held the book, and pointed to the copyright page, as he had done so many times in his life. "St. Ignatius" was stamped there, and he said that meant it was owned by a Jesuit (of course) house in Ireland. When St. Ignatius dismantled its library, rare book collectors had a field day. After showing me the copyright, he carefully turned to the title page. This was really what he wanted to show me. An epigraph from *King Lear* was printed under the title:

The weight of this sad time we must obey;
Speak what we feel and what we ought to say.
The oldest hath borne most; we that are young
Shall never see so much, nor live so long.

My father pointed at the epigraph and had me look closer. There in pencil was a marking: "and" in the second line was crossed out, replaced with "not." A month from his death, he chuckled and whispered, "Here's this Jesuit — he hasn't even gotten into the book yet — and he notices a typo on the title page ..."

And what a typo! "Speak what we feel not what we ought to say" is totally different from "Speak what we feel and what we ought to say." "And" prioritizes polite niceties. "Not" does not. What you "ought" to say has no place in the "weight" of a "sad time." It is the difference between living deeply and refusing to do the same. Perhaps my father understood the note would be balm for me in the difficult years to come. Maybe that is why he wanted me to see it.

After my father's death, his massive book collection was organized for donation to his alma mater Boston College by his best friend, Barry Scott, a rare book dealer. Barry told us that if there was anything with personal meaning for us we could just put it aside. The only book I wanted was the copy of *The Passing Chapter* with the Jesuit's penciled correction.

My father had multiple copies of the book and I looked through them all but none of them were The One. Where could it have gone? I finally had to admit defeat. I never found the book. It's taken on a bit of a mystical meaning for me, like it vanished with my dad, once he showed me what he needed to show me. The gift wasn't the object. The gift was my father's mind, his appreciation for a one-word editorial change and the deeper meaning that it italicized, and also his certainty that I would appreciate it, too. In a chaotic world, where memories are monetized, where ownership is meaningless, where objects are crushed by a giant metal press and we are supposed to call it progress, a ghost book I can no longer put my hands on is even more of a precious object. Its tactility is spiritual.

I have sometimes wondered if I imagined that early morning conversation with my father. Or imagined the book. But no. I know that book existed and now you know about it, too. And I just can't believe none of this matters.

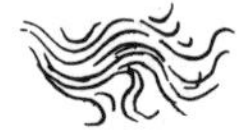

CLOUD HOARDERS

JULIA KIESERMAN

For nearly a decade, *Clean House* television host Niecy Nash would start each episode standing on a stoop or in a driveway to introduce "the show that rescues families from a cluttered home." In a series of cuts rich with delightfully harsh commentary ("how did two little ladies make such a big mess?") her team turned barely functional spaces into livable homes. The message was clear: clutter is wrong, it is embarrassing, and it is no way to live.

Today clutter creeps beyond the home. We are constantly bombarded with digital clutter — emails, texts, and voice messages from every realm of life. And we create our own, snapping photos or jotting down notes, likely with the intention of allowing these creations to "sit" in seemingly infinite "spaces" in perpetuity, mostly out of sight and mind. When we run out of storage space, companies are more than happy to trade gigabyte-sized slices of The Cloud for dollars, and so our digital footprint swells. We may have people like Niecy Nash to save us in the physical world, but who is coming to rescue us from our digital stuff?

To classify someone as a digital hoarder is a challenging exercise. Without the physical junkyard, it is difficult to distinguish between excessive and normal twenty-first-century accumulation. An unexpected event helped me begin to see the physicality of my own digital footprint as something resembling clutter; it disappeared.

On the morning of the Great North American Eclipse in 2024, I woke up to find that all my digital files were gone, in what felt like a fitting cosmic event. After a few moments of panicked research, I learned that I had been a victim of a process known as offloading — an unintuitive term that "frees" my files from the confines of a $2,000, three-and-a-half-pound machine. The process has good intentions; laptops come with a set amount of storage space, some of which is needed in order for basic machine functionality and the rest of which stores the same files that might be sent to The Cloud, such as photos and documents. My laptop had nearly run out of storage and so, in an effort to help keep my device functioning, Apple had copied some of my data from my laptop to The Cloud and then removed my own copy, which is why I no longer saw my files.

Practically, no data was lost; it was as if a company had moved most of my stuff to a storage locker for me to free up space to dance around my home. But as I tried to understand all that I had lost, I couldn't recall even a fraction of what I had been storing on my laptop, let alone what lived in the additional 871.72 gigabytes of data that I had spread across three accounts in The Cloud. My amnesia reminded me of conversations that Niecy Nash had with embarrassed homeowners who couldn't recall the contents of overflowing closets. When I did start to go through my folders and files, I found items both meaningful and utterly useless. It took me as long to find old photos shared by my now-deceased grandmother as it did to stumble upon a flimsy high school resume.

How did I let my digital home get so messy, so full of meaningless items? Part of the blame surely rests on the gatekeepers of The Cloud themselves. The word "cloud," a brilliant marketing coup cooked up by tech companies, paints a powerful image. In 1994 an advertisement for AT&T introduced The Cloud in much the same way many of us picture their namesake; peaceful and expansive, dotting clear skies, of the fluffy cumulus variety. Thanks to that word, when I try to visualize my digital self in a room that needs decluttering, I am instead transported to an idyllic, expansive view seen through the oval of an airplane window.

To cleanse my imagination of this conception, I attempted to visualize my data as approximately one hundred eighty-five standard single-layer DVDs (for those who can still visualize them), four hundred thousand photos, or nearly eight hundred thousand books of approximately five hundred pages each. This is not just a theoretical exercise — ultimately the digital is physical. Data lives on real tangible pieces of metal alloy excavated from Earth, but knowing that isn't enough to rewrite my relationship to things I never experience in physical space.

The way I do experience digital items is likely part of the problem. It is as simple as navigating to a website in my browser (for me, Google Drive) and clicking on a document icon, the same way I might pick up a paperclip. Behind the scenes things are a little more complicated: my browser makes a network request to Google, which then performs a series of tasks like validating that I am in fact Julia, fetching the document metadata (i.e. discovering who owns the document, who has access), loading it from storage, and then streaming it back to my browser. Technically the document is never even in my possession (unless I download it or configure offline viewing) in the same way that the paperclip is; it remains in Google's possession and any edits I make get sent to Google servers where they apply my changes.

But I need to be able to picture where my files are actually, physically, stored, to start to understand my own clutter scale. I am on the East Coast of the United States, so my first guess is (relatively) local; several Google data complexes in Virginia, South Carolina, or Ohio. To get on the grounds, in the building, and on to the server floor would require authorization through many checkpoints — what Google describes as a "6-layer deep" security model. So instead, I take myself on a Google Maps tour of just one of them, in Moncks Corner, a suburb of Charleston, South Carolina. It is home to approximately thirteen thousand people, the historic Santee Canal, a Piggly Wiggly grocery, and a sprawling Google data center campus. According to Google Maps, the campus has streets with names like The Faster Way, The Users Way, and Reboot Road. It is here, in one of possibly seven data center buildings (according to Aterio, a real estate insight company), behind an anti-climb fence and under around-the-clock security watch, that my high school resume likely spends its days. Nor is this the only copy of a document that has not been accessed in over a decade. In order to make good on its promise that data is available 24/7, Google, and other companies that offer storage in The Cloud, usually keep multiple copies in different locations around the country or world.

That is The Cloud. It is made up of hundreds of millions of square feet scattered across cities around the world in places like Changhua County, Taiwan; Fredericia, Denmark; and Quilicura, Chile. It lives in campuses with servers stacked in neat towers the height of a human, or even taller, casting perpetual green light on concrete floors (at least according to the virtual tour, which requires no authorization to visit). Perhaps it should be more fittingly named The Data Bunker: to store data in The Cloud is to store data on countless machines in locked-down facilities, likely echoing with a soft hum, communicating with others around the world on countless tasks beyond retrieving my stored documents.

Visualizing my data in The Data Bunker is a good start, but it still leaves more questions than answers; am I taking the equivalent of one, two, or three boxes in a single server rack? What number is equivalent to a minimalist apartment and what number is closer to a family home littered with relics? This matters because data centers are resource guzzlers, relying on vast amounts of electricity to keep things humming and millions of gallons of water to keep things from overheating. Understanding that the prolonged life of an old document plays even a small role in the environmental health of our planet should be enough to make me consider pressing the delete button.

But it also matters because what we choose to keep should mean something. That which we cherish enough to hold on to through time can become an extension of the self, representative of our experiences and values, and what we leave of ourselves for future generations. When we default to keeping everything, we risk hiding gems in the mass. This is easier to see in the physical world than the digital one, as it was for a woman on *Clean House*, whose deceased grandmother's treasured hat collection became a significant feature of her home only after decluttering the closet that they were buried in. For anyone who knows the feeling of a thumb tired from prolonged scrolling through saturated photo albums, or who cannot easily access one of the likely small number of emails that have truly made them smile, this should be something to consider.

Changing our relationship to digital things isn't easy, but by imagining it as a metastasizing heap of incalculable, forgotten junk and occasional treasure, we become more cognizant of the real tangible limits of what feels like infinite storage space. Tech companies make it all too easy for us to expand the space we take up without ever considering why or what we are keeping and what it means to do so. Perhaps we can rely on the guidance of organizers like Marie Kondo and her call for things to "spark joy" in order to become more intentional about our digital closets. The cost of failing to do so is both a fractured relationship to our memories and a less livable planet within which to make them. Our stuff remains our responsibility whether we can see it or not. It is our job to clean house.

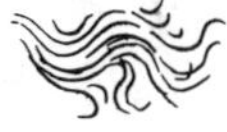

AGNES CALLARD

In Search of the Leisure Class

If you want a surefire way to incite hostility on social media, I suggest flaunting the fact that you work nights and weekends — or complaining about those who do. The sea of humans will suddenly part before you into two angry mobs: the workaholics, who are prepared to sacrifice their lives at the altar of capitalism, and the restaholics, whose highest ideal is slacking off and who seethe with resentment at those ruining the curve. Or so the two groups understand one another.

Do we work in order to rest, or do we rest in order to work? Neither answer is very appealing. Working in order to rest sounds like a paraphrase of Freud's death drive: as though, in an ideal world, we would just be sitting quietly, motionlessly, imitating corpses. Resting in order to work suggests the equally depressing thesis that the goal of a human life is to become a well-oiled cog in some kind of machine, a tool for the use of the leviathan called society.

We need to work, because survival demands it, and we need to rest, because work is tiring, but are those two possibilities really exhaustive? Isn't there a third state — one that we don't need but freely choose?

When I teach book ten of Aristotle's *Nicomachean Ethics,* I explain to the students that if they want to understand Aristotle's concept of leisure — *scholē* — they need only look in the mirror. As students, they are leading scholastic lives, which is to say, lives of leisure. They balk at this: it might be true that the Greek word *scholē* is the source of the English "school," but they cannot see how a lifestyle centered around grades and exams and being forced to read chapter after chapter of Aristotle's *Nicomachean Ethics* could count as leisurely.

Like the workaholics and the restaholics, my students fail to leave room for a third possibility: when they deny that school is leisurely what they really mean to deny is that school is restful. And they are right about that, even on a capacious understanding of rest, one which extends well beyond sleep to include everything they classify under "self-care" — exercise, meditation, "me-time," therapy, unplugging — as well as humor, games, trivial amusements or hobbies, vacations, and all those activities whose attraction lies in being "fun." School is not like any of those things; it might sometimes happen to be calming or relaxing or amusing, but it is not that way essentially.

But school is also not like work, not even if we have a capacious understanding of "work," inclusive of training for work. We forget almost everything we learn in school, and even if we didn't forget it, little of it would be useful to us in our jobs. Some people claim that school trains you in "analytical skills" or "critical thinking"; others say it instills the obedience and the conformity and the submission necessary for most modern jobs. If school does those things, it does them behind the scenes, while you are busy learning not how to be submissive or critical but how to understand calculus or economics or the causes of World War I. Just as playing video games would not be work even if it turned out that (unbeknownst to the players), it trained someone to have fighter pilot reflexes, school is not work even if you do end up with some abilities that are relevant for work.

Aristotle is not stymied by our chicken-egg problem. Faced with the work-rest cycle, he sees a clear teleological winner: fun and relaxation are all for the sake of returning to work, and the reverse is simply not the case.

> Now to exert oneself and work for the sake of amusement seems silly and utterly childish. But to amuse oneself in order that one may exert oneself, as Anacharsis puts it, seems right; for amusement is a sort of relaxation, and we need relaxation because we cannot work continuously. Relaxation, then, is not an end; for it is taken for the sake of activity.

Aristotle chalks up our affinity for relaxation to the lamentable fact that mortal beings are incapable of continuous activity: we need to take breaks from doing what matters to us. A person who worked in order to relax would be getting the proper order of things backwards, like a person who cooks dinner in order to go grocery shopping again. We shop in order to cook, and not vice versa. Likewise, if we see a person working, then relaxing, then working, and so on, the charitable interpretation, says Aristotle, is to assume that she is relaxing in order to get back to work. Relaxing activities may, at times, feel more enjoyable than the work they relieve us from; nonetheless, proclaims Aristotle "no one would live for the sake of trivial amusements." The point of life can't lie in the breaks we take from it.

But now consider work — and I am using the word broadly, as a catchall to describe both what happens in the office and also all the various forms of biological or social necessity that show up in our lives as problems needing to be solved. Getting young kids dressed in snow gear, deciding which chores to do in what order, maintaining a friendly face at a social gathering: those can all be forms of work. Work is activity that manages constraints and tradeoffs to pursue goals of social value — which means the story can't end there. The question remains: what are we working for? The answer cannot be more work, because that simply postpones the question, much less rest, which is done for the sake of work. There must be a human activity that is done for its own sake, and this activity has got to serve as the teleological lynchpin of the whole system. Aristotle calls it "leisure," or *scholē*.

What is leisure? The phrase "leisure time" is familiar enough, as is the fact that there is a big difference between having to spend such time on business or chores or other needful activities, on the one hand, and getting to indulge in an entertaining or restorative respite from activity, on the other. We can use leisure to work and we can use leisure to rest. What is less familiar is that there is, in addition, a native use of leisure as leisure. Aristotle speaks of a "serious" or "zealous" (*spoudaios*) use of leisure. We use our leisure in a serious way when we *don't* convert it into work, as the workaholics do, or into rest, as the restaholics do.

The serious use of leisure, according to Aristotle, is what life is all about. He says that the reason we put servants in charge of our household is leisure: "[the steward] is procuring leisure for the master, in order that he may not be hindered by necessary cares and so shut out from doing something that is noble and befitting." Ignore the elitism for now — we will come back to it in a moment. The insight here is that the point of being elite and aristocratic and rich is leisure: "you must have regard to wealth, in order to secure leisure." Wealth is not valuable for itself, and being elite and aristocratic are not valuable for themselves. There is something they are for. That is why, if legislators have to choose between the two, Aristotle's instructions are clear: "And even if the legislator does not care to protect good men from poverty, he should at any rate secure leisure for them when in office."

I think that we cannot help but read these passages of Aristotle through the lens of Thorsten Veblen. In *The Theory of the Leisure Class*, he writes:

> From the days of the Greek philosophers to the present, a degree of leisure and of exemption from contact with such industrial processes as serve the immediate everyday purposes of human life has ever been recognized by thoughtful men as a prerequisite to a worthy or beautiful, or even a blameless, human life. In itself and in its consequences the life of leisure is beautiful and ennobling in all civilized men's eyes. This direct, subjective value of leisure and of other evidences of wealth is no doubt in great part secondary and derivative. It is in part a reflex of the utility of leisure as a means of gaining the respect of others, and in part it is the result of a mental substitution. The performance of labor has been accepted as a conventional evidence of inferior force; therefore it comes itself, by a mental short-cut, to be regarded as intrinsically base.

Leisure activities, according to Veblen, are a signal of social status; they are performed in order to show off one's membership in the (superior) group of people who have been freed from manual labor. My conspicuously wasteful consumption of time demonstrates to others that I am the sort of person who counts as better or nobler or more honorable simply on the grounds that I do not need to work.

When I describe education, or academia, or humanistic learning as calling for "leisure," people routinely ask me to pick a different word; they tell me that "leisure" sounds elitist. That suggests to me that Veblen is currently winning the battle over the word. Still, I don't think he can win the war over the concept. Although Veblen insists that he is not making the mistake of conflating leisure and rest —

> ...the term "leisure", as here used, does not connote indolence or quiescence. What it connotes is non-productive consumption of time. Time is Consumed non-productively (1) from a sense of the unworthiness of productive work, and (2) as an evidence of pecuniary ability to afford a life of idleness

— in fact he is making exactly that mistake. Leisure, as Veblen understands it, involves a distaste for work, and, far from being easy or relaxing, often involves a difficult and elaborate performance of idleness. But if the third thing involves constructing a certain kind of appearance of the second thing, it is not really a third thing. It is just another version of the second thing. Yes, sometimes the freedom from work is wasted, either in idleness, or in the performance thereof, but isn't there another possibility?

Veblen has glued "leisure" to "class," thereby tainting the former word with elitism. For an antidote, consider John Maynard Keynes' position: in his essay "Economic Possibilities for our Grandchildren," he predicts that within a century increasing productivity due to capitalism will solve "the economic problem" — of subsistence — with which human beings have (almost) exclusively occupied themselves. The result, he thinks, will be a massive reckoning: when people only need to do, say, fifteen hours of work in a week, what will we do with the remainder of our time? Notice that if we cut down on work time, we will also cut down on how much time we need to spend resting and recovering from work, so the leisure problem grows in both directions. Keynes describes the aristocrats of his own time as the canaries in the coal mine:

> It is a fearful problem for the ordinary person, with no special talents, to occupy himself, especially if he no longer has roots in the soil or in custom or in the beloved conventions of a traditional society. To judge from the behavior and the achievements of the wealthy classes today in any quarter of the world, the outlook is very depressing! For these are, so to speak, our advance guard — those who are spying out the promised land for the rest of us and pitching their camp there. For they have most of them failed disastrously, so it seems to me, those who have an independent income but no associations or duties or ties to solve the problem which has been set them.

Keynes is no more pleased than Veblen by the sight of the deliberately wasteful customs by which the aristocracy signals their ability to engage in them. But unlike Veblen, Keynes did not take such behavior to illustrate the inherent impossibility of using leisure well. He admitted that people had not yet found a way to "solve the problem which has been set to them," but was optimistic about our prospects:

> I feel sure that with a little more experience we shall use the new-found bounty of nature quite differently from the way in which the rich use it today, and will map out for ourselves a plan of life quite otherwise than theirs.

Keynes was writing in 1930 — in the year after the stock market crashed he begins his essay, "we are suffering just now from a bad attack of economic pessimism" — so it has been almost a hundred years since he made his predictions about the two problems. Neither one seems to be coming true. We have not solved the economic problem — most of us work more than fifteen hours a week — and we have not solved the problem of how to use leisure, either. The straightforward explanation is that the first problem is harder to solve than Keynes anticipated, and thus we haven't even properly encountered the second one. When I reflect upon the economic history of my own family, I come to doubt this theory.

My parents, my sister, and I immigrated to the United States in the 1980s, refugees from communist (and antisemitic) Hungary. We arrived in New York City with very little, but my parents were extraordinarily hardworking and thrifty. I remember one time my dad and sister and I were out for a walk in Central Park — usually it was my dad who took care of us on weekends, because my mom, in addition to her day job as an oncologist, took on a second job as the doctor at the maximum security prison on Riker's Island — and we came across someone who was handing out free samples of yogurt. My dad made us circle around multiple times, and I think each of us ate at least four samples of yogurt; such was the allure of free food. My mom bought one queen-sized comforter for my sister and me, because that was cheaper than two twin comforters.

She cut it in half, lengthwise, and sewed up each one with a raggedy stitch. My parents worked and worked and worked and slowly made their way up in the world, moving often, having two more kids, exchanging a small apartment for a small house, then a small house for a bigger one, and next for one with a pool. The richer they got, the less thrift they had to employ — I still remember the thrill of getting *my own drink*, instead of having to share with my sister — but the one thing that never changed was how hard they worked. If they had been happy with what counted, in Keynes' day, as a decent standard of living — a radio, a gas stove, a few changes of clothes — my parents could have worked far less than they did.

Even rich people choose to work quite a lot. We have become wealthier than Aristotle ever dreamed we would, yet we do not buy ourselves much of what, according to him, wealth is for. The more wealth we have, the more desperately we seem to hunt for ways to convert leisure into work or rest. Some economists accuse Keynes of underestimating how much people like both working and spending money. Tyler Cowen writes that

> It may well be that a significant proportion of individuals have kept on working as much as they have because a) they really enjoy earning and spending money, and b) they consider their jobs to be relatively attractive ways to invest their time and energy. In that case economic progress would in fact seem to translate into very real forms of human satisfaction.

But that does not really answer Keynes' question, which is: why haven't we found anything we like more?

Are we caught in a work-rest cycle where we force ourselves to work harder, so as to spend more money, so as to work harder, intentionally exacerbating the economic problem ("rising standards of living") so as to delay our confrontation with the leisure problem?

Aristotle did us the favor of pointing the spotlight at the concept of leisure, and the disfavor of failing to turn that spotlight on. I'm going to be blunt and claim that Aristotle's descriptions of leisure activity — what you are actually doing when you are at leisure — borders on incoherent. Aristotle is not given to Platonic flights of fancy; to the contrary, he is usually refreshingly sensible, so when he tells you that the paradigmatic use of leisure is disembodied thinking which takes only itself as subject matter — thought thinking itself — you know he has stumbled into some tricky territory. I understand what thinking is when you are thinking about something so as to accomplish some end, but I do not understand what it is to be thinking only of thinking. (What is the second thinking thinking about? The first thinking? Is this supposed to be a circle of thinking?) Thought thinking itself is, supposedly, in Aristotle's theology, what God does, or rather, what God is, and you are certainly at leisure when — (literally only) God knows how — you imitate that. Aristotle calls this "contemplation," and he says that when you engage in it, you participate in the divine activity that moves the universe. I do not know what this means, and I have doubts whether even Aristotle did.

As evidence, consider Aristotle's life. Embarking on a detailed naturalistic study of every animal under the sun. Comparing tyranny, oligarchy, and democracy. Researching spontaneous generation. Refuting Platonism about mathematics. Cataloguing the various kinds of error in sophistical argumentation. Inventing logic. Role playing a battle with someone who denies the law of noncontradiction. Exploring the ways in which actuality is prior to potentiality — and vice versa. Lecturing to others about all of these topics. Tutoring Alexander the Great. None of these activities are thought thinking itself, they are all thought thinking about something, and *accomplishing* something.

Because contemplation epitomizes the serious use of leisure, Aristotle declares the contemplative life to be the happiest possible life a person can live. So why didn't he live one? Why did he choose, instead, to live an intellectually productive life of inquiry, argumentation, discovery and education? Aristotle's God outputs nothing: why didn't Aristotle imitate that?

I think that we have to assume that work *was* Aristotle's best shot at leisure. His intellectual efforts yielded contemplative moments when, caught in the beauty of a sudden realization about dolphins, or logic, he could feel that he was approximating the divinely perfect leisure activity. And this can be generalized to other kinds of work: when we view our work not in terms of what we can exchange it for — survival, or money — but instead simply take pride and pleasure in a job well done, that is leisure rearing its head in the world of work.

It is one thing to demand pure leisure and another to seek after the type of work or rest that we hope will, at least occasionally, take a leisurely form. If we make room for impure leisure, we will suddenly find leisure everywhere around us. When someone doesn't want to do just any job in order to survive but insists on finding what she will consider "meaningful work," she is saying that she wants her work to be (at least somewhat) leisurely; likewise, when someone resists "guilty pleasures" of entertainment in order to engage with something she finds challenging, she is demanding leisure in her rest time. The home is a place where we do tedious chores, and a place where we enjoy simple pleasures and needed rest, but it is not only those things. Sometimes we manage to spend time with families in a serious and energetic way of which we can be proud.

The work-rest cycle is the solution that we developed for our old problem, the economic problem, and it stands to reason that we would repurpose it when confronted with the newer problem, the leisure problem. In lieu of finding a third thing, we retool and offset, balancing out the overly instrumental form of "contemplation" available to us in the context of work with the overly passive form of "contemplation" available to us in the context of rest. Demanding that our work be rewarding and engaging and that our vacations be learning experiences may be the best that we can do, at the moment, to steer in the direction of what Aristotle called "serious leisure." If you look around you, however, you will see that our best is not good enough.

We are living in unleisurely times. The internet and phones and social media offer up many insistent work-like demands on our attention, many rest-like temptations for entertainment, and few opportunities for leisure. Social media alternates between occasions for worry and outrage, on the one hand, and the promise of relief — in the form of humor, cute pictures, and the mindless scroll — on the other. Between working ourselves up and calming ourselves back down, we have created a loop that forecloses the possibility of leisure.

The opinion pages — where we go to take a break from the news — have exploded, competing with one another for your attention by scolding you for your lapses of attention. The message of most op-eds is, "you cannot justify no longer paying attention to whatever this op-ed is telling you to pay attention." Fearmongering, hatemongering, worrymongering — these are all ways of laying claim to attention. The claim that something has failed to have received its allotted share of concern keeps coming at me from surprising new places, and the form of praise that encapsulates our era is: underrated. The internet is always whispering to me, "what are you overlooking?," launching me on a quest to shift my attention to a worthier target.

Academia, once the proper home of leisure, is now the place where we play whack-a-mole with the ever elusive "gap in the literature." Is something understudied? Is there some topic we don't talk enough about? Have we failed to pay enough attention to some time, place, or group? Do some voices need to be uplifted? Being constantly on the lookout for what we are not seeing creates an anxious, neurotic, even paranoid mood — the opposite of being set free to explore the world of ideas.

Those who are deeply impressed by the world's structural injustices — against black people, or trans people, or poor people, or fat people, or indigenous populations, or nonhuman animals — often describe themselves as "tired." I can well believe it. Constantly attending to what you'd be a bad person if you stopped attending to sounds exhausting. But it is important to distinguish what a plausible claim to tiredness can justify — namely, a concession that one has done enough of "the work" — from anything having in any way to do with leisure. You may deserve a break, but you can't *deserve* the leisurely use of that break. When you make serious use of leisure, you don't treat it as a relief from anything.

The serious use of leisure is intrinsically inegalitarian and intrinsically ruthless. The person who is to use their leisure for leisure is necessarily disengaged from the plight of those unfortunate enough to lack it. Notice that even if suffering and misfortune were evenly distributed among humans, the serious use of leisure would still be inegalitarian, as long as that distribution were not perfectly time-synchronized. While you are at leisure, you ignore their suffering; when it is their turn to be at leisure, they will ignore yours. Those at leisure are neither embroiled in the struggle nor resting up so as to rejoin it. They have opted out of the struggle, too busy enjoying their lives to allow themselves to be pained by the fact that others cannot. To an activist, this indifference is unjustifiable.

A different flavor of unleisureliness is to be found in the ethos of the tech world, which valorizes an optimistic, can-do, progress-oriented, problem-solving attitude. Let's cure disease, let's extend human life, let's simplify online payment, let's make everything faster, cheaper, and more efficient — and let's compete to get to be the ones who get to do these things. The backdrop to this world is the talent tournament, because so many aspects of it are structured as a series of competitions to enter later stages of the competition. Venture capital asks: can you prove that you have what it takes, that you will give your all, that you are presently a future winner? Whether one views this sector of the economy cynically, as being at bottom just an expression of unmitigated greed, or as sincerely seeking improvements in the human condition — probably there is some of both — the overall tenor is one of nonstop instrumental activity, a hubbub of busyness and scurry and conspicuous productivity.

Though tech founders talk the talk of "vision" and "creativity" and "innovation," they have a tendency to confuse medium-sized ideas with big ideas. Increasing human lifespans is a medium- sized idea, decarbonization is a medium-sized idea, blockchain and smartphones and social media and ChatGPT are all medium-sized ideas. The idea that a technology like blockchain — which allows for strangers to transact in the absence of a centralized authority — could make possible a new form of social organization is the idea of a big idea, but you haven't got the big idea itself until you specify what that form is and explain why it is good. One can dream of a future in which social media, for example, facilitates instead of impedes deep human connection, but a dream is different from an idea. If ChatGPT improved to the point where we wanted to count what it was doing as "thinking," that would still only be a medium-sized idea. If ChatGPT could engage in leisurely thought, that would be a big idea. A big idea is not the kind of idea that wins competitions, because a big idea has no peers.

The social justice activist conscripted into a forever war against the forces of oppression and iniquity has something in common with the tech founder piously sacrificing on the altar of progress and innovation: neither understands leisure. But if leisure is so difficult to appreciate, can we really be sure it is something that we want? I think the answer is yes.

Derek Parfit noticed that, on a utilitarian calculus, if given the choice between a world with many poor people and one with few rich people, we should choose the former as long as the number of poor people is large enough, and as long as their lives meet the (fairly low) threshold of being worth living. He called his conclusion — that we should trade our wealthy, prosperous society for one teeming with people living just on the edge of subsistence — "repugnant." But he doesn't say why it is repugnant. I think the intuition of repugnance marks the fact that something inside of us is attuned to the value of leisure, and feels a deep resistance to allowing the world to be drained of it. Effective Altruism, which typically denies the repugnance of the repugnant conclusion, is a philosophy of leisurelessness: while you were at leisure, three babies drowned. If you are only allowed to take breaks from altruism so as to do more altruism, there is simply no room for leisure.

Having disparaged Aristotle's account of pure leisure, let me point out that we can learn a lot about leisure from what he says on other topics. For example, on selling or eating eyeballs:

> One can use each thing both for its natural purpose and otherwise, and either per se or again per *accidens*, as, for instance, one might use the eye for seeing, and also for falsely seeing by squinting, so that one thing appears as two. Both these uses are due to the eye being an eye, but it was possible to use the eye in another way — per *accidens*, e.g. if one could sell or eat it.

Aristotle thinks that there is such a thing as the native use of an eye as an eye — we can call this "pure seeing" — but he also wants to grant the possibility of impure forms of seeing. Squinting is still seeing, even if it is not the perfect kind of seeing. And then there is simply treating the eye as a means to some other end in disregard of its native use altogether — when one sells it or eats it. These uses are not "due to the eye being an eye;" they are not any kind of seeing.

What Aristotle says about eyes, I want to say about time. One can use time for external ends, working joylessly under possibly miserable conditions for the sake of mere survival, and using rest merely as a way of recuperating from and forgetting work. That way of using your time is like selling the eye or eating it. One can also use time in a way that imperfectly reflects its native use, when one pursues rewarding and engaging work and when one spends one's rest time in the sorts of guiltless pleasures that make a person proud to have pursued them. That is like squinting. Aristotle's point is: eating the eye and squinting with it are not the whole story, there has to be a third thing you can do with the eye, with reference to which we understand the other two, and that third thing is *seeing*. We should believe in the possibility of pure, undistorted leisure for the same reason that we believe in the possibility of pure, undistorted seeing. And that means there must be such a thing as a use of time that is not structured by external pressures but solely by the engine of our own efforts and desires, something that human beings do with their time when it is truly their own. Yet Aristotle didn't know what that was, and I don't know what it is, and you don't know, either. And this, to quote Keynes, is a "fearful problem."

You might reply: yes, but at the moment there is a more fearful problem, namely Keynes' economic problem. Before we worry about how we might be misusing our leisure, we should worry about all the people who aren't anywhere close to having any. That reaction is empathetic, but it is also evasive. George Orwell once observed that "every revolutionary opinion draws part of its strength from a secret conviction that nothing can be changed." Serious concern with injustice means not indefinitely deferring the question of what one will do after it is eliminated.

In the Marxist utopia, "it is no longer labor time that is the measure of wealth, but rather disposable time." But how should we dispose of it? That quotation from Marx's *Capital* appears in Martin Haggelund's book *This Life*, which celebrates the prospect of a world in which we "reduce the necessary labor of society to a minimum," so that people can have as much "socially available free time" as possible:

> We can affirm as a feature of our freedom that all the members of the household now have more time to lead their lives: to pursue their education or chosen profession, to connect with people who matter to them, to engage in sports or dancing, to observe nature, to read or paint, to learn new skills, or to engage in some other way with the question of what they ought to do with their time.

Haggelund cannot be accused of wholly ignoring the question of how to use one's free time, given that he lists some possible uses, and goes on to grant that merely having the time to "engage in some way" with the question "cannot guarantee" that the way will be "productive." But he doesn't explain why the uses that he cites are good ones and not just his own preferences, or what "productive" means, possibly because "there are no given answers to these questions of our practical and existential identity, which is why the actualization of freedom requires that we have the time and the material resources to engage them as the demanding questions that they are."

I am not sure what Haggelund means by "no given answers" or "existential identity" or "the actualization of freedom," but I fear that what he is really saying here is that there is no way to solve Keynes' second problem, the problem of free time; that each person just has to come up with a way — any way — to dispose of his time; and that the name for these inventions is "freedom." If that is indeed his view, he is in esteemed company: in the past century, many philosophical houses have been built on the foundation of existential despair.

Everyone understands the economic problem as a social problem, and just about everyone thinks that gradual collective progress on it has been, and is continuing to be, made. If individual human beings are to survive, if the species is to sustain itself into the future, then we must work together both to acquire knowledge, and to create the institutions and technology and laws that support our continued shared existence. That much is obvious. What is less obvious is that the problem of free time is also a social problem, one on which we can also make real progress, over time, if we work together. The problem of leisure is both harder and more social than the economic problem: whereas surviving on your own is difficult, finding meaning on your own might just be impossible.

When it comes to the problem of leisure, I believe the battlefield has shifted. Perhaps in 1930 the idle rich aristocrats were "our advance guard — those who are spying out the promised land for the rest of us and pitching their camp there." Today's idle rich, however, have no cultural significance. No one even knows who they are. The prominent rich people in our world are obsessively hard-working; they are the rearmost part of the rear guard. I return, thus, to my initial assertion, which is that today it is the students who are on the front lines. *Scholē* means school. At any rate, that is what it ought to mean.

Imagine that we go back in time and inform Keynes of the upcoming higher education explosion: in a hundred years' time the number of students in higher education in the United Kingdom will rise by 5,000 percent, although the total population will not even double. His response might be to credit us with a creative approach to the leisure problem: "Ah, I see! Instead of bringing work hours down over a lifetime, you have given people four years of intense leisure early in their adult lives." How sadly mistaken he would be.

At a recent event on campus, about a hundred of my undergraduate students were gathered together and one of them said: "Let's be real, the reason we're here is to get a job." Everyone nodded. But if you "have to" go to college to get a decent job, that makes school work-like. Enemies of higher education are likely to make the opposite complaint, which is that it is too rest-like. They are eager to paint students as deadbeats who could be doing something more productive with their time. Recall when Ted Cruz disparaged "that slacker barista who wasted seven years in college studying completely useless things..." or when Rick Scott, then the governor of Florida, declared that "we don't need a lot more anthropologists in the state... I want to spend our dollars [on] STEM... so when they get out of school, they can get a job." Similarly in Britain, Rishi Sunak declared that "too many young people are being sold a false dream... a poor-quality course... that doesn't offer the prospect of a decent job" and Nigel Farage instructed that "uni should be free for STEM... For the rest, folks, too many of you are going to university. You'd have been better off learning trades and earning real dough." These sentiments have been echoed by politicians and education ministers all over the world. College education has become the epicenter of our discontent over the rest-work cycle, occupying a place in the culture wars that would have been unthinkable in Keynes' day. And yet, as much as we are at each other's throats over education, I think we might not be disagreeing enough.

When did everyone decide to accept the premise that the goal of college is to make students more productive? Even the defenders of the humanities object only to a narrowed understanding of "productivity," insisting that college trains you for more than just a job — it prepares you for being a democratic citizen or being a cultured person or leading a fulfilling life. Not even the champions of humanism consider the possibility that college might not need to be construed as a preparation. Instead of thinking of humanistic learning as a prequel to real life, what if we conceived of it as real life? What if college is *scholē*?

Leisure, it must be sadly or angrily recognized, is not a large part of life for most people. Some people do not go to college, and some of those who do go to college do so under exceptionally unleisurely circumstances. Even students lucky enough to have a paradigmatically scholastic college experience will go on to spend most of their lives outside of school. Am I saying that they are all necessarily deprived of serious leisure? Not necessarily, not any more than someone is necessarily deprived of artistic experience outside museums. But there is a reason why, when people engage in serious leisure later in life, they often think of themselves as "going back to school." We dedicate a place to some value not because you cannot find it elsewhere, but because the task of finding it is hard enough to warrant specialists. Students are supposed to be the specialists. If you find this suggestion absurd, I challenge you to improve upon it. The problem of leisure is upon us, and it is not going to solve itself. Someone has got to be on the front lines. If not the students, then who? Do you prefer the landed gentry?

My oldest child was four or five years old when I first started taking him to museums. I struggled to get him to pay attention to the paintings — he would just rush past them — so I developed the following strategy. I would pick a painting and tell him, "In this picture, there is a secret. It is our job to figure out what it is." When this worked, we would spend a long time staring at the painting, discussing what was unusual about it, floating various theories of what its secret could be, and walk away with a sense of pride: it had yielded its treasures to no one in the room but us.

We live all our lives in the museum of reality, rushing past blurry wonders until one day someone forces us to stop. We find ourselves gathered together in a group in front of one of the paintings, and there is someone who tells us: "here, there is a secret." And then we find we can look for a long time, with a look that is energized instead of sated by what it finds, so that the more we see the more we want to look, because what seemed like a surface turns out to hide a whole world behind it—or none of that happens, and we go through the motions of cooperating with the group, bored and disaffected and impatient to keep moving. Perhaps this was not the painting for us. School does not always work, but when it does it works by tapping into a source of human energy and motivation that is, if not bottomless, at least as profound as the reality it seeks to know.

ROSANNA WARREN

Divination I

God god god I heard the word
rattling and buzzing in the cubicle
of the elevator car, thwacking the walls
and rebounding as it rode
relentlessly up and down in the School of Theology
every day, every evening, season after season;
it escaped, too, down the fluorescently dazzled linoleum halls
when the door slid open, it dizzied into seminar rooms
and offices, befuddled blue books and tenure reviews.
And sometimes the small, dry exoskeleton,
two parched consonants and one shriveled vowel, lay
on the elevator floor before the janitor
swept it up. But a new
god-word always flitted in and resumed the hurtle,
the bluster, the thrum, by which we knew
business would survive, livelihoods were
assured, and we would keep being pestered
by an alien vocable no one could seize on the wing
and which might, in an instant, sting.

Divination II

But what to do with the body—
the body in the city, bare buttocks on Third Avenue,
flesh in morning light, a human crouched
in the gutter, shitting—having nowhere else—
face hooded, just the pale sagging melons exposed as trucks
clank past:
"There be many that say,
who will shew us any good?" The
pavement glints under my feet. Glamour
streaks the East River, whorls
in conflicting currents. I am at odds
with myself. Above us soar
glass and steel towers, brute vertical rule,
crypto-ledgers piercing poisoned air:
Moloch's this furnace. And the molten prayer.

The Cabin (Partita)

With the power out, we worked
by candlelight, you setting
mousetraps with peanut butter dabbed
and the metal bar
hinged back and balanced
not to snap your fingers, I asquint
over my notebook, trying to form
letters in the near-dark. Which is how we
work, even in electric light. A shadow
nibbles the mind: will your numbers
line up to catch the conjecture, will my
words touch anything alive? In the
solstice pit of December
you climb to the attic where you play
the Bach partita on the frigid keyboard until
your fingertips bleed. Art isn't meant
to comfort. But
it can bring us into the hot
real: the rare, the treasured
shock when the notes line up and then
flip upside down reflecting
perfectly as if they remembered
a conjecture backwards. When I wake
deep in the night,
moonlight lies across the meadow as starkly as snow.
And it is snow.

Rosanna Warren

MELANIE W. SISSON

Against Nuclear Stoicism, or the Wisdom of Fear

"May you burn in hell like you are going to burn here."

SECRETARY OF DEFENSE CASPAR WEINBERGER, UPON ORDERING A MASSIVE NUCLEAR STRIKE ON THE SOVIET UNION AT THE CONCLUSION OF A PENTAGON NUCLEAR WAR GAME IN 1983

For eighty years, the world has lived with the knowledge that a small number of nations have it in their power, in an instant, to commit genocide, to destroy civilization, and to eradicate most forms of life on Earth. In the main, international society has accommodated itself to this fact of the nuclear age in much the same way people accommodate themselves to the fact that they might be run over by a car, bitten by a shark, or attacked by an ax murderer. These events are all possible, of course, but none is felt constantly to be likely or imminent, and so each occupies space in dark precincts of the mind, emerging only occasionally through an act of the subconscious or when called forth by a tragic news report or a popcorn horror show.

For the average global citizen, this coping mechanism is both understandable and necessary. For what is someone in Gabon, or Sri Lanka, Costa Rica, Russia, or Pakistan really to do? Even in the United States, the successes of the peace movement of the 1980s had to do only with how many nuclear weapons the country would have, whether it needed to keep testing them, and where it would put them. Not trivial matters, to be sure, but matters that still had very little to do with what makes nuclear weapons so catastrophically dangerous. It is not, after all, strategy — numbers of warheads, projectile throw-weights, the placement of delivery systems, or their targets — that suspends humankind on the cliff-edge of oblivion. The danger isn't physics and it isn't politics. The danger is that nuclear restraint is a miracle, and the world is choosing to believe in it.

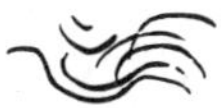

In the early 1700s, a teenaged David Hume became captivated by the moral philosophy of the Stoics. Not satisfied simply to improve his intellect by consuming the works of Cicero, Seneca, and Plutarch, he determined also to put their teachings into practice — to follow their instructions about how to achieve happiness through the mastery of emotion and the honing of virtue. And so he embarked upon training his mind, living simply and exercising rigid self-restraint, engaging in deep introspection, and otherwise seeking to cultivate his ability to reason such that it would inure him to the pains and pleasures of life on earth. As he reported in a lengthy retrospective missive in the mid-1730s, this experiment not only cured him of his attraction to ancient moral philosophy, but also convinced him that the Stoics' theory of human nature was bollocks. He had not emerged happier or more virtuous, as had been the promise. The victory of the rational over the emotional, in his experience, was Pyrrhic.

This realization awoke in Hume the conviction that there was a need for a new theory of human nature, one on which a philosophy of how to live well could be built — a philosophy that, contrary to Stoicism, did not believe that happiness required negating corporeal sensations and internal passions, but that instead gave them their due. And so he set about to produce a "science of man." He would use newly emerging techniques of scientific discovery — experimentation and observation — to uncover and explain the relationship between feeling and reasoning. This empiricism, he believed, was the necessary foundation for philosophy to have any chance of pointing the way to human happiness.

The outcome of Hume's inquiry was *A Treatise on Human Nature*, which he produced in his twenties. In it, Hume concludes from his own experiences together with his observations of the experiences of others, that reason and emotion are not severable from each other. What it is that humans experience as reason is the product of what they have felt, are feeling, and anticipate that they will feel. These feelings first are immediate sensory experiences, or what Hume calls the "violent passions" — fear, joy, anger, love, and so forth. They then are rendered down, through memory and reflection, into such "calm passions" as morality, sympathy, compassion, and justice.

These passions, violent and calm, he says, are the forces that move people to act. Reason on its own, unmatched with a passion, is inert. It can identify facts and make associations, and so it can calculate which actions are more or less likely to make a person sad or happy, to satisfy greed or generosity, inspire fear, or call forth pride or shame. But reason alone cannot impel action; it cannot offer the purpose, only the means. And so, he says, reason "is and ought only to be the slave of the passions, and can never pretend to any other office than to serve and obey them."

Hume thus patently rejected the ancients' assumption that reason and emotion are in constant battle with each other, and that virtue is achieved and happiness is the reward when reason wins. And while he passed no judgment on the righteousness of it, he did consider instances in which it was the calm passions that motivated action to be evidence of "strength of mind." Like the Stoics, however, Hume acknowledged that it was common for it to go the other way round — for the violent passions, which are felt immediately and vividly, to overpower the calm. This fact of human nature meant that strength of mind was not a talent to be exercised but a craft to be practiced; absent cultivation, the calm passions are too easily overrun.

In 1945, the United States of America detonated two nuclear weapons over Japan, the first over Hiroshima and the second over Nagasaki. The extent and the duration of the devastation that those weapons caused was not immediately clear. It has since become very much so. The horrors that the people in those cities experienced remain terrifying because what happened to them then was minor compared to what the world's nuclear arsenals can make happen to anyone, anywhere, now.

Many of the scientists who built those first two atomic bombs and some of the policymakers who directed their use concluded from Hiroshima and Nagasaki that no reasonable person could consider nuclear weapons anything other than a last resort. They are weapons, that is, for employment only *in extremis,* when the population for which a leader holds ultimate responsibility is at imminent risk of being politically overtaken or physically destroyed — and perhaps not even then. Indeed, in his final State of the Union address, President Harry Truman — the same man who had made the decision to bomb Hiroshima and Nagasaki, and to dramatically expand the U.S. nuclear arsenal, and to create thermonuclear weapons — told the nation that "the war of the future would be one in which man could... destroy the very structure of a civilization that has been slowly and painfully built up through hundreds of generations. Such a war is not a possible policy for rational men."

This essential conclusion, however, arrived at by the person most intimate with the responsibility for the use of the bomb, is absent from the eighty-year history of official U.S. nuclear strategy. That history is instead a record of how analysts, policymakers, and military officials have attempted to convince potential adversaries of precisely the opposite. For eight decades, the United States has tried to make the world believe that the United States can wage nuclear war; that in certain circumstances it will wage nuclear war; and that it will win nuclear war. An adversary so persuaded, the logic goes, would not dare attempt an attack against the United States, or any other state to which it has extended its protection. This is the theory of nuclear deterrence that the United States has implemented through a sequence of nuclear strategies — decisions about how many nuclear weapons the United States should have, of what types, where they should be placed, and what they should target— since 1945.

Like all strategies, the nuclear kind are at least nominally designed to solve a problem. Between 1945 and 1949, the practical nuclear problem was one of anticipation. There was very little doubt that the Soviet Union would build its own arsenal of nuclear weapons, it was just a matter of how quickly. The goal of American nuclear strategy, therefore, was to ensure that the United States, for as long as possible, would have more of them. This strategy succeeded; for years after the first Soviet demonstration of nuclear capability, it did, indeed, have fewer of them than the United States — though fewer was still plenty.

The more nettlesome problem thereafter was to figure out where these weapons fit in American defense strategy — the ways in which and the purposes for which the United States would use the threat and application of violence to secure the homeland and protect the nation's vital interests abroad. Both the Truman and Eisenhower administrations puzzled over whether to treat nuclear weapons as occupying a special category and therefore being something apart from regular, conventional weapons, or whether such treatment reflected a layperson's artificiality more than it did a military reality. Eisenhower settled the matter by determining that there were two immediate problems that the

American nuclear arsenal, and only the American nuclear arsenal, would solve. The first was to defend the United States against the possibility of a nuclear attack. The second was to remove any temptation for the Soviet Union to invade Europe. The USSR, at the time, was bristling with soldiers, airplanes, tanks, and other means of land advance that the United States and its European allies simply could not match.

The solution was that if Moscow did either, then Washington would respond by dropping nuclear bombs on the Soviet Union itself. The United States would implement a strategy of "massive retaliation." This strategy, based as it was on the threat not of initiating but of responding, required the United States to be able to strike back even after absorbing an attack itself — to have a secure second-strike capability. If the Soviets thought they could destroy the U.S. nuclear arsenal with a surprise "glorious first strike," however, then Massive Retaliation was a massive misnomer. It would have no deterrent effect and in fact might tempt Moscow to try for a knock-out blow.

Massive Retaliation thus turned wholly on making Soviet leaders fear that launching a nuclear strike would guarantee receiving one. To achieve this in implementation, American nuclear forces were designed to have four characteristics meant to degrade the Soviets' confidence in their ability to destroy the full complement of American nuclear weapons. First, they would be defended against attack. In the great plains the United States built an expansive network of silos — cavernously deep tubes made of heavily reinforced concrete and covered by multi-ton blast doors — within which its land-based intercontinental ballistic missiles (ICBMs) were suspended on massive shock absorbers.

Second, American nuclear air forces, its long-range strategic bombers, would be dispersed across the country and kept in a perpetual state of readiness. This imperative of rapid deployment was taken so seriously that some aircrews lived underground, in "mole-holes," an arrangement that would allow them to scurry directly from quarters onto the taxiway and into their airframes for speedy takeoff.

Third, the United States would have nuclear-armed submarines constantly roaming under cover of the globe's three-hundred-and-twenty-one million cubic miles of salty, murky, noisy, rocky, and vastly deep ocean water. And finally American nuclear forces — the "strategic redundancy" of the triad of ICBMs, bombers, and submarines — would be plentiful. Together, these characteristics would confront the Soviet Union with a set of targets that were numerous, widespread, defended, mobile, and hidden.

By the time Eisenhower left office, the United States had fielded its first of what would grow to forty-one ballistic missile submarines, initiated development of more than 1,000 ICBM silos, maintained a fleet of more than 1,500 strategic aircraft and amassed upwards of 18,000 nuclear warheads with which to arm them. Although the warhead stockpile has changed in size and composition over time, the basic contours of the structure that began with Eisenhower, the nuclear triad, has remained solidly in place ever since.

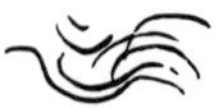

One could be forgiven for thinking that this complement of bombs, rockets, airframes, and underwater vessels, which provide the United States with as much confidence in its second-strike capability as it is possible to have, surely was then and remains now an adequate and durable approach to securing the United States against all external threats. And yet between 1960 and today there have been successive rounds of intense academic and political debate about whether the United States does, in fact, have enough nuclear capability and, if so, how it can prove it.

Under the Kennedy and Johnson administrations the having and the proving were bundled into what has been called the strategy of "flexible response." Although analysts and historians have since demonstrated that "flexible response" was more rhetorical than actual — the Department of Defense did not, in fact, reshape its nuclear war plans to be less massively retaliatory and more flexible and responsive — it did reflect a growing suspicion that massive retaliation would not solve the problem of the day. That problem was not the possibility of a glorious first strike or sudden invasion of Europe, it was the probability of inglorious first bites — Soviet incrementalism, salami tactics, and small territorial incursions that were contrary to American interests but that would hardly merit an all-out nuclear response.

Flexible response, therefore, was meant to offer policymakers options for nuclear use that were more proportionate to a range of potential offenses than reflexive and indiscriminate destruction of military and urban industrial targets and, with them, population centers would be. The intent was to arrive at more reasonable alternatives that, by merit of being more reasonable, would make the Soviets less likely to transgress in the first place. What the doctrine of flexible response began in theory the Nixon administration extended into practice in a pursuit of reasonableness that they called the doctrine of limited nuclear options (LNO). By the time Nixon and his team entered office, the United States had amassed 30,000 warheads in sizes that ranged from an artillery shell to a massive gravity bomb. The core of America's nuclear capability was located in the United States, with intercontinental ballistic missiles and strategic bombers distributed around the country. But its fingers were buried in Europe — the continent was home to more than 7,000 U.S. nuclear weapons — and its toes in Asia, which housed nearly 1,000 of them. So, too, were American nuclear-tipped missiles constantly winding through the global bloodstream on quieted submarines.

LNO didn't seek to reshape the body of this arrangement, but it wanted to substantially rewire its central nervous system. It sought to change what the American arsenal targeted and how the decision to fire on those targets was made. The point of massive retaliation had been to enable uncontrolled nuclear disaster; the point of LNO was to enable controlled nuclear disaster. Under massive retaliation nuclear war was a cascade of dominoes, a rapid gravitational progression toward an inevitable cataclysmic conclusion. The Nixon administration wanted LNO to be a game of chess, with leaders making sequential choices over time, and the final outcome the product of negotiation through extreme violence. And so LNO invested in improving the accuracy of delivery systems and sought to change operational plans to give decisionmakers more discretion over which weapons to fire, on what targets, and when.

Although subsequent presidential administrations made adjustments around the margins and added their own rhetorical flourishes to its name, the essential concept of LNO has been a persistent feature of American nuclear strategy ever since. Each president from Nixon forward, that is, has accepted the premise that fighting nuclear war will be like playing a chess match. And together they have bet trillions of American taxpayer dollars on the belief that the leaders of all other nuclear-armed states accept that premise, too.

Hume was just as inclined to apply empiricism to other fundamental spheres of life — commerce, politics, ethics, and social order — as he was to human nature. Central to his treatment of each was his insistence that belief, whether in a promise of payment for work completed or in a threat of punishment for breaking the law, arises from the conjunction of thought with feeling as shaped by experience. To be believed, that is, a promise or a threat must provoke a passion. Thus Hume believed a person is moved to sign a contract only when past experience generates the feeling of trust that it will be paid. And threats of consequence for breaking the law motivate compliance through the apprehension generated by the experience of having seen punishments carried out.

Although he largely left the matter of religion alone, Hume makes this argument most sharply in his discussion of miracles. A miracle, after all, is definitionally abnormal. A departure from the expected. A breach of order. Therefore to believe in a miracle is to believe in an occurrence that is contrary to all human experiences, except as reported by a small few. The inevitable conclusion, then, is that to believe in a miracle — all miracles, not just particular ones under particular conditions — is unreasonable. This is so because those who are not themselves witness to the miracle have only the testimony of others upon which to rely. And no matter how reliable, how serious, how consistent a person that witness might be, his testimony must be taken in context with the volume of experiences — the millions of contrary observations, repeated throughout history — that are "against the reliability of the report." For Hume, no person's reputation for honor, honesty, or integrity can overcome this test. Belief can only accord with the steady weight of experience.

The theories of flexible response and limited nuclear options were efforts to address the central dilemma of nuclear weapons, which is that they aren't very useful for anything other than annihilation. The scientists, strategists, and military officials who ushered in the atomic age recognized this fact early on. But rather than satisfy themselves and the policymakers they counseled that these weapons could only be used as an insurance policy — that their possession was the closest any state could have to a guarantee of not suffering surprise attack or invasion — some of them determined instead to resolve the dilemma. They wanted to make the case that nuclear weapons could, in fact, be useful for defending allies, and even for prevailing in lesser conflicts of interest.

This drive to tame nuclear weapons and bend them to political will found its expression in game theory, a field of study that had been gaining traction among economists since the 1940s. In 1954, the RAND Corporation, the defense research and analysis outfit, introduced the discipline into military matters as the "Theory of Games of Strategy," in a monograph entitled *The Compleat Strategyst.* Game theory is obsessed with solutions. More specifically, it is obsessed with winning solutions, whether winning means not doing worse than the status quo, accruing gains in absolute terms, accruing gains relative to an opponent, or decisively defeating that opponent. Game theory proposes that these winning solutions are discoverable through the elaboration of chains of logical if-then reasoning. It quantifies what decision-makers value — which outcomes they desire and which they disdain; it maps, as a decision tree, the courses of action available to each actor given the courses of action chosen by the other, and it represents how likely each outcome is to occur, given the possible combinations of those choices.

The argument for game theory in nuclear strategy is that it is the method through which the "priestly mathematical activity of the professional scientist" (as it is described rather cheekily in *The Compleat Strategyst*) can provide policymakers with a purely rational guide to action. So long as decision-makers are scrupulous in following its mathematically derived moves, uncontaminated by emotion, the guide will direct them towards winning solutions: the right decisions to make, given the decisions already made by, and in light of the next steps available to, the opponent. What stoicism prescribed as the path to human happiness, game theory prescribed as the path to nuclear victory. Adhering strictly to its logics, undistracted and unimpeded by the passions, game theory would, for the president with the great misfortune to have to ask, answer the question of whether it was better to bomb Minsk or Magnitogorsk in response to a Soviet attack on Tokyo or Toledo.

The answer to this and many other such questions — and there were many, given that the United States and the Soviet Union had interests that bumped up against each other all around the world — would dictate which weapons the United States would need to have, and where it would need to put them, to make the tree's branches available to the President in the event of war. These choices concerned which U.S. nuclear forces to posture and where they would be visible to the adversary; the Soviet Union generally knew where the United States was putting its warheads and which areas of Soviet territory those weapons put at risk, and the United States knew the same about Soviet forces. This mutual knowledge, together with public and private pronouncements of policy, strategy, and doctrine, were to be used by both sides to anticipate what the other could do and to prepare to impose a punishment if they did it. This meant that each side could calibrate its own moves to keep wars from escalating beyond a few, limited nuclear detonations to all-out nuclear exchange.

Converting nuclear dominoes into nuclear chess, in other words, could be achieved through sterile quantification, ruthless rationality, and careful step-wise progression through an intricate sequencing of threats. All policymakers needed to do to prevent Armageddon was to follow mathematical instructions about what to threaten and when. So long as they did, the United States could prevent nuclear war or, if it came to it, get out of one with a winning solution.

This promise of control, nestled in protective math, is nonetheless battered by an ocean of corroding experience. The whole history of U.S. nuclear strategy is a record of nonperformance. All that holds each intricate construction of threats together is the testimony of a small number of officials, some of whom are people of honor, honesty, and integrity and others not, who claim they will do something that none of them has ever done. And no person, taking this testimony in context with the steady weight of experience, the millions of contrary observations that are against the reliability of the report, could reasonably believe it. The only reasonable conclusion, in fact, is that nuclear restraint doesn't have anything to do with U.S. nuclear strategy at all, that the carefully pruned decision trees with branching equations and calculus-laden leaves, this whole anti-empirical business of nuclear stoicism, is bollocks.

What that leaves as the solution to the world's nuclear problem is the solution that human nature reveals intuitively and viscerally: fear. Fear, in the first instance, that the terror and suffering and death inflicted upon the people of Japan will be inflicted upon one's own. Fear, in the second instance, that even if a first strike is survivable, the war will not in fact be controlled and there will be a next strike, and a next, and a next. Fear that the actual human beings in charge in the moment — Kim Jong Un, Vladimir Putin, Donald Trump, Xi Jinping, Benjamin Netanyahu, Narendra

Modi, Asif Ali Zardari, Emmanuel Macron, and Keir Starmer, and those who will follow tomorrow — will have their calm passions overrun by their violent ones. Fear that the reasonableness of American nuclear strategy really is nothing more than a laughable fiction, because nuclear chess, no matter how rationally played, doesn't come to much if just one participant succumbs to the urge to make the dominoes fall.

Hume often and rightly is credited with having advanced the application of empiricism in domains that for centuries had been dominated by metaphysics. But this alone is insufficient to explain his lasting influence not just on philosophy, but on almost every discipline in the social sciences, from moral psychology to anthropology to economics and political science. More than the application of a new method, what distinguishes Hume, what gives his works this special breadth and durability, are the conclusions to which his use of that method led.

From Hume comes an account of human nature that reflects the reality of living in bodies that are embedded in and constantly experiencing the world. His is an account that opens the door to philosophies of the good life that do not demand the constant, arduous, and in his experience far from rewarding attempt to make feeling — sensation or emotion — subordinate to logic. By elevating the passions to be co-equal with rationality, giving the motivational "why" to reason's mechanical "how," Hume suggests that the good life can only ever be achieved through their partnership. More than this, however, his work suggests that it is the mutual dependence of feeling and thought that make it possible to act in ways that are intrinsically human and, if one so chooses, humane.

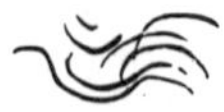

The idea that the more than 5,000 nuclear warheads and almost 1,000 delivery vehicles in the nation's nuclear arsenal might not be enough capability, that the United States needs to prepare to make more, to have more, and to prove it, is again gaining traction in Washington. Vladimir Putin's unprovoked invasion of Ukraine and his nuclear hints and allegations during its course contribute to a general unease about nuclear affairs. But the primary driver of renewed complaints about the inadequacy of the American nuclear arsenal is China.

China entered the nuclear club in the 1960s as a minimalist, creating and maintaining the smallest possible nuclear force needed to ensure it could strike back if it was struck first. In 1990, China was estimated to have approximately 200 nuclear warheads. In 2010, it was estimated to have approximately 200 nuclear warheads. In 2016, it was estimated to have approximately 200 nuclear warheads. In 2020, it was estimated to have between 200 and 300 nuclear warheads. In 2024, it was estimated to possess approximately 600, and what was then called the U.S. Department of Defense predicted that by 2030 it will have 1,000.

China's recent nuclear expansion, of course, did not occur in a vacuum. Since the latter years of the Obama administration, the U.S. national security apparatus has been increasingly captured by the view that China is aggressive and of malign intent — toward Taiwan, toward its neighbors, and toward the United States of America. This was not a position invented from whole cloth. China had spent the prior decades making significant investments in modernizing its military by increasing the number and sophistication of its planes and ships, advancing the technologies behind its command-and-control infrastructure, and reorganizing and retraining its forces.

The first Trump administration, recognizing that American military dominance in East Asia was no longer assured and disliking that fact, pointed the limousine of state firmly in the direction of confronting China as a strategic rival. The Biden administration stepped on the gas. Between 2016 and 2024 the United States generated multiple national security and defense documents identifying China as an adversary. It imposed tariffs on trade and export controls on advanced technologies. The then-Department of Defense oriented itself around preparing to fight a war over Taiwan, and U.S. officials regularly shuffled through East Asia, the small islands of the Western Pacific, and Europe to enlist allies, partners, and friends into the effort. The D.C. establishment engaged in debates, sometimes with an unseemly relish, about whether this was the dawn of Cold War 2.0 and about what needed to be done to win it. It did not seem dismaying, to some, that the bad old days might be here again.

Yanking off the dust cover and ginning up the Cold War engine to crank out new game- theoretical solutions to nuclear problems surely appeals to a wide constituency — to the professional researchers and strategists inside and outside of government who will be paid to do the gaming and the theorizing, to the defense industries that manufacture the bombs and the next generation of platforms to get them where they will need to go, to the policymakers who take comfort in being able to offload onto the branches of a decision tree some of the weight of responsibility for choices about nuclear employment, and to the citizen who is reassured by the thought that the people in charge know what they are doing.

But China's nuclear arsenal is a responsive force. It is not, as had been the Soviet Union's, designed to hit first. It is designed to hit last. And so its sizing should not be expected to be static but rather elastic; what Beijing holds in its arsenal should be expected to change as its perceptions of the likelihood of suffering a first strike change. It should be expected to continuously calculate how much of an arsenal it needs to secure its second-strike capability to make sure it can keep fear alive.

The United States could very well choose to do the same. But giving fear its due and making it the center of nuclear strategy produces only a policy of moderation, one that says that in a world in which nuclear weapons cannot be uninvented the country must have enough of them, and that enough of them can be enough. And so it galvanizes neither the nuclear abolitionists nor the nuclear maximalists, and has no direct constituencies unless one counts remuneration to the small number of reporters and authors and artists — the late William Langewiesche, Kathleen Kingsbury, W. J. Hennigan, and Katherine Bigelow notably among them — trying valiantly to remind Americans of just how very afraid they really ought to be.

Attachment to the myth of nuclear stoicism, to the idea that nuclear decision-making achieves its highest form when it is game-theoretical, exsanguinated of the passions, is a tragedy. It is the fig leaf that pretends to prevent the eye from seeing that in nuclear war what is logical is also profoundly inhumane, and that what is humane is only so because it is emotional. So, too, has the pretense of nuclear stoicism made the atomic age grievously wasteful. Treasures have been ill spent. Environments have been contaminated and people harmed by nuclear tests and nuclear runoff and nuclear accidents. Talent and ingenuity and even genius have been frittered away devising how nations can most efficiently destroy one another rather than on how to tend to the health, wealth, and well-being of their own citizens. Presidents, premiers, and prime ministers have lit diplomatic capital on fire negotiating the placement of missiles in wealthy nations rather than on figuring out how to get food to the famine-stricken in poor ones.

And it has allowed generations of policymakers not to take responsibility for the unconscionable hubris of a nuclear strategy according to which attempting to perpetuate America's political ideology, however cherished it may be, could one day justify the premeditated murder of millions of people as it has already justified the knowing endangerment of humankind. A trite litany of sins perhaps, but being trite makes it no less true, and certainly no less shameful.

EVAN PARKS

Up To The Gate of Mercy: With Celan at Columbia

In the spring of 2024 I taught a comparative literature class at Columbia University called Unland: Writing Utopias. The word *Unland* is a neologism of the German-Jewish poet Paul Celan, from his poem "Hawdalah" from 1963. *Unland*, in my reading, could refer to a decimated postwar geography that is no longer recognizable as itself. It could refer to the ghoulish moral transformation of a polity like Germany, whose population had become "unpeople" (*Unmenschen*) — people who commit heinous acts and deny them, who are haunted by their crimes. The German word alludes to the Greek etymology of utopia, *ou topos*, a no-place that is ever-emergent, unconnected to any existing political entity. *Unland* struck me as connoting a tentative "not yet," a place in formation, like the nascent State of Israel in 1963 and perhaps more aptly like poetry, a place where one exists as if "dreamed." Here one can convene with murdered friends and family, parlay with an inscrutable divinity, hold and cherish words independent from their worn-out everyday use. Through this sacred intentionality the post-Shoah poet grasps for scraps of healing in the face of unspeakable loss. The poet in the rubble strives for new realms, where contradiction hangs together, where life and justice are honored, while at the same time casting critical, even satirical aspersions at the apocalyptically failed politics of the present.

In other classes I taught, Celan appeared in the context of German postwar writers, in a larger arc of German-Jewish writing from the Enlightenment to the present. But in this class I relished the opportunity to place Celan in a culturally heterogeneous and transhistorical context, in which science fiction mingled with highbrow literature. We read speculative writers whose depiction of reality was touched by dystopian or utopian alterations, who found refuge in writing itself as a realm suspended from the invariable violence of the real world to which they respond. Touching off from Celan's poem, we read *The Castle* by Franz Kafka, "Uqbar, Tlön, Tertius Orbis" by Jorge Luis Borges, and works by Georg Büchner, Shakespeare, Theodor W. Adorno, Italo Calvino, Ursula K. Le Guin, Stanisław Lem, Samuel Delany, and Donna J. Haraway.

I found the syllabus to be one of the most rewarding and intriguing I had ever taught, and I had a sensitive and highly engaged group of eighteen students representing many academic disciplines and countries of origin. After teaching in Columbia's Core curriculum I found it gratifying to work closely with texts by Kafka and Celan, paying careful attention to the violent antiJewish context that shaped their writings, while also engaging both of them as "world" writers who set formal and thematic precedents for writers in many languages. Celan, as I was coming to see him, offered a unique link between canons that were deeply Jewish and deeply Western. He was not a Jew who had shed his "accidental" biography in order to join a wider discourse; rather, the precision and subtlety of his Jewish references, the delicacy of his language, and the necessity for clear context about the Holocaust seemed to make his writing *more* rather than less universal.

Yet the spring of 2024 was one of the most challenging and painful semesters I ever spent in a university setting. As the war between Israel and Gaza worsened in the Middle East, Columbia's campus became a global flashpoint for its vociferous protest movement, whose organizers possessed a newfound faith, in the wake of the brutal Hamas attacks of October 7, 2023, that "anti-colonial" violence was not only justified, but a most effective tool for bringing a just future to Israel-Palestine. In addition to the protest movement, the university's administration was under scrutiny for its failure to set a tone of civil, compassionate, and informed discourse, at a moment when students connected to all sides of the war were in deep pain. They pursued a strategy of police crackdowns that incensed the university community and escalated the conflict between protesters and the administration.

On April 30, 2024, this escalation came to a head when activists forcefully occupied Hamilton Hall, the home of my department at the time, draping a banner that renamed the building for Hind Rajab, a six-year-old girl who had been killed by the Israeli military in January. Banners were unfurled from all sides of the building, including "Free Palestine" written in English and Arabic, "Intifada," and "Glory to the Martyrs: *Tortuguita Vive, La Lucha Sigue*," referring to the police killing of Manuel Esteban Paez Terán, an environmental activist in Atlanta. The police presence was high around campus, and an atmosphere of chaos, confusion, and joy spread through Morningside Heights. There was a feeling that the orderly rule of the university had been breached and, for a short while, the protest movement had wrested control.

Around 3 PM that afternoon, I stood at the corner of Amsterdam Avenue and 116th Street, steps from my office in Deutsches Haus, and looked on dumbstruck as a crowd of some three hundred protesters congregated at the base of Hamilton Hall outside the campus gates and erupted in ecstatic cheers as a masked protester appeared on the roof with a billowing Palestinian flag. Helicopters circled above and dozens of newscasters documented (and helped to comprise) the spectacle.

That evening the New York Police Department was called in

for a massive evacuation, with many hundreds of officers in full riot gear. Students who came to see me later in the week expressed deep fear, even trauma, from having witnessed a swarm of police envelop the campus and the SWAT team break down the doors to Hamilton Hall, throwing flash grenades and — as we later found out — accidentally firing a bullet. Around this time of the semester we had been reading *The Futurological Congress* by Stanisław Lem, a dystopian satire of totalitarian police violence in the face of earth's crippling overpopulation, including bombing campaigns that drop drugs to neurologically wire the population to experience happiness.

From this point onward, the social and infrastructural fabric of campus was so torn that it was impossible to teach as usual. Classes had been moved to Zoom and many students were no longer coming to campus. The precarity of my position as a fixed-term postdoctoral lecturer was intensifying as I navigated the anemic job market: I hesitated greatly, given my conflict-averse temperament and my disappointment in the university, to lead a frank or revealing discussion with my class about the conflict in the Middle East and on campus. Events featuring Israelis and Palestinians in conversation had been vigorously protested. A few months earlier the Boycott Divestment Sanction movement had called for the boycott of a prominent grassroots movement of Palestinian Israelis and Jewish Israelis organizing in opposition to the war in Gaza, the occupation of the West Bank, and the Hamas captivity of Israeli hostages in Gaza. Friends seeking to bring members of this group to Columbia decided to do so only on an unadvertised, invitation-only basis, out of fear that a publicized event would attract disruption and condemnation.

I held several strange "hybrid" sessions, with a group of students on the screen and a group at the table in our windowless basement classroom. Around this time one of the leaders of the most active protest group, Columbia University Apartheid Divest, was expelled from campus for one of its members saying, on camera, "You're lucky that I'm not just going out and killing Zionists." It was then that I decided, reluctantly, no longer to avoid the subject and to hold a discussion with my class, to share some of my own views, which I had not often seen expressed by faculty or campus leaders. I knew I had students in the course with a range of perspectives — some active in the protest movement and some not. After the encampments had been created one student wrote to me to plead that we move the class to Butler lawn in solidarity ("It's time to take a stand," he exhorted). I felt respect, admiration, and even affection for this eclectic group, and for the seriousness they had brought to our discussions of challenging, often abstract texts.

With reference to Kafka and Celan, I tried to explain the metaphysical and political significance that the creation of the State of Israel holds for most Jews, including me, while also expressing my profound reservations about the way that Israel was conducting the war, and my anger toward the cynicism, opportunism, and religious extremism that propelled the governing coalition. I expressed concerns with the protesters' explicit and implicit appeals to violence, and I emphasized that refusing to stand in solidarity with them does not mean that one is complicit with war crimes in Gaza, or that one doesn't care. I emphasized that the language used by protesters is consequential; that I felt the need to cultivate a new and productive language — perhaps connected to the poetic dimension of *Unland* — that can allow roughly seven million Jews and seven million Palestinians, in some configuration, to peacefully share a land. In my view, the callous language from Columbia protesters risked inflaming and entrenching the wounds of violent conflict.

I was surprised by how sensitive and open my students were, how genuine their questions and observations were, as if they had begun to absorb our writers' delicate approach to language. A Jewish student thanked me profusely for my words, particularly on the importance of careful nonviolent language. I was approached by several students who had been involved with the protests, including the person who had implored me to "take a stand" but had become increasingly disillusioned by the movement's militant tone and incendiary actions. My words seemed to have opened up a space for them to voice their discomfort. One student expressed dismay that in order to enter the protest encampment, guards demanded that visitors pledge that they "are not Zionists" and that they are "committed to the liberation of Palestine." She was thinking especially about the exclusion of Zionist-identifying friends who she strongly disagreed with but valued as interlocutors. Some of the students, I am sure, were confused or angered by what I had said. But my general perception was that it was a relief (rather than another burden) to air and discuss these issues.

It was disconcerting to me that even with the multiyear humanities Core Curriculum, and with some of the world's leading experts on Israel-Palestine on faculty, members of the Columbia community seemed to hold such a flat understanding of the historical and cultural meaning of Zionism. Columbia takes pride in the rigor, the nuance, and the heterogeneity of its discourse, and in the wake of the murder of George Floyd in 2020 the humanities underwent a period of profound self-reflection, resulting in a commitment to greater representation, context, and sensitivity toward oppressed and marginalized peoples. As much as I learned during that period — and as much as I appreciated the attempts at greater inclusivity — I harbored reservations that the charge toward representational parity was being conducted with a sense of moral panic, even cynicism. At their worst, the sweeping interventions in the humanities approached literature as a flat conduit for sociological and historical information. The preoccupation with categorizing texts by their author's identity — something we *know*, and that we know we know — risks losing touch with facets of the text that we continuously do not know: their multifariousness, their emergent and retrograde tendencies which reveal themselves across time, their fundamental mystery.

Throughout those years, Jewish experience, the history of the Shoah, and the intellectual history of Zionism were not considered worthy subjects for inclusion or "rehabilitation." Outside Jewish studies, the concept of Zionism was not allotted anything close to the wild multifariousness that, for instance, Derek Penslar elaborates in his fine book *Zionism: An Emotional State* — as an ideology that continues, like many ideologies, to shift meaning over time, and can simultaneously span from far-left binationalism and Jewish fascism, fervent religiosity and staunch secularism, political and cultural forms of self-determination, and often odd mixtures of these poles.

I was also not confident that students had a robust understanding for the massive and violent antisemitism that Zionism developed alongside in the nineteenth and twentieth centuries. Throughout my years as a graduate instructor at Columbia, I felt increasingly less confident that students would come into my classes on German language and literature or my first-year Core Humanities classes knowing basic details about the murder of European Jews during the Holocaust. My subjective impression was that this knowledge was decreasing during the roughly ten years I taught at Columbia, from 2015 to 2024.

This knowledge gap felt especially conspicuous in Core Humanities classes where, in 2021, significant syllabus changes had been instated to remediate the "Great Books" with representation by female, LGBTQ+, African American, Asian American, Latin American, and Arabic Islamic authors (a strategy that I felt was at once necessary and dubious). Kafka, added as a representative of "East European Jewry," was included in the overstuffed syllabus, but many instructors remarked that they did not understand why he had been chosen and that they were dropping "The Metamorphosis." An executive decision soon followed to drop Kafka, leaving this version of the class with no Jewish authors, and no reference to the Shoah. (And, of course, no Kafka!) In 2020 a faculty petition that helped to catalyze these sweeping revisions bore down on the "Judeo-Christian" bias of the curriculum, a sentiment that I believe was common, in spite of the fact that the course sequestered the Hebrew Bible as a precursor text to Christian and Western literature. In my experience, the Core provided instructors-in-training and their teaching community with only a few resources to identify and engage with anti-Judaism, specifically in readings from the New Testament and Augustine, and generally in relation to the supersessionist teleology of the syllabus, which synthesizes the Greek tradition with the Hebrew Bible.

Over the four years I taught Literature Humanities, I added Celan's poem "Death Fugue," from 1948, which, in its grave juxtaposition of two women, the Aryan-Germanic-Greco Margarete and the Hebraic Shulamit, and in the historical context necessary for studying it, was the only text that challenged and undermined the christological Greco-Hebrew synthesis. In the late spring of 2024, as I navigated topical discussions with my upper-level *Unland* seminar, I also played Celan's haunting recitation of "Todesfugue" for my first-year students in the Core, which ends with the unforgettable lines:

your golden hair Margarete
your ashen hair Shulamit

dein goldenes Haar Margarete
dein aschenes Haar Sulamith

Shulamit, a stand-in for the Hebraic tradition, finally and ironically, in the wake of unfathomable death, gets the last word. Celan referred to the poem as an "epitaph," a grave for those who had none, including his mother. Yet in my reading — and one that especially emerged with my Core students, who had studied both the Song of Songs and Goethe's *Faust: Part One* — the story of Margarete and Shulamit is not closed. The absence of punctuation makes us think about what could have been between these female-personified traditions, and what could yet be.

By including Celan's poem — perhaps the greatest work of literature to emerge from the Shoah — I hoped to render legible the violence that had been committed against Jews in the catastrophe, and the legacy of antisemitism, but also to ask about how we can rewrite the relation between the Greco-Christian and

Jewish traditions. Is there any way that Margarete and Shulamit can come into relation in a manner that is not determined through violent hierarchy? Can one find the possibility for an authentic relationship between these traditions, one that now must frankly acknowledge the mass violence committed against Jews? The figures of Margarete and Shulamit echo the centuries-old anti-Jewish archetypes *Ecclesia* and *Synogoga*, two women incorporated into Christian iconography from at least the fifteenth century onward to reinforce the inferiority of Judaism. *Synogoga* is typically depicted as a promiscuous ugly woman, often with a broken staff, bending against the crowned, glowing, and golden-haired *Ecclesia*, representing the righteousness of Christianity.

Faust: Part One and the Song of Songs were two other texts that had been taken out of the curriculum, but I continued to teach them, at least in part for how they set up our reading of Celan. Margarete, in *Faust: Part One*, is of course a female victim of male violence, someone who is catastrophically manipulated and misled by Faust. Shulamit of the Song of Songs is also a female character who is abused, who is beaten by the "watchmen of the walls" of Jerusalem, whose sexual chastity is smugly policed by her brothers. Both texts can plausibly be interpreted as sympathetic portraits of women striving for sexual autonomy in the face of brutal and hypocritical male chauvinism, which operates on a personal and social level.

These literary connotations invite links between the Jewish Shulamit and the German Margarete; they indicate a shared thread, one that invites new points of connection. The histories of these women hint at a female solidarity that cuts across violently imposed racial and ideological categories, suggesting alternate ways that stories can be told; connections that can be broken or linked. Like the geographical metaphor of "Meridian" that Celan later took up, the women are points that can be brought into relation variously. However much the poem rebukes the canon, represented by grim references to Bach, Goethe, and the Bible, at a moment of seemingly irrevocable historical violation, the ending leaves a gaping ambiguity — a faint sense that the attempt to hold these archetypes in relation cannot and must not be in vain.

"Don't Split off No from Yes," Celan would later write, a sentiment that is perhaps already incipient in "Death Fugue," which accompanies its resounding rebuke of anti-Judaic canonicity with an aura of uncertainty, a refusal to give up on tradition as a site for ever new relationships, ever new (and perhaps ever unfulfilled) connections. The poem lays bare the violent governing binary of German and Jew, yet it also refuses to capitulate to this binary, tentatively imagining different ways in which these identities could be (or could have been) configured.

My German department was not much stronger than the general curriculum in its engagement with the Holocaust, the history of anti-Judaism, and the rise of Zionism in the German-speaking sphere. The Jewish German experience was not always but frequently subordinated to the Marxist and anti-fascist tradition, the legacy of eighteenth- and nineteenth-century German humanism, or discourses such as affect studies, media archaeology, and, increasingly, environmental humanities. Over my years of doctoral study there I was mentored by professors who modeled delicate close reading, made the pleasure of reading and critical thinking feel contagious, and indelibly conveyed how much literature matters. Yet I was concerned that, as a whole, the department tended toward a redemptive reading of German culture, regarding the Nazi era either as noncentral to their intellectual interests or an aberration from an intact German critical theory-humanist legacy. My readings of Celan, whose writings are anything but intact — fragile, skeptical, in a shaken multilingual German — drew me ever further afield from the department, and from a coherent German language tradition. My feeling was that positive Jewish theology was frowned upon; Judaism was invited when it fit into existing canons and agendas, often as an identity-card that lent moral weight to the critique of fascism, or anti-humanism.

A figure such as Gershom Scholem, the German-Jewish-Israeli scholar of Jewish mysticism and a titanic cultural thinker and critic, was never taught, in spite of having produced an extensive body of German-language philosophical, theological, and literary-critical writings. However Zionistic or theological his ideas, Scholem in my opinion should be considered as part of the same intellectual milieu as his friends and interlocutors Walter Benjamin and Theodor Adorno, rather than an aberrant appendage on this club. I was told by a professor whose perspective I valued immensely that Benjamin's late-life turn to theology was a metaphor, not to be taken literally, and perhaps also a sign of his despair, an implied intellectual lapse. Benjamin and Adorno were figures who were embraced at Columbia, and with abandon, as long as they were engaged as predominantly secular, left-associated Jewish critics. By leaving Scholem out of our syllabi, our faculty missed an opportunity not least to explore a crucial aspect of Benjamin's writings; and more largely to understand how Zionism and a commitment to Jewish tradition emerged within the context of German literature and thought.

By the time the department's graduate students had erupted into a fevered, hectoring anti-Zionism in the spring of 2024 — demanding statements and petitions from their faculty — I couldn't help but feel that this was a volatile return of the repressed, the politicized eruption of a taboo topic. Had Jewish perspectives, including a frank and nuanced account of the cultural history of Zionism, been more thoroughly integrated into the curriculum — perhaps a responsibility for German Studies — we might have found pathways to a more constructive and inclusive mode of activism in the aftermath of October 7, and amid ongoing Israeli violence.

After the police raid on Hamilton Hall, emails from the administration about university policies were scattered and incoherent. No one knew if we were supposed to cancel finals or keep them. For the last seminar of my *Unland* course, I decided to hold class as a picnic in Morningside Park. While it was not originally on the syllabus, I taught selections from Paul Celan's posthumous volume *Zeitgehöft*, or *Homestead of Time*, from 1976.

My intuition was that these poems could contextualize aspects of Zionism but also model a different mode of political and interpersonal discourse, one that relished slowness, allowed pain to resonate, and invited space for contradiction. *Zeitgehöft* includes poems written in the aftermath of a trip to Israel in October 1969 and in reference to the love affair that had taken place on this trip with Ilana Shmueli, an acquaintance from his native Czernowitz whose family escaped Romania for mandatory Palestine in 1944. Several of my students had already left New York City. It was a still Thursday morning with a clear blue sky. After eating fruit and bagels, we sat in a circle and quietly started to work through the packet of poems.

Celan's oeuvre is marked by at least two historically and politically resonant extramarital affairs, one, toward the beginning of his career, with the Austrian poet Ingeborg Bachmann, the daughter of an early member of the Austrian National Socialist Party, and later, shortly before his death, with the Israeli poet Ilana Shmueli. Celan's correspondence with each of them, published posthumously, reveal the great extent to which his poetry was composed in the intimate context of these relationships. In an early poem dedicated to Bachmann, *"In Ägypten"* ("In Egypt"), the speaker seems to suggest that an erotic connection to a "stranger woman" is necessary for memorializing murdered Jewish women, represented by the biblical names "Ruth, Noemi, Miriam." Now, in preparation for his trip to Israel, Celan explores what kind of memory — what kind of poetry — is (or is not) possible in an endogamous romance with an Israeli woman from his birthtown of Czernowitz.

Shmueli and Celan reconnected in preparation for his trip to Israel, his only one, where she served as a metaphysical and touristic host, especially in their walks around Jerusalem. Their letters, and the poetry they exchanged, reveal a powerful yearning, but are marked by a sense for the relationship's inherent impossibility. Writing shortly after returning to Paris from Israel, Celan suggests an oscillating ability to give himself over to their love: "I wanted to start a longer letter, to warn you, about me and about us — but then your face appeared, as I saw it in Jerusalem and in Neve Avivim, and I know: what brought us together is a first and primary thing — Your face, Ilana. Your Jewish face. Your face." Perhaps an indication of his mental unwellness, he conveys longing matched with reticence.

Celan's reservations echo Adorno's concerns about whether someone can "live after Auschwitz," erotic passion serving as a metonym for life itself. Giving oneself over fully to love could be understood as a betrayal of the murdered dead. On the other hand, this formulation to Shmueli, emphasizing an *Erstes und Vorerstes,* a "first and primary thing," indicates exactly the kind of singular Jewish affiliation that a thinker such as Adorno (or Derrida) would eschew. Both of them challenge a unified "first thing," Jewish or otherwise — something that Celan clearly longs for, even if he is incapable of embracing it.

As several scholars have noted, Shmueli becomes for Celan a proxy for the State of Israel itself. His hesitancy in regard to their relationship can perhaps be understood as analogous to a general hesitation toward Israel as a site of Jewish manifestation. In formulations that, at worst, essentialize myriad modes of Judaism, Amnon Raz-Krakotzkin has argued that the advent of the State of Israel is a betrayal of the longstanding Jewish orientation toward withheld messianic promise. "Exile," he writes, "is what distinguishes Jew and Christian, indeed the Jew who is loyal to his exile negates the claim that the world has entered into the age of Grace and salvation... choosing to be a Jew is the same as choosing exile." In such a view, the Jewish state erroneously reconfigures a perennial messianic horizon as the material and historical present. For Raz-Krakotzkin and the other post-Zionist and anti-Zionist "exilists," "choosing exile" is an essential imperative of Judaism. From this perspective, the mainstream Jewish embrace of political Zionism could be seen as a betrayal of something fundamental about Jewishness. This is an ideology that tips Judaism closer to Christianity.

In his attraction to Shmueli, and to the terrain of Israel, Celan reveals the strong appeal, even the importance of manifestation. Even if Celan tends towards "choosing exile," his poetry also explores post-exilic Zionist Judaism as a legitimate mode of expression. This understanding is apparent in expressions like "your Jewish face," written to Shmueli, but also in words like *Sabbatglanz* (Sabbath-radiance) and *Wimpel* (pennant), a German-Yiddish wordplay that connotes the orienting, tentatively national masthead pennant of a ship, as well as the Jewish ritual cloth band that swaddles a circumcised infant or a Torah scroll. An affinity for Jewish nationalism can also be heard in his taciturn address to the Hebrew Writer's Association in Tel Aviv, which expresses "a thankful pride in every green thing planted here that's ready to refresh anyone who comes by" and "joy in the newly earned, self-discovered, fulfilled word that rushes up to strengthen those who turn toward it."

Celan's writing thus entails an unusual and interesting ideological ambiguity. Its various articulations of irrevocable exile make his poetry appealing to strong critics of Zionism, such as Derrida. At the same time it has a decided interest in Jewish materiality; it engages with, even partakes in the symbolic imagination of Zionism in ways that distinguish it from a principled, coherent embrace of Jewish diasporism.

Poetry, for Celan, is a site that holds contradictions. In regards to the Zionist imagination, Celan sought to uphold the figurative and liturgical potential of Jerusalem, in accompaniment to its political rebuilding. As a poet, Celan is not apophatically committed to the figurative Jerusalem (and the withheld messiah), against the materialism of Zionism — the position that has become increasingly popular among American Jewish Studies academics and Diasporist critics. His inclinations are oscillating, and he finds room for multiple paradigms simultaneously.

In the context of conversations about Zionism in the

aftermath of October 7, 2023, I see this as an unusual, and unusually valuable approach, one that honors the Jewish attraction to Zionism while also keeping in mind the dangerous and corrosive effects of tipping a theological paradigm of the withheld messiah into one of manifest reality. What seems most salutary to me is Celan's passion for unresolved attraction rather than firm conviction — for impulses, thoughts, feelings, tendencies, explorations, hauntings, wavering along a spectrum, rather than hardened, didactic principles. The poetry is remarkable for the way that it combines thinking with feeling, conviction with not-knowing.

However much there is to praise about Celan's approach to the notion of Zion, his writing to and for Ilana Shmueli is flagged by the same male prerogative that wounded Ingeborg Bachmann, and which she protested in several strident unsent letters. Here his writing takes on an especially problematic dimension, as the male question of whether the divine promise of "Israel" can ever be embodied is pursued with Shmueli's female body as conduit. Responding to Celan's lines in a love poem — "*es stehn / die Geträumten für / die Mitternachtsziffer* (the dreamed ones stand for / the midnight numeral)" — Bachmann asks, "*Sind wir nur die Geträumten?* (Are we only the dreamed ones?)," possibly reading: don't we also have bodies? Are we not selves whose boundaries remain intact, in spite of so much poetic dissolution? Are you not obligated to attend to me as a woman, as a human being, as a writer? In the case of Bachmann and Shmueli one wonders if a particular woman, the object of Celan's creative imagination, can withstand the pressure to stand in for any independent metaphysical anchor that affirms life. Is there room for Ilana as a complete, human interlocutor — one who shares the male lyric subject's boundlessness — or can she only ever serve as a metaphysically charged foil for the poet?

THE POLES
are within us,
insurmountable
while we're awake,
we sleep across, up to the Gate
of Mercy,

I lose you to you, that
is my snow-comfort,

say, that Jerusalem *is*,

say it, as if I were this
your whiteness,
as if you were
mine,

as if without us we could be we,

I leaf you open, for ever,

you pray, you lay
us free.

DIE POLE
sind in uns,
unübersteigbar
im Wachen,
wir schlafen hinüber, vors Tor
des Erbarmens,

ich verliere dich an dich, das
ist mein Schneetrost,

sag, dass Jerusalem i s t,

sags, als wäre ich dieses
dein Weiß,
als wärst du
meins,

als könnten wir ohne uns wir sein,

ich blättre dich auf, für immer,

du betest, du bettest
uns frei.

The poem "Die Pole," translated here by John Felstiner, was written in November 1969, part of a suite of poems composed in Paris after Celan's return from Jerusalem. Felstiner interprets the poles as "all the opposites pulling at [Celan] — female/male, sexual/sacred, present/past, Israel/France, passion/reason, love/loss, free/unfree — " In German as in English, poles connote charged opposites, in electricity and magnets, but also of course the (magnetically charged) nodes of the planet, which are crucial for navigation and orientation. These poles seem to create an untenable tension, one that is "insurmountable," yet poles in the plural also connote balance, a dialectical force. This balance is impossible to configure "while we're awake," in the conscious world, the world of deliberate action and literal language, of "light" that pressures phenomena into complete knowability. But Celan implies that these wrenching poles — personal, political, and psychological — hang together with some kind of balance in the sleep-world of Jerusalem.

The sleep that allows "the dreamed ones" to be dreamed is now associated with the *Unland* of Jerusalem, especially the Gate of Mercy, *Sha'ar Ha'Rachamim* in Hebrew, a stone-shut gate on the eastern wall of Jerusalem's Old City that is associated with the arrival of the messiah in Jewish, Christian, and Islamic tradition. It is the filled-in gate that you see clearly from across the top of the Mount of Olives. The Gate of Mercy is a bizarre site that is at once indelibly physical — such that it can be fought over and won — and metaphysical, as in several traditions it links the world as it is to the world beyond. Christians and Muslims generally believe that this is the gate through which Jesus arrived to Jerusalem in the lead-up to his crucifixion, on a donkey, to the adulation of Jerusalemites. In the Islamic tradition, there is an association between the eastern wall of Jerusalem and the "Last Day." The Arabic name for the gate, *Bab al-Rahmah*, symbolizes a gate in paradise, or an entry to Mercy. An alternate Arabic name means "The Gateway to Eternal Life." In the Jewish tradition, this is the gate through which the messiah will enter when he arrives in Jerusalem. The historian and geographer Zev Vilnay mentions, in his *Legends of Jerusalem*, the famed Jewish traveler Petahiah of Regensburg, who visited Jerusalem in 1187 and left a Hebrew account of his travels.

> At Jerusalem there is a gate, and its name is the Gate of Mercy. The gate is full of stone and lime. No Jew, much less a gentile, is permitted to go there. One day the gentiles wished to open this gate, but the whole of Palestine shook from one end to the other, and there arose a great tumult in the city until they ceased. There is a tradition among the Jews that the divine Presence first departed through this gate, and that by the same gate the divine Presence will return...

In the story of Rabbi Petahiah — his name means "God

opened" — the Gate is associated with the precursor and successor of historical time; it is a means through which our entire temporal framework is bracketed.

In a way that echoes parables of Kafka or Agnon, the story indicates a rumbling, violent power associated with an untimely attempt to open the gates. Humans, the story seems to suggest, must not hubristically dismantle the blockages. They comprise our worldly existence, which is altogether threatened when we attempt to clear them. And yet this is a physical location that implies an end to the order of the world as it is; in which the imagination of divine Mercy, a Paradise that is unattainable in the world as we know it, becomes so palpable as to form a presence, one that can shake reality at its foundation. In Celanian fashion, the gate is a stoppage that paradoxically implies an opening, and vice versa. The Gate takes us up to the limits of human experience, exhorting us to hold multiple realities in simultaneity. These realities are blocked from one another yet abut one another so closely that slippage could occur unexpectedly, even unknowingly.

Celan's odd use of prepositions and lineation emphasize a blockage that is never, almost, and always an opening. "*Wir schlafen hinüber, vors Tor*;" "we sleep across, up to the Gate." The German adverb *hinüber* implies a passage over, a crossing to the other side. This is also the etymology of the Hebrew word *ivrit*, which became the name for the language itself, related to *avar*, a crossing or a traversal, which could refer to Abraham as a migrant who constitutively crosses over the Euphrates river. *Hinüber* colloquially is associated with a passage into death, an appropriate connotation given the Gate of Mercy's connection with the "Last Day" and the end of times.

Celan's *Hinüber* unavoidably implies crossing, yet the successive preposition *vors* indicates a motion up to the seemingly blocked gate. Here we have been merely taken to the gate's edifice — the crossing of *hinüber* was perhaps a crossing that preceded the Gate, that only took us to its edge. The combination of the two prepositions leaves us with the strange impression of the

Gate remaining both blocked and crossed. This is accentuated by the enjambment of *Tor / des Erbarmens*, as if Mercy almost does not come. The splitting of the two prepositions echoes the Gate of Mercy's two blocked doors, which are traditionally the Gate of Repentance and the Gate of Mercy, implying a procession in and out of this Gate to Paradise; a ritual rhythm for crossing the uncrossable.

Shmueli and Celan avoided visiting the Western Wall of the Temple Mount complex. She writes that Celan referred to "too much sacredness" in regard to the sites that they did not visit, including the Western Wall. Celan's reference to the Gate of Mercy strikes me as a surrogate reference to the Western Wall, whose symbolism risks a dangerous conflation of liturgy and territorial nationalism. Yet the Gate of Mercy is nevertheless a physical holy site located in post-1967 occupied East Jerusalem. Celan shifts the onus from locations that are fraught with Jewish national significance to one that has an array of messianic symbolism in all the Abrahamic traditions. The Gate of Mercy is material and political, yet it offers room for the messianic to remain withheld. The implied shift from the Western Wall to the Eastern wall of the city betrays a different orientation from mainstream Jewish nationalism, one perhaps associated with a rising, unknown possibility that crosses between Abrahamic faiths.

Reading with my Columbia students in our exterritorial classroom in Morningside Park, the poems were not mere cultural documents of Zionism, used to expand students' historical understanding of this movement at a time when it was grievously, even perniciously maligned (although perhaps they did serve this function in that they allowed students to understand, experientially, the spiritual significance of the state of Israel for a Holocaust survivor who finds few scraps of hope and meaning in the postwar period). As deeply ambivalent poetic documents, the texts are not an endorsement of Zionism, neither from the 1920s of Celan's childhood in

Romania, the late 1960s of his visit to Jerusalem, nor the war-torn 2024 in which we encountered them. Celan circles around Zionistic images, seeking nourishment and buoying solidarity, while also eyeing them with suspicion.

These poems, and perhaps "The Poles" in particular, simply do not fit into the binary categories that were constructed daily on campus that spring: Zionist/anti-Zionist, terrorist/genocidaire, antisemite/social justice fighter. Students had been encouraged to see Zionism and anti-Zionism as a simple matter of right and wrong. The poems open the possibility for multiple simultaneous timelines, multiple simultaneous narratives of suffering. They invite and model how to hold a belief but also to step outside of it, to counter it, to approach a phenomenon from several angles at once, with varying degrees of proximity and sympathy. Moreover, like the tentative solidarity implied between Margarete and Shulamit, the poems beckon for threads that cross between poles and allow for configurations that eschew today's broken dyads.

Reading against the backdrop of the raging, lethal, and seemingly unceasing bombardment of Gaza, and the seemingly hopeless fate of the scores of Israelis held hostage, I was inclined to treat the poem as offering a messianic alternative to worldly Jewish-Israeli and Palestinian suffering. Like Yehuda Amichai's poem "Why is Jerusalem Always Two?," "The Poles" is today impossible to read without thinking about East and West Jerusalem, Israeli and Palestinian Jerusalem. Writing about another poem in the series that plays with the image of the Gate of Mercy, Galili Shahar suggests that references like the Gate of Mercy are shadowed by the Israeli "security barrier" that bisects Palestinian villages and segregates Palestinians and Israelis. "The cry of the poem, the prayer for an opening...is now also associated with these fences and barriers." Shahar has described the unspoken "third person" of Arabic that appears when German and Hebrew are at play, implying that Celan's work — so attuned to presences and absences — holds a latent invitation to consider the Palestinian perspective, one that must now be fulfilled.

The messianic dream world that Celan associates with the Gate of Mercy demands a poetic imagination, one distinct from the world of waking thoughts — of statements, arguments, the will to semantic fixity. This is a world of "wandering words," of words that hold open their capaciousness — their capacity for hope, for refuge, for endogamy, for exogamy, to be weaponized, to have magic and healing. These are words that we find when we sleep *hinüber*, when we sleep across to the other side. These are words that cross divides and poles, but they remain within a determinate political state — the territorial location of the Gate of Mercy. Yet Israel-Palestine and specifically East Jerusalem could well be deemed an indeterminate political state, one associated with Abrahamic mythology. The Gate triggers a religious imagination in which tribal and historical distinctions are maintained but can dissolve into ever new formations.

The poles "are in us": they are in our human communities, our tribes, but they are also in each of us readers. They can be insurmountable, even the prerequisite for violence, if we think only in the logic of separateness, of the daytime, of wakefulness. But there is a mysterious and poetic capacity for them to mingle, through a closed gate that is not really a gate. The gate is associated with God's mercy, a mercy that allows the violence of human distinction to be released. The Gate allows us, somehow, to maintain the aspect of distinction that gives us meaning, while relieving the aspect of distinction on which violence is propagated and received. Like Celan's neologism *Atemwende*, or Breath-turn, a breath that returns, waking and sleeping must continuously circle and accompany one another. The goal cannot be to only live awake, or to only live in possibility, asleep, but for the shadow of each realm to challenge and accompany the other.

In the aftermath of October 7, 2023, I see these poems as subtly (yes, too subtly) imagining a shared Palestinian and Israeli society. This shared society is a possibility that is as tangible and present as stone, yet as closed shut as the gate of Mercy. Another poem that refers to the Gate is *"Der Königsweg"* ("The Kings Way"), translated into Hebrew as *Derekh HaMelekh*. In addition to its monarchical association, the Hebrew connotes an ideal way of living, perhaps in the sense of the *Tao Te Ching*, an ancient mystical Chinese text that Celan read closely in German translation. Like the elusive Tao, the King's Way is *"hinter der Scheintur,"* or "behind the shine-door, or apparent-door" — meaning it is perennially inaccessible, blocked behind the bricked Gate of Mercy. Yet "behind the door" could also indicate just over there, almost present, about to be with us.

THE KING'S WAY behind the shine door,

in front, deathed
round by its counter-
sign, the Lion sign,

DER KÖNIGSWEG hinter der Scheintür,

das vom Gegen-
Zeichen umtodete
Löwenzeichen davor,

The "Scheintür" is a door that appears to exist (and does not), but it is also a "shining" door, a royal door poised at the threshold of new realms, and new secrets. The King's Way, in its Taoist sense, has many connotations, of holding memory and presence bound together, of a speech that does not "split off no from yes." It also connotes a polity where the distinctions that predicate Israeli and Palestinian violence have softened. The realm of poetry, love, and memory is, through the Gate of Mercy, woven into an interdenominational hope that the world as it is, ravaged by violence, can be otherwise. Life must find a "counter- / sign [*Gegen- / Zeichen*] " — another realm to accompany it, to enrich and to goad it, to not let it sink into the merely literal.

While there is disagreement about dating the present-day

Gate of Mercy, it is generally thought to have originated in the late Byzantine or early Umayyad period, in the sixth or seventh century. The standing structure is presumably sited on a similar location as the gate that holds messianic significance for Christians of the Second Temple period, and to Jewish legend preceding that time. One archaeologist has argued that the current structure is sited on top of another gate that could be seen if the entire area was excavated. The notion of a (closed) Gate with messianic associations that covers over another unknown gate could uncannily echo the layers of language in Celan's poetry, where German often stands on top of or adjacent to Biblical and modern Hebrew. This relationship is oppositional and obfuscatory, but the archeological proximity could imply a connective point, a site of confluence.

The Gate of Mercy archaeologically echoes Celan's irritating yet productive polysemy. It is indeed a double gate, whose messianic doubling is mirrored in two material portals. In the case of Celan's Jerusalem poems, I believe that Christian and Islamic messianism, and Christian and Islamic claims to Jerusalem, are invoked as a co-presence with the Jewish claim, in a way that invites new models for political cohabitation and new orientations that move beyond sacred ownership. The messianic realm is associated with a poetic language that both allows for and abrogates distinction. The line "*als könnten wir ohne uns wir sein,*" or "as if without us we could be we", often seen in an erotic context, could also be understood as a reorientation toward tribal identities — a hypothetical in which we lose our distinguishing marks yet keep them.

Celan acknowledges the human importance, even the existential necessity, of both cherishing identity and remaining aware of how identity propagates violence. In a poem that is regarded as his most Zionistic, "*Denk Dir,*" or "Just Think," written after the Israeli victory in 1967 and broadcast on Israeli radio, Celan uses the problematic German word *Heimat*, which connotes a territorialistic sense of home. "Just think: / the Peat-Bog Soldier of Masada / makes a homeland [*Heimat*] for himself, most / ineffaceably," Here ostensibly Hebrew soldiers are praised for recovering *Heimat*, a celebration of Israeli victory that has unavoidably ominous Germanic overtones.

Celan is too aware of the pernicious connotations lingering in nearly all words, and the lingering residue of the Third Reich across the entire German language, to use a word such as *Heimat* in a Jewish nationalist sense without keeping in mind its link to the most murderous instantiations of German nationalism. This is not to say that Celan compares Israelis to Nazis in a one-to-one, literal way as his acquaintance Erich Fried did (something he greatly took issue with), or in the manner one finds common on anti-Israeli activist posters after October 7. He creates a set of unresolved associations around words which connote their different possibilities, one of which, in the case of Israeli *Heimat*, is the possibility for identitarian and territorialistic violence. Few writers that I am aware of were able to follow the Zionist imagination so deeply, to partake in a sense of Zionist political and metaphysical refuge, while also remaining outside it — not only with ambivalence, but with suspicion, even grave fear, of what nationalism can devolve into. The frame of mind that these poems cultivate is not one of righteous and indignant anti-nationalism, nor can it be one of tribalistic pride and belonging. The poetry has meanings that are both manifest and withheld. It takes on new resonance in relation to the beliefs of its interlocutors, and in relation to an unfolding legacy of European and Middle Eastern violence.

Celan's poems attempt a language where contradiction remains possible, and, hopefully, from this language, a reality where contradictions can coincide. But as with the *Scheintür*, it is not clear if such a language can ever be siphoned into in the real world or if it must remain a painful, tantalizing dream.

In their slow, cryptic style, as the sun shone on our circle in Morningside Park, the poems enabled a different discourse, one attuned to the sacredness and the consequentiality of language. This was, if only very briefly, an instantiation of the King's Way that lies behind the *Scheintür* — a way that I found my young students leading. The King's Way, in Morningside Park at least, occurred in a circle, with the poems seemingly shining out of the middle, through everyone's different, confused questions; we peeled off lines, almost like the delicate layers of an onion. The discussion was nonlinear in its spatial blocking but also in the sense that the poems were not "accessed;" they were ambiguous configurations that we skewed in different ways. This group included students who had participated in the Gaza encampments and others who had been disturbed by language emanating from the protest movement.

In a creative reflection, one student described the experience of reading Celan in the park, using a roman numeral dating taken from Lem's *Futurological Congress* — a dating that chronicles the protagonist's journal entries after his brain has been surgically inserted into a new body, which wakes up years into to the future.

> *2 V 2024*: Jess and I walk to Morningside for our make-up class where we are discussing selected poems by Paul Celan. The weather is perfect. Warm, summery, and picturesque. After a quick bite, we all gather on the picnic blanket, and Professor Parks has printed out the poems for us to look at. I sit, listening, chiming in when I feel like I have something to say, but most of all just existing. It is the first time I've felt truly present in weeks (months?). It's my first time in Morningside Park and it's beautiful. There's a slight breeze and not a single cloud in the sky. The commotion from the previous days seems to have faded in this moment and things are still. I don't understand a lot of what Celan's writing about, but I don't think that matters too much. If you had asked me what I thought or perhaps hoped Columbia was going to be like when I was first accepted, I believe an image like this one would've come to mind.

This was the last class I taught at Columbia. The student's reflection corroborates my profound belief in the capacity of poetry to create experience at a moment when the university gates were literally locked. What happened around the poems felt like a small opening, a window into what study, community, and reading can be. The gathering embodied Celan's notion of a "missed encounter," between a semester that was and a semester that could have been, or could yet be.

Celan's poems did not pick a gated lawn, did not take a side at Columbia in 2024. But neither were they silent. They were attuned to the unprecedented scope of Israeli and Palestinian suffering and loss in 2023-2024, and to the Jerusalem of seemingly insurmountable divides. They were documents of Zionism, demonstrations of what Israel meant to someone who survived unthinkable catastrophe and arrived there in 1969, looking for threads of life to hang on to. The poems challenged us to expand and rethink the scope of how we approach Jerusalem; to invite many co-present Jerusalems, sacred and profane, material and figural, Jewish and Palestinian.

The lived, relational dimension of teaching, of reading in a circle: in the classroom beneath the sky, history is present but it does not overdetermine the poetry's meaning. We keep trying to figure out what's going on, keep finding possibilities for words that seem to speak in ever new ways. This is a poetry that calls its readers into a sustained not-knowing as a mode of experience. At the same time it calls us into a relation of commitment — to ourselves, to others, to healing the ongoing wounds of history.

ANDREW BUTTERFIELD

La Dolce Vita

Sometime during the year 1337, the Sienese painter Ambrogio Lorenzetti began planning one of the most innovative works in the history of European art. Frescoed on three of the four walls of the executive council room of the Palazzo Pubblico in Siena, the painting is huge — almost twenty feet high and a hundred and twenty feet in total length. It is even more colossal in ambition than in scale. The picture is the first naturalistic landscape in Western painting, and the first detailed cityscape. It also portrays a number of allegorical personifications of virtues and vices. Taken together, all these elements combine to provide one of the most acute depictions of the contrasting characteristics of tyranny and justice ever made. The earliest known title for the painting is *Peace and War*, but today it is commonly referred to as the *Allegories of Good and Bad Government*. What it has to say is still pertinent today — alas, especially today — almost seven hundred years later.

The painting has three sections, each corresponding to one wall. The central portion depicts an allegory of Good Government. It is an intricate representation consisting of some sixty figures, chief among them personifications of Justice, Peace, Concord, and Commonwealth. On the wall to the right is a picture of the blessings of Good Government; we see the city of Siena and its countryside flourishing; people are at work, study, and play; and a watchful personification of Security flies above in the sky. By contrast, on the wall to the left is an allegory of Bad Government and a portrayal of the destruction it brings. There the central allegorical figure is Tyranny, who holds court among vices, including Pride, Greed, Anger, Fraud, Cruelty, and Divisiveness. In this picture, Justice is shown cast down, and Siena is coming apart. Buildings are aflame, crime is in the streets, and Fear hovers over it all.

A poem running along the bottom of the frescoes, supplemented by scrolls with inscriptions held by Security and Fear, and two short texts below Peace and Tyranny, explain the meaning of the images, in case the viewer was in any doubt. Under the rule of a just government, citizens as long as they respect the common good will be free to go forth and pursue the life they seek. They can achieve the good life; the poem calls it the *dolce vita* — one of the earliest known uses of the term. By contrast, under tyranny, "Justice is bound," "each seeks only his own good," and "the land lies in waste." Quoting the Book of Wisdom, an inscription in the central allegory of Good Government dictates the frescoes' major command: "Love Justice ye who govern on earth." These words were meant to instruct the council members who sat in the room — the so-called Nine — as well as all other citizens of the city.

It is in the details that the image comes to life, and its analysis of justice and tyranny gains strength. Near the center of the Allegory of Good Government, for instance, stands a group of twenty-four men. They vary in age, from young to old, and we can see by their clothes that while all are well-off, they come from different professions; the group includes merchants, physicians, knights, judges, and a law professor. Each of the men holds with one hand a cord that runs between them; this cord extends from the personification of Justice at the upper left in the image, down to Concord (which literally means "with cord") below her, and then across the picture to the allegory of *Bene Comune* at the upper right, a bearded figure sitting on a throne like a king, and flanked by the Virtues. This venerable man represents Commonwealth or the Common Good, and he is also meant to personify the city and government of Siena.

The metaphor that the bond of Concord was what held society together was an ancient one, going back to Cicero and Augustine, and it was still much discussed in political treatises in fourteenth-century Italy. The poem below the painting explains that the twenty-four men represent the "*animi molti*" who together make the Common Good the ruler. It is standard in English to translate *animi molti* as "many souls," but as Gabriella Piccinni stipulates in *Operazione Buon Governo*, her excellent book on the frescoes, in Italian the word *animo* means mind, not soul, and has connotations of understanding, opinion, or thought. What we see therefore is a group of men of different stations and many opinions who all voluntarily agree to live in concord for the sake of peace and the common good. When we do so, promises the poem, "every public benefit ensues — useful, necessary and pleasurable."

The poem invites viewers to turn their gaze to the right wall to see what the republic of Siena can look like in this blessed state of peace and abundance. The captivating picture that occupies this wall is naturalistic in detail but idyllic in mood. It divides evenly into two sections. At the left is the city of Siena, easily identifiable by the presence of several landmarks: the cathedral, with its distinctive dome and campanile in green and white marble; the tower of the Palazzo Pubblico, which is shown under construction, as it was at the time; and the southern gate of the city, the Porta Romana. The streets of the city are spacious and filled with light, and the buildings are brightly colored in rose, lavender, and silvery grey. Shops are open for business: we see weavers and wool merchants, a goldsmith, a shoemaker, a grocer. Snuggled between the stores there is a window into a classroom where a professor is instructing students, who are concentrating on what he says.

It is a city alive with pleasure and delight, not just industry and commerce. In a piazza in the foreground, nine young women in long flowing dresses are dancing and singing; in the background a group of men are playing a game (damage to the painting makes it impossible to say whether it is dice or something else); and near the left edge of the picture a bride is riding on a horse to her wedding, accompanied by a small cortège. The loggias and windows of the apartments above the streets are decorated with flowers and adorned with marble columns and beautiful tiles. One apartment has a pet bird, another a cat, adding to the air of domestic bliss.

The view of the countryside at the right in the image is equally rich in lovingly observed details. We see merchants and farmers bringing their wares to sell in the city; workers in the fields, sowing and threshing wheat; men hunting with crossbows to keep the rabbit population down in a field of grain; someone is fishing in a stream. In the background there are vineyards scattered over the rolling hills, and carefully depicted buildings: a country inn; a villa with a pergola; a small hamlet; a church and a few castles in the more distant elevations. The land is observed with so much care, you can even see changes in the color and the composition of the soil, depending on which side of a hill, or how close to a stream, the ground lies. The countryside in the Allegory of Bad Government is likewise depicted with assiduous attention. Damage to the wall sadly makes this section difficult to read; still, we can see that the land is barren; villas are burning; and the sky is dark and grim.

Nothing like this had ever been painted before. Compare, for example, the depiction of the city in Giotto's fresco *The Exorcism of Arezzo*, part of the mural cycle in the basilica of San Francesco in Assisi. In that picture, the artist portrays the city from outside the walls; no streets are depicted, and the simplified buildings are shown squished together in an impossible tumble. Or look at the landscape in Simone Martini's fresco of the soldier Guidoriccio riding on horseback to two castles in the Sienese countryside. This was painted in the early 1330s, in the Sala del Mappamondo in the Palazzo Pubblico — literally on the other side of the same wall from Ambrogio's frescoes — and yet there the representation of the land is nearly devoid of any distinguishing features. No fields, vineyards, workers, hunters, hamlets, streams, and so on.

Ambrogio Lorenzetti's pictures are works of staggering creativity, and of staggering preparation, too. The elements of his frescoes are so varied and finely described there can be no reasonable doubt that he spent many days or weeks going around Siena and the countryside making hundreds of preliminary drawings. If true, as I think it must be, it would be the first time in the history of European painting where we can confidently infer that an artist studied *en plein air* directly from nature. The practice by which painters from Leonardo to Cezanne trained themselves began here.

Born in Siena around 1295, Ambrogio Lorenzetti was celebrated as a genius of the first order who greatly expanded the boundaries of the visual arts. He was said to be a brilliant draftsman (alas, none of his drawings survive). He was praised for his almost single-handed invention of the depiction of the ephemera of weather — we catch a glimpse of this in the decorated band above the Allegory of Bad Government where there is a personification of Winter, who is shown as a man who stands in thickly falling snow and holds a snowball. Lorenzetti also made the most important explorations of the pictorial representation of space in the fourteenth century; indeed, the image of the streets and the buildings of Siena in the Allegory of Good Government was the most accomplished use of perspective before Masaccio's frescoes in the Brancacci Chapel in Florence nearly one hundred years later. And Lorenzetti also had a gift for the portrayal of interior states of mood and thought. In the first history of Italian art, written by the Florentine sculptor Lorenzo Ghiberti around 1450, he praised Lorenzetti's capacity to convey "fervor . . . anxiety

... breathlessness ... fear" and other intense emotions.

In the *Allegories of Good and Bad Government*, Lorenzetti's power of characterization is especially evident in the figures of Tyranny and the Vices. They are hybrid creatures who mix human and animal features in fearful combinations. Tyranny has horns and tusks, and is crosseyed, owing to its excessive self-regard. Cruelty is threatening a child with a snake. Vanity is bedecked in pearls and silks and stares into a small gold mirror to admire its blond hair. Anger is a centaur-like beast, holding a dagger and a stone, which historians see as a reference to the potential for street violence by mobs and factions. Betrayal has in its lap a strange animal, whose front half looks like a lamb, but whose tail is that of a scorpion. Greed carries money bags, clamped shut, because it never spends. And above the head of Tyranny flies Pride, the central vice. In the place of the scales of Justice, it has in its left hand the yoke that formerly held it under control, and the yoke swings unbalanced, one end higher than the other, to emphasize Pride's essential difference from Justice. Directly below Pride, on the same axis, we see the real personification of Justice, bound, afraid, and thrown to the ground beneath Tyranny's feet. Rape, torture, kidnapping, murder, and robbery take place nearby.

Ambrogio Lorenzetti was said to be highly learned, and at least once in the records of a governmental meeting he was praised for his wise counsel. Yet modern historians are unanimous that he must have had guidance in devising the complex program of the Allegories of Good and Bad Government. It has been argued that the most likely candidates for this role were the panel of legal experts who were at that moment also advising the government of Siena on a new draft of its constitution. These included several professors of law and two men identified in documents as "judges and professors of civil science" — an astonishingly early use of the term. This hypothesis seems persuasive, since a preamble to the new constitution these men were drafting contains imagery and language similar to that of the anonymous poem under the frescoes.

One may wonder why the government of Siena felt it needed a new constitution as well as a new series of frescoes reminding the members of its executive council and other citizens of the dangers of tyranny and the duty to love justice. To suggest an answer, we must look both at recent history of the city and the changes in political theory around 1300.

The city had enjoyed self-rule since around 1125. It was the nobles who first obtained political rights, but with the rapid increase in wealth and population, "the people" ("*il popolo*") also fought for inclusion in government. In 1287, after a long series of struggles, a new system of sharing power was established, known as the regime of the Nine, which featured an executive council of nine governors who served in two-month terms, and a general assembly of as many as 450 citizens who served for one year. Participation was limited by profession, income, and social standing. By law, only merchants of "middling" wealth — a broad definition then as now — could serve on the executive council of the Nine. All others were barred, not only the poor but also lawyers, doctors, artisans, guild members, and the nobles, including the largest landowners and the richest bankers in the city. These groups, however, could participate in the general assembly, although half of its seats were reserved for members of "the people." These rules were meant to constrain the predominance of the nobles, some of whom were vastly richer than everyone else — it has been estimated that four noble families owned twenty percent of the total wealth of Siena. Moreover, in Siena as elsewhere in Italy, the nobles were seen as the main source of societal disorder, owing to their attacks on the poor as well as their endless vendettas against one another. Modern historians have often referred to the Sienese government as an oligarchy and a plutocracy, but these words tend to oversimply a complex reality whose details are not fully understood. Yet it is generally agreed that Siena under the rule of the Nine enjoyed a period of relative peace and stability.

In the Middle Ages, Siena was a boom town, whose explosion in wealth arose largely from silver-mining and banking. It was a happy combination since the silver, once minted as coin, became capital and could be loaned out by Sienese banks throughout Europe. But in the fourteenth century both industries began to contract in Siena. The yields of the mines grew more unpredictable and the city's preeminence in international finance began to slip. The Sienese firm of the Bonsignori family was once the largest bank in Europe, but it ran into trouble in 1298 and collapsed in 1309. Other Sienese companies, too, had to close in the following decades. There were also conflicts over political representation, as the nobles and others sought a greater place in government in 1315, 1318, and 1325.

In 1338, moreover, at exactly the same time that Lorenzetti was finishing the frescoes, there was a run on the banks in Siena. This was triggered by the outbreak of the Hundred Years War, which led investors to fear that the huge loans by Sienese banks to the French and English kings would never be repaid. Some got their money out in time and suddenly had huge sums to invest or spend. Others got nothing. There was also a crisis in managing the city's debt. The government of Siena, while dedicated to the interests of business, also fervently believed in doing good works, by supporting art patronage all over the city, as well as helping the poor and misfortunate in countless ways, and other public projects. These many endeavors, against the background of economic uncertainty and constant troubles over food supply — an endemic problem in premodern Europe — led to considerable speculation and inflation. Some of the rich got immensely richer — we hear of wealthy women in 1338 paying absolute fortunes for luxurious handbags. But many others struggled as rarely before.

The great experiment in representative and republican government had begun in the cities of Tuscany and Lombardy around 1100, but everyone knew that it had a fundamental weakness: a tendency to factionalism. Violent struggles for political control plagued city life throughout the peninsula. Street battles were common, and the losers sometimes were killed or exiled and had their houses burned to the ground. To avoid such wearying chaos, many cities eventually chose to give up self-government, and instead be ruled by a *signore*, often a count or a duke, like the Visconti in Milan or the d'Este in Ferrara. Yet Siena, like Venice, tried a different path: to have an elite who governed, in principle at least, for the common good. This was the ideal under strain in the 1330s, and tyranny was the feared outcome, should it fail. It was this threat the Sienese magistrates had in mind when they commissioned Lorenzetti's mural cycle.

To understand the program of the frescoes, it helps to remember two points. First, that in fourteenth-century thought the contrast between tyranny and good government centered not so much on constitutional form — monarchy, oligarchy, or democracy — but rather on whether the rulers worked for their own benefit or for the common good. If a government truly sought the common good, it was by definition good, whether it was one person, a few people, or the many who ruled. Conversely, a government was a tyranny, no matter what form it took, if it did not seek to rule for the benefit of all. It was with this principle in mind that Bartolus Sassoferrato, one of the most important authorities on political philosophy in mid-fourteenth century Italy, could write that Siena was legitimately governed, even though only a small number of citizens held office.

Moreover, the frescoes express a relatively new idea about the purpose of government: that it should serve to help human life flourish on earth, not just in heaven. The efforts in self-government that began in Italian city-states in the 1100s, permanently transformed political thought in Europe, and eventually around the world. Many of the principles of civil life that we take for granted were first clearly enunciated in Italy in this era, including popular sovereignty, personal freedom, the right to property, freedom of speech, and the separation of church and state. As is well known, these developments in the ideals of liberty greatly accelerated following the rediscovery and translation into Latin of Aristotle's *Politics* in the 1260s.

The study of this work by Thomas Aquinas and his pupils

and followers, chiefly Italians, changed the basic idea of the role of government. Previously, it was seen as a necessary evil, rooted in the fallen state of mankind, whose sinful nature required oversight and restraint. But in the wake of Aristotle and Aquinas, philosophers began to argue that the purpose of government was to help mankind achieve its full human potential — in the words of Dante, to obtain "happiness in this life." Among the exponents of this new attitude were Bruno Latini, Dante's teacher; Ptolomy of Lucca, who was both Aquinas's confessor and the prior of the Dominican convent of Santa Maria Novella in Florence in the early fourteenth century; and Marsilio of Padua, author of the *Defender of Peace*, which was completed in 1324. The *dolce vita* depicted in Lorenzetti's frescoes is an attempt to show what such happiness could look like.

There is often a tendency among modern historians to emphasize the place of Florence in this advance, no doubt owing to the importance of Dante, and later Leonardo Bruni, Machiavelli, and Guicciardini, for political philosophy. Yet it would be a mistake to overlook Siena, which in the fourteenth century was described by the great jurist Cino da Pistoia as a "city of ideas." A profound concern for freedom and good governance was a long tradition in Siena. It was there — or to be more precise, in the country hamlet of Rocca d'Orcia, some forty miles southeast of the city — that "equality, justice, and liberty" were first invoked as a trio of interrelated rights. This occurred in a Charter of Liberties that freed the serfs in 1207 — eight years before the Magna Carta. Government documents in fourteenth-century Siena still regularly expressed its commitment to justice, equality, peace, concord, liberty, and protecting the poor from the predations of the rich.

It was also likely in Siena around 1288 that one of the earliest translations of Giles of Rome's *On Good Government* was made. This astonishing book — *De Regimine Principum*, to give its Latin title — has been described as among "the most widely read books" and "the most successful attempts at mediating Aristotle's moral and political philosophy" in the Middle Ages. It was enormously popular: hundreds of copies survive in Latin as well as in French, Italian, German, and Castilian translation. Giles of Rome — sometimes also called by historians Aegidius, Egidio Romano, or Egidio Colonna — had a brilliant career: he was a pupil of Aquinas; the tutor to King Philip IV of France; the head of the order of Augustinian Hermits; the Archbishop of Bourges; and advisor to Pope Boniface VIII. He also lived in Siena in 1295.

While there can be little doubt that the men who devised the program of the Allegories of Good and Bad Government knew this book, I do not mean to use it as a key to decode the pictures. Instead I want to draw attention to it because it serves so well to illuminate the general terms of the discussion of tyranny, justice, and good government in early fourteenth-century Italy. The following remarks are based on the late thirteenth-century Italian translation. I have not read it in Latin; I do not believe an English translation exists.

The first thing to note is that the author describes the book as a work of political science — *scienza della politica* in Italian — which must be one of the earliest uses of this term. Another is that while Giles of Rome is a staunch defender of monarchy, he does so because of its putative capacity for justice and the defense of the common good, rather than appealing to tradition or some divine right. Moreover, following the example of Aristotle, the political unit that he most often describes is the city, not the realm, province, or kingdom. Whereas in the Bible, cities are often seen as entrepôts of evil, for Giles they are the polity wherein citizens can best attain their full humanity. The book is a paean to the city and civil life.

Invoking the authority of Aristotle, Giles says that cities should be arranged and governed to obtain several specific goods for its citizens, the first of which is to have "joy and pleasure" ("*goia e sollazzo*") — the *dolce vita*, indeed. This can be most readily achieved in a city because humans are by nature social animals, and it is there that you have the best chance for exchange and companionship, a source of great cheerfulness. Cities also encourage mutual defense, the growth of families through marriage, the growth of wealth through trade, and other benefits. "Therefore," Giles writes, "if someone asks you what a city is, tell them it is nothing other than a gathering of people brought together to live well and virtuously, according to law and reason, and to have a perfect and sufficient human life."

To promote these ends, a good ruler or government must ensure that the people "have the things which are necessary to happiness, which are three things: knowledge, virtue, and material wealth" ("*scienze, virtù e beni temporali*"). For this reason, he continues, the ruler must make sure that the realm is full of many wise people who are knowledgeable in different fields ("*diverse scienze*"), and that the population is well educated. If the ruler does not seek this outcome, this alone is enough to determine he is "not a king but a tyrant."

The book is full of passages contrasting the characteristics of a king and a tyrant, so that the reader will be prepared to tell them apart. One astonishing section (book three, chapter nine) is dedicated to the theme of the actions which a real king undertakes, but which a tyrant only pretends to do. Item number one is that the king "must procure the common good . . . and must spend the resources of the realm for the benefit of the people; this the tyrant pretends to do but doesn't do. Instead, he gives gifts to flatterers" and spends money on things that bring no benefit to the people. The second characteristic of a real king is he "guards the wealth of the country and the common good, but the tyrant does the opposite; that is to say, he takes goods from others and does not guard the fiscal and moral integrity ["*drittura*"] of the country." Another is that a good king never dishonors, dispraises, or scorns his subjects, but a tyrant does.

The next section of the treatise, which Giles says is loosely based on book five of Aristotle's *Politics*, concerns the steps that a tyrant takes to stay in power. For example, the tyrant wants his subjects to be so foolish that they do not know what he is doing, and therefore he kills the learned and destroys the schools. He also "wants to make his subjects poor so that they will be too busy making a living to think about organizing against him." By contrast, says Giles, a real king "loves and takes care of the learned and supports the schools and studies in his land, and wants that the subjects to love one another . . . nor does he want them to be poor, but rich." Giles sums up his analysis thus: "Those who rule for and desire the common good . . . create good government . . . but those instead who aim for their own good and not the common good are tyrants."

Similar ideas can be found in other contemporary treatises on government by the likes of Ptolemy of Lucca, Marsilio of Padua, and Bartolus of Sassoferrato. It was common wisdom in the fourteenth century. And it was in the same spirit that verses from the poem that accompanies Ambrogio Lorenzetti's *Allegories of Good and Bad Government* declare (in this modified translation by Julian Lubbock):

> Turn your eyes to admire Justice,
> You who govern...
> Look how many benefits flow from her,
> And how sweet and tranquil is the life
> Of the city where this Virtue,
> More resplendent than all others, is maintained.
>
> She guards and defends
> Those who honor her, she feeds and nourishes them;
> From her light are born
> Rewards for those who do good,
> And she punishes the wicked as they deserve....
>
> But where Justice is tied up
> No one ever accords with the common good
> Nor keeps things in line,
> Therefore, Tyranny triumphs....

Tyranny hounds out those intent on good
And summons each one who intends harm.
It always protects
Those who use force, who rob, who loathe peace
Whence the entire territory is laid waste.

...and as a result,
Where there is Tyranny there is great mistrust,
War, pillage, treachery and deceit.

Defend against Tyranny
And spur your mind and your intellect
Always to hold each citizen subject to Justice
So as to avoid certain harm,

And overthrow tyrants.
Whosoever tries to destabilize Justice
Shall be for his actions
Banished and shunned
Together with every one of his followers,
So that Justice may be strengthened
For the sake of peace.

Despite the crisis of the 1330s, and then the Black Death in 1348 (which killed half of the population of Siena, including Ambrogio Lorenzetti), and the replacement of the Nine with a more broadly based magistracy in 1355, and a pair of political crises in the fifteenth century, the republic of Siena survived for another two hundred years. May we do as well, and for longer.

AMIR GILBOA

In Darkness

If they show me stone and I say stone they will say stone.
If they show me wood and I say wood they will say wood.
But if they show me blood and I say blood they will say paint.
If they show me blood and I say blood they will say paint.

Translated from the Hebrew by Leon Wieseltier

MARK EDMUNDSON

We Need Robert Frost

A boy is out doing a man's work with a chainsaw, when his sister comes to call him in for supper. Suddenly, the chainsaw leaps and cuts deep into his hand. The boy looks at the bleeding gash and begs his sister, "Don't let him cut my hand off— / The doctor when he comes." But before long the boy's pulse begins to drop: "Little, less," soon "nothing." And the boy is dead. There's "no more to build on there," so his family turns away: "And they, since they / Were not the one dead, turned to their affairs."

That is the narrative that Robert Frost unfolds in "Out, Out —" and it is, I believe, emblematic of his understanding of life. Danger is everywhere; the darkness is always crowding in. You cannot rely on others to sustain you. They have their own lives to live, and they return to them readily, no matter what sorrows might befall you. You have only one pillar of sustenance in this world: yourself.

Frost elaborates his view of the world with considerable art.

In the long run, I think that Frost will prove to be our most consequential and most read twentieth-century poet. Though interest in poetry overall is dwindling and rather rapidly, Frost continues to draw readers and top-flight critics. Adam Plunkett's recently published *Love and Need: The Life of Robert Frost*, for example, is a deeply thoughtful blending of reflections on Frost's life and his work. It testifies eloquently to our culture's need to continue reading and brooding on the poems of this profound and often misunderstood man.

Born one hundred and fifty years ago, Frost writes the poetry of the isolated and often threatened individual. He is our prophet of post-Emersonian self-reliance, our most inspired chronicler of its joys and of its costs. Whitman, the greatest of democratic poets, writes memorably about the joys of being in groups. He loves the collective, the mass, the everyday. Frost doubts all groups. In "Neither Out Far nor In Deep," he describes people looking blankly out to sea: they cannot look out far or in deep, "But when was that ever a bar / To any watch they keep?" Most people and most crowds are numbly uncomprehending; they offer little or nothing to the individual. But the individual does have the power to go his own way and sculpt a life worth living outside the rule of the majority. In his best poetry, Frost shows how to live a self-reliant life far from the noise of the crowd. He also is committed to showing what self-reliance can cost. Nothing is got for nothing in Frost's world, and though self-reliance has its joys, it also comes at a price.

We know Frost as a New England poet and a poet of rural life, though he was born in San Francisco and lived for some time in the city of Lawrence, Massachusetts. Eventually he moved north to farm in New Hampshire and Vermont. Frost had a difficult time getting his early work published. When he was nearly forty he finally found an appreciative editor, and a group of literary allies (including the very unlikely Ezra Pound) in England. Frost returned to America in 1915 and thrived. He won the Pulitzer Prize four times, and was poet in residence at Amherst, Michigan,

Harvard, and Dartmouth. He read — or tried to read: the glare of the bright winter sun defeated him — at John F. Kennedy's inauguration. He went to Russia as a goodwill ambassador for the United States, and apparently charmed Nikita Khrushchev. Frost died in 1963 at the age of eighty-eight, having written well into his final years, and reigned consistently as the best loved poet in America. He could also be what Lionel Trilling, in a revisionist speech delivered in the presence of the poet, called a "terrifying poet."

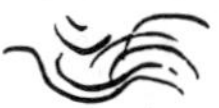

Frost is a poet for all seasons, but he is especially apt now for those of us who are weary of the current forms of collective identity. We look around and see that the joy that Whitman found in groups is no longer readily had: groups now are acrimonious, conflict-ridden, nasty. The happiness that Whitman found in collective life is hard to locate, if you can find it at all. But we do have another path. Enough of the romance of community, which can curdle quickly: the freedom that democracy dispenses to the individual can also be vitalizing if we know how to use it. Whitman taught the way to general happiness: it is free, unguarded. Its emblem is the open road. Emerson, whom Frost greatly admired, launched the discourse of the free if beleaguered democratic individual. In essays and addresses such as "Self-Reliance" and "The American Scholar," he wrote the prose of the independent man or woman, though he could not, despite his efforts, write the poetry. That had to await the next century. A hundred years and more after Emerson's great period in the 1830s, Frost came along to do precisely that. Frost can teach us what it might *feel* like day to day, to follow one's own path, go one's own way. For those who do not care for the present-day pressure to join, profess, represent, and conform, Frost can be a resource and an inspiration.

Frost's world is constantly dangerous; rarely does anyone in it care about you and yours. "Out, Out — " is an allusive title. It refers to Macbeth's famous speech after his wife dies of guilt and grief:

Out, out brief candle!
Life's but a walking shadow, a poor player
That struts and frets his hour upon the stage
And then is heard no more. It is a tale
Told by an idiot, full of sound and fury
Signifying nothing.

Obvious allusion is not common in Frost, though his work is drenched in the English poetic tradition, as Plunkett demonstrates; and so an open allusion to Shakespeare, and to what may be his darkest speech, carries weight. For Frost this is what life is, or too often can be. And if this is the case, what is to be done?

In "Acquainted with the Night," Frost finds himself walking disconsolately down city streets late:

I have been one acquainted with the night.
I have walked out in rain — and back in rain.
I have outwalked the furthest city light.

I have looked down the saddest city lane.
I have passed by the watchman on his beat
And dropped my eyes, unwilling to explain.

Then the walker hears a cry from far away. He pauses hopefully. But alas, the cry is not meant for him. It is not sounded to call him back or say goodbye. Whatever he has left broken behind him will stay broken. No one comes to save him from his sorrow. No one comes because no one ever comes. It is up to you to do what you can to help yourself.

A life of solitude has its pleasure (we will get to those), but it also creates fear and longing. In "Desert Places," Frost stares off into a "blank whiteness of benighted snow / With no expression, nothing to express." His world has gone as inscrutably and frightfully white as Ahab's whale. Salvation? Solution? There is none ready to hand. All Frost can say is that this is familiar territory: "I have it in me so much nearer home / To scare myself with my own desert places." Frost's comfort is that he possesses "a violence from within that protects us from a violence without," to cite his rival Wallace Stevens.

The writer whom Frost most admired was almost certainly Emerson; but his chosen philosopher was Schopenhauer. Schopenhauer took his understanding of life from Buddhism: life is largely pain. And pain hurts far more than any pleasure pleases. "Pleasure is never as pleasant as we expect it to be," Schopenhauer declared, "and pain is always more painful. If you do not believe it, compare the respective feelings of two animals, one of which is eating the other." Frost would probably nod in assent.

Is there anything to be done to mitigate a life largely defined by pain? Whitman's answer — merge ecstatically with the democratic mass — was never on the table for Frost. He knew himself to be different. He speaks of "the exception I like to think I am in everything," and though he seems to be boasting, he is also aware of the vulnerability that the sentiment entails. He would surely have concurred with an observation that I heard Harold Bloom make frequently, "He who would be all in himself risks becoming nothing in himself." Put off by the poisoned and futile group life of our day, in which people too often define themselves through hatred and opposition, any number of us will end up choosing the path that came naturally to Frost, the path of the individual who tries to live on and find meaning on his or her own.

Religion cannot solve Frost's problems for him. Though he respects Christianity — probably as Schopenhauer does, for its tragic view of life — he could never conform to an institutional or catechismic faith. He cordially disliked T. S. Eliot, who he thought relied too heavily on religious consolation in his poetry. "I play euchre," Frost said. "He plays eucharist."

So what is there for the solitary individual unmoored from the traditional stays and props? To begin with, you can go off and make something. Frost called his poems momentary stays against confusion. He was speaking not on behalf of the reader but on behalf of the poet. You make something that is sturdy and well-crafted and resilient. You capture the play of human speech; you find just the right metaphor; you round the work off with a dose of wisdom, however ambiguous it may be. Frost particularly wished to be praised for his power to make metaphors: he wanted to be applauded for his capacity to be reminded of this by that, of that by this. The chainsaw story sends him to Shakespeare; climbing a tree delicately in "Birches" — "I'd like to go by climbing a birch tree, / And climb black branches up a snow-white trunk / Toward heaven, till the tree could bear no more . . ." — recalls what it is like to fill a glass to the top and then, ever so slightly, over the top. A white spider on a white flower takes him to Aquinas' argument about how the perfect design of the world proves the existence of God. A bounteous woman reminds him of a graceful silken tent standing alone and poised in a field.

To keep confusion at bay and the night from taking over, you make things, well-formed, useful things. Frost was not referring only to poems: he made that clear. He said that to make a horseshoe, with perfect symmetry, tough and durable, was a kind of making that could hold off confusion. Make things, make them right, and you put darkness at bay and maybe do a little good in the world.

You should also hold onto what gives you sustenance. In "Two Tramps at Mud Time," a pair of ragged men emerge from the woods while Frost is chopping wood. He reads their minds: they want to do his job for pay. But Frost will not hand over his axe. Thoreau observed that he hoed beans to get sustenance, but also to cultivate tropes for his writing. The farm and the chores that sustain it are practical necessities for Frost, but they also provide him with substance for his art. Frost writes about country life — farming and husbandry — because he feels deeply that rural life is where reality is most potently concentrated. "My object in living," he proclaims near the close of "Two Tramps," "is to unite / My avocation and my vocation / As my two eyes make one in sight." My students are often disappointed when it becomes clear to them that Frost is not going to give up the axe or even hand a few charitable dollars to the men. But in Frost's world you need to take care of yourself, for no one — at least no one creditable — is going to provide for you. It's not that Frost does not feel the social sting of not handing off his axe. He does. It's just that such a gesture makes no sense in his fragile but competent individualist world.

There is a recorded clip of Frost reading a hyperbolic poem about putting away resources for old age. The poem is called "Provide, Provide," and it's a fable about a one-time starlet, called Abishag, "the picture pride of Hollywood," scrubbing stairs in old age to get by. Do not let it happen to you, Frost says.

No memory of having starred
Atones for later disregard
Or keeps the end from being hard.
Better to go down dignified
With boughten friendship at your side
Than none at all. Provide, provide!

After he's done "saying" the poem — Frost never recited his verse or read it aloud, he "said" it — he pushes his face toward the camera and remarks, with dark gusto, "Provide, provide — or someone else will provide for ya. How would you like that?" Someone else being your neighbor, the town, the government.

Frost takes another memorable swipe at groups and groupthink in "Departmental." Ostensibly it is a poem about ants, and in particular the death of one ant, the noble forager Jerry McCormic. "The word goes forth in Formic / 'Death's come to Jerry McCormic.'" (Calling ant-talk Formic is a marvelous touch, no?) The disposal of Jerry's body is cold and standardized:

Will the special Janizary
Whose office it is to bury
The dead of the commissary.
Go bring him to his people.

It is all routine, all unfeeling. Jerry is an anonymous creature, characterized only by his work, not mourned for when he passes but submitted to a scripted interment. How much is Jerry's fate like that of the human factory worker, rendered faceless by the industrial machine? His funeral protocols "[C]ouldn't be called ungentle / But how thoroughly departmental."

The factory worker: in "A Lone Striker," Frost tells the story of a man locked out of the factory gates when he is late for work. He doesn't immediately reject the factory and its regimented (ant-like) life. But as he stands outside waiting, a fresh impulse takes him, and surprising both himself and the reader, he considers taking off for the woods:

> He knew a path that wanted walking;
> He knew a spring that wanted drinking;
> A thought that wanted further thinking;
> A love that wanted re-renewing.
> Nor was this just a way of talking
> To save him the expense of doing.
> With him it boded action, deed.

Note that the lone striker is not a member of a union, striking for better wages and conditions. He is striking for freedom and for no one other than himself. At the end of the poem, he seems on the verge of discovering it.

The lone individual — the one who says no to the ant-life of groups — can find joy in beauty, though Frost's idea of beauty is not entirely conventional. Schopenhauer believed that beauty saved you from inner turbulence by creating a contemplative calm. You could stand and stare at a landscape or a painting for hours and achieve some manner of ease. For Schopenhauer, life was walking a fiery path: beauty gave you a cool spot to rest, for as long as you could sustain your gaze. But Frost loves, and brilliantly evokes, *transient* beauty. Listen to him praising a hillside thaw:

To think to know the country and not know
The hillside on the day the sun lets go
Ten million silver lizards out of snow!
As often as I've seen it done before
I can't pretend to tell the ways it's done.
It looks as if some magic of the sun
Lifted the rug that bred them on the floor
And the light breaking on them made them run.

The poet claims that it is the sun that makes the magic here, but it is the poet who knows to compare the shimmer on a snowy hillside with the glow of lizards running wild.

Beauty passes in Frost, and even at its most dramatic it submits to constraints. It's as though Frost were somewhat suspicious of beauty and joy. The more transient the beauty, the more Frost loves it. Consider the short and quite wonderful poem "Blue Butterfly Day":

It is blue butterfly day here in spring,
And with these sky-flakes down in flurry on flurry
There is more unmixed color on the wing
Than flowers will show for days unless they hurry.

But these are flowers that fly and all but sing:
And now from having ridden out desire
They lie closed over in the wind and cling
Where wheels have freshly sliced the April mire.

The blue butterflies are magnificent, more vibrant even than the spring flowers will be. Yet their magnificence lasts only a short time — blue butterfly *day*. Soon they are folded over, clinging to the mud. The poignancy of this portrait of transience brings to mind the classical Chinese poets and their blossoms.

Beauty is splendid, but sustain contact with it too long and you will inevitably be left vulnerable. You become mesmerized and can be taken unawares. Life is dangerous, life is fraught, as the boy in "Out, Out — " learns. Frost commends vigilance: there is too much out in the world that can ruin you if you are besotted by its wonders. In *Studies in Classic American Literature*, a book that has itself become something of a classic, D.H. Lawrence observes that "the essential American soul is hard, isolate, stoic and a killer." Frost is no killer, and though he is often hard he has a capacity to open himself up, albeit cautiously, to beauty. But "isolate and stoic": that is Frost to a T.

What about love? You might, if you are very fortunate, find one other person to share your solitude fruitfully. (Frost often thought that he had found such inner companionship in his formidable wife Elinor.) Frost wrote some wonderful love poems, the best of which manage to be both joyful and prudent. Prudence, of course, is not a common theme in the poetry of love. Perhaps the most touching of them is "Putting in the Seed," a sonnet (Frost wrote many of those) that runs this way:

> You come to fetch me from my work tonight
> When supper's on the table, and we'll see
> If I can leave off burying the white
> Soft petals fallen from the apple tree
> (Soft petals, yes, but not so barren quite
> Mingled with these, smooth bean and wrinkled pea),
> And go along with you ere you lose the sight
> Of what you came for and become like me,
> Slave to a springtime passion for the earth.
> How Love burns through the Putting in the Seed
> On through the watching for that early birth
> When just as the soil tarnishes with weed,
> The sturdy seedling with arched body comes
> Shouldering its way and shedding the earth crumbs.

Anyone with an acquaintance with gardening will recognize the feelings that infuse the poem. In the springtime, people fall in love with planting, and with imagining the bounty to come. It is the time of hope for the gardener, before pests or bad weather interfere with the dream of plenty. Frost himself was a gardener and knew the passion for growing well.

Yet the poem is about more than gardening. "Putting in the Seed" is also about the act of love, putting in the seed that leads to pregnancy and birth. But "Love burns through the Putting in the Seed": life begins with sex, passion inspired by love. (Note the quasi-metaphysical capitalization of the central terms.) But love continues on past the moment of lovemaking, into the days of pregnancy, when husband and wife together wait for the birth. And then comes the seedling, the child, sturdy and strong, "shouldering" away the earth crumbs. The poem, then, is about fidelity. The husband is there for the act of love, yes; but he will remain there through the pregnancy and on to the birth. The transformation that his wife undergoes will not rattle or alienate him. Love will abide into the future. This is a marriage poem, about a love that goes beyond simple passion into regions of care, compassion, steadfastness, and respect.

But Frost was also the author of a stingingly bitter marriage poem, "Home Burial" A newly married couple's child has died, and the death has put them horribly at odds. Amy, the wife, is mourning her child furiously, and she makes it clear that her grief will never stop. Her husband, unnamed in the poem, is a practical countryman, who cannot understand the depths of Amy's grief. "What was it brought you up to think it the thing / To take your mother-loss of a first child / So inconsolably — in the face of love?" He thinks that his wife's grief arises from conceit and over-refinement. Amy finds her husband crude, empty, hopeless. The poem is composed with grim conviction. For the strong individualist, like the husband in the poem, marriage can provide some succor, but it can also be a trap, a chainsaw waiting to jump.

The poem that seems to me most completely to capture Frost's view of life is called "The Most of It." In its way it is an anti-marriage poem. It is an allusive poem, with a submerged mythical theme. A man finds himself alone in the world, not unlike Adam before Eve. He is lonely. He cries out in frustration and sorrow, but all he hears in response is an echo. He wants more. He cannot live with a mere reflection from the world. He wants what he calls "counter-love, original response." He wants Eve, or someone like her, someone who will give him more than "copy speech," and talk to him in an idiom of her own. But he never gets it. The kind of Romantic love that helps a poet like Shelley burn imaginatively through received feelings and thoughts, and discover, if only fleetingly, a paradise on the other side of them, is not available to our man.

What he sees instead is a shape plunging into the waters on the opposite bank. It makes its way toward him, and emerges,

> Instead of proving human when it neared
> And someone else additional to him,
> As a great buck it powerfully appeared,
> Pushing the crumpled water up ahead,
> And landed pouring like a waterfall,
> And stumbled through the rock with horny tread,
> And forced the underbrush — and that was all.

Not a woman, not Eve, but a magnificent buck, that appears as though in a dream-vision and then is gone. Our Adamic individual is left alone.

Yet he does receive something. Or as he puts it in another poem about the unlikelihood of fulfillment: "For once, then, something." He receives the buck, who is potentially an image of majestic self-reliance. Adam can embrace that vision of himself or he can go on pining. To save himself, and affirm his solitary dignity, he is going to have to learn to read in the way that Frost commends. He is going to have to see a metaphor when it arises and understand how far he can ride it out. As Frost says in *Education by Poetry*, "Unless you have had your proper poetic education in the metaphor you are not safe anywhere. Because you are not at ease with figurative values: you don't know the metaphor in its strength and its weakness. You don't know how far you may expect to ride it and where it may break down with you." Our protagonist will have to begin by seeing that nature has offered him a potentially illuminating image, if he is ready himself for such an illumination — if he can then understand what he can make of it. He will need to grasp and embrace his solitude, even if he wishes things were otherwise.

The poem's title, "The Most of It," can be puzzling. The most that we can even be given in the way of consolation — a warning of a limit? Or, as I would prefer to read its inexplicit meaning, Make the Most of It, in the old American phrase. Can our man do so? Can he read the metaphor that life has offered him? And then can he live it out, taking some joy in his solitude? Can he be satisfactorily alone in the world, savoring the beauty of nature and the dignified, difficult pleasures of work? Is his life a diminished thing for the lack of others? Not, I suspect, if he knows what his path is and how to follow it.

Frost steps into our militant age of groupthink and tribal rage and makes a path for the individual who does not care for any of it. Make sturdy useful things; contemplate beauty in nature, but not for too long; consider marriage, but acknowledge the dangers; learn to be at home in the metaphor, and when the image arises that embodies your fate do not be afraid to embrace it. Take the hits as they come, for they *will* come. Chart your own course, cut your own path, to the best of your abilities; and be prudent and wise. Learn to rely on yourself and do for yourself. Think twice before you surrender the axe.

STEVE WASSERMAN

The Rise and Fall and Rise of American Publishing

I knew the jig was up when one day, in the fall of 1995, my boss and publisher Peter Osnos asked me to lunch. I was then editorial director of Times Books, an imprint of Random House. Previously, I had been publisher of Hill & Wang, a nonfiction division of Farrar, Straus & Giroux. I'd had some success during my years there in the late 1980s, publishing *Innumeracy* by John Allen Paulos, Hill & Wang's first bestseller since Elie Wiesel's *Night* in 1960. Wiesel's slim and scorching account of his torment at Auschwitz and Buchenwald had been rejected by more than fifteen American publishers before Arthur Wang took it on. It was not an immediate success despite glowing reviews. Over time, however, it would sell more than ten million copies and become a central text in the world's moral education, such as it is. Paulos' polemic pressing the case for mathematical literacy was unlikely to find similar favor, especially given the one-hand-clapping review buried in the middle of the *New York Times Book Review*. Yet to my surprise it vaulted to the upper echelons of bestseller lists all over the country, including the *Times*, largely, I came to believe, because of its brevity — it was more essay than full-length jeremiad — written with engaging wit, and so it didn't feel like homework. It did a lot to help many people overcome their allergy to numbers.

My phone was soon ringing with offers from other publishers, who perhaps felt I had some mojo, some secret sauce, that might help them out. They offered to double my salary and to give me the keys to their respective bank vaults so that I might dangle larger and more substantial advances to authors whose books might similarly sell well. Plus giving me a larger playing field to run around on, with all the presumed market clout that a larger, more corporate concern might provide. I took the bait. What could go wrong?

There I was, on the eve of publishing a revisionist history of the American Revolution by Theodore Draper, one of the most independent and formidable historians in the country, a public intellectual *avant la lettre*, a man I had long admired and whose defenestration of the Iran-Contra scandal I had published at Hill & Wang. His new book was the work of a lifetime of study, just over five hundred pages of brilliantly argued scholarship, an original account of the causes and nature of the revolutionary process that resulted in the final rupture with England and, as Draper put it, in a struggle for power, whatever its ideological conceits. I rounded up praise — read: blurbs — from a clutch of worthies, including R. R. Palmer, Esmond Wright, Edward Countryman, and even Gore Vidal, who had long ago anointed himself an expert on American history. He called it a book written "with an acuity and balance worthy of the late (and until now unequaled) Richard Hofstadter." I arranged a paperback edition with the head of Vintage Books at Random House, to follow our hardcover. Our first printing was ten thousand. The pump was primed. I was excited.

Osnos waited until dessert to deliver the bad news. He said that we could no longer publish the Drapers of this world. First printings of ten thousand copies were killing us. It was our obligation to find books that could command first printings of forty, fifty, even sixty thousand copies. Only then could profits be had that were large enough to feed the behemoth — or more precisely, the more refined and compelling tastes — that modern mainstream publishing demanded.

It was a dark moment, but still I was game, except for the sad fact that almost never had I — or Osnos — acquired books that warranted such large printings. To be sure, we had published books that had "done well," going back to press, some in numbers that ultimately far exceeded sixty thousand copies sold. But, I pointed out, if such a principle were raised to the level of dogma, none of the several books that were then keeping Random House fiscally afloat — Paul Kennedy's *The Rise and Fall of the Great Powers*, John Berendt's *Midnight in the Garden of Good and Evil* (eventually spending a record two hundred and sixteen weeks on the bestseller list, and adapted into a film by Clint Eastwood), and Joe Klein's *Primary Colors* (published anonymously and made into a movie by Mike Nichols in 1998) — would ever have been acquired. None had been expected to be a bestseller, and each had started out with a ten-thousand copy first printing.

Osnos would soon decamp to start an independent press called PublicAffairs, and I accepted an offer in late 1996 to edit the *Los Angeles Times Book Review*, one of only three separate Sunday sections devoted to books left at the country's major metropolitan dailies. Four years later, I organized and published a symposium on the state of American publishing. More than thirty distinguished editors (Robert Gottlieb, Robert Loomis, Jason Epstein, Robert Weil, Marion Wood), publishers (Alberto Vitale, André Schiffrin, Richard Seaver, Roger W. Straus Jr.), literary agents (David Black, Sandra Dijkstra, Morton L. Janklow, Gloria Loomis, Betsy Lerner), and booksellers (Andy Ross, Barbara Meade, Douglas Dutton) participated. They represented both mainstream trade publishers (Alfred A. Knopf, Random House, Simon & Schuster) and independent houses and university presses (W. W. Norton, Farrar, Straus & Giroux, Seven Stories, Harvard, Oxford, Walker & Co., The

Overlook Press, Verso). Today a third of the respondents are no longer with us. The important, and stinging, question remains: Is their publishing world still with us? Or has the business — which, like all cultural enterprises, has effects beyond its own profits or losses — evolved beyond recognition, for better or for worse?

When, in that Pleistocene era, I invited a broad spectrum of industry veterans to share their individual and collective wisdom, the twenty-first century had just begun. It was plain that for some time several issues had been plaguing those of us fortunate to work as midwives to the birthing of books. None of us were naïve. We had always known that working at the intersection of art and commerce was inherently fraught. Publishing had always required an admixture of idealism and cynicism. Many were temperamentally Chicken Littles, fearing that however difficult the old ways of acquiring and editing and selling books were, the new ways were worse. The Golden Age, as usual, was in the past — a time synonymous with our youth — and of course we were convinced that it had been much better. (And there were, we soon discovered, some good reasons for thinking so.) The future was now fast upon us, and whatever else might be said about it, we knew one thing: it would not include us.

We had entered a new world of painful — even, for many, unimaginable — challenges. Among the more acutely distressing trends were the conglomeration of nearly everything, a sovereign obsession with the bottom-line and the pressure to reap short-term profits, and the near-universal enrollment in the junk cults of celebrity, sensationalism, and gossip, which made it harder for publishers to successfully maintain a commitment to literature and the public discourse — to be a serious publisher. Complicating the picture even more was the advent of electronic technologies that threatened to significantly transform old ways of both producing and distributing books. The swift rise of Amazon was a critical factor, transforming the landscape of bookselling, putting to the sword hundreds if not thousands of independent bookstores even as Jeff Bezos built with a single-minded determination both admirable and appalling a digital juggernaut that made it possible for millions to gain access at remarkably cheap prices to a more diverse array of books than ever before. Bezos got big fast and was soon able to dictate the terms of the entire trade. Publishers reeled. And so did the noble bookshop owners. By 2010, the number of bookstores in the country fell from a high of about four thousand in 1990 to fifteen hundred. (Thirteen years later, against all expectation, it had rebounded by about 1,000 bookstores.)

The rise of digital communication and book-buying caught Hollywood's imagination and swiftly became the basis for a hit movie, Nora Ephron's *You've Got Mail*, a glamorous tale of the unglamorous reality of the independent American bookstore. Worry deepened that these trends would alter even how people read. The growing proliferation of screens raised the specter that the habits of attention necessary to absorb extended narrative — the new term "long form" was itself an expression of the jitters — would fall victim to the seductions of a culture hostage to velocity and instant gratification. The patience necessary for the lasting pleasures of a more contemplative, slower approach to both knowledge and entertainment was at risk.

Perhaps it was delusional on our part, but optimism dies last. We felt ourselves to be a species defined by our opposable thumbs and an inherent need to tell each other stories. For this was the principal way in which we extracted meaning in an otherwise inchoate world. Surely technology could not destroy or replace this essential human quality. We might debate the many ways the industry had resisted opening itself up to the stories of others and what should be done about it. We could argue about how a world of ostensible privilege and presumed entitlement had too often shaped who got to be the "gatekeepers" — another shibboleth of digital culture, though of course it applied most precisely to Bezos and Zuckerberg and the other tech mandarins — of our literary culture. We might decry the dismal fact that American publishers, with notable exceptions, had long been allergic to translating works from other languages. We might blame the manifold failure of our experiment in public education to advance literacy so that we now have an electorate in which fully half are unable to read at a level higher than fourth grade, thus enfeebling the very idea of an informed citizenry that is so essential for a healthy democracy.

Book people are nevertheless temperamentally given to a persistent idealism even while constantly complaining that everything is doomed. Almost uniformly they will insist that any glass filled halfway with water (or more likely, vodka) is half empty, but they will behave almost without exception as if it were half-full. They live to hear a new story by a new writer, or a fresh gloss on an old truth. The main worry, as the late Marion Wood, a veteran of many years in New York publishing, insisted to me in early 2001, wasn't "the conglomerate or a celebrity-hungry culture or the technology, or the idiocies of the last thirty years. The biggest problem is keeping reading alive as a passion — and finding ways to reach those passionate readers with the news of a great new writer." The renowned Robert Gottlieb, who died at the age of ninety-two in 2023, told me: "Every few years since I've been in publishing — that's since 1955 — we've been told that it's all over. There's always a new reason: remember 'The medium is the message'? Meanwhile books go rolling along. The very golden age that young and middle-aged people are looking back at so romantically was forcefully (and frequently) described to me by Alfred Knopf as 'the age of the slobs' — for him, everything after 1939 represented the death of publishing. I thought he was mistaken then, and I think today's doom-criers are mistaken, too."

The venerable literary agent Georges Borchardt is still working at age ninety-seven. When I met with him not long ago in his Manhattan office, he saw no reason to revise his sober assessment rendered a quarter of a century earlier, reminding me that good and daring writers had almost always had a hard time getting published by big established houses, long before the mergers and the conglomerates came into being: "William Faulkner was turned down by the legendary Maxwell Perkins (Scribners); Elie Wiesel was turned down by the original Knopf (Mrs. K herself); Samuel Beckett was turned down by just about every publisher in New York. Both Wiesel and Beckett were then picked up by small publishers with little capital, but good instincts, Hill & Wang and Grove Press respectively." (Borchardt represented both writers.) "So put me in the camp of the guardedly optimistic." It was inspiring to have pessimism dispelled by someone who has seen so much.

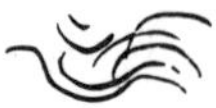

Still, twenty-five years into the new century, something has changed; an ill wind is blowing through publishers' suites. One wonders if those rosy sentiments are more a treasured conceit — editors and publishers have always mythologized themselves — than an unsentimental acknowledgment of a more disturbing reality. The big surprise is less the manifold ways in which Brobdingnagian publishing has come to dominate the ecosystem of publishing generally, but — this is the good news of our day — the consequent and unexpected resilience of an entire galaxy of small independent publishers. You would have thought that as big publishers battened on economies of scale, merging back-office bureaucracies, outsourcing entire departments of copyeditors, shedding aging (and expensive) staff, and kicking an entire generational cohort to the curb, the result would be leaner, more efficient, more profitable publishing machines ever more deft at discovering the quirky writers whose daring imaginations would be well served by publishers skilled in the alchemy of promotion and marketing. More: that as the big companies merge and consolidate the small fry would be snuffed out, deprived of oxygen, unable to compete. But you would be wrong.

With conglomeration came cowardice. Turns out, mass wasn't synonymous with class. A culture of timidity soon set in among the corporate overseers, and invertebrate behavior quickly became a striking hallmark of the merger mania that characterized much of mainstream publishing dealmaking and practice. (Beyond the economic realm, one must not forget the shabby fear with which mainstream publishing greeted the fatwa against Salman Rushdie.) Most publishers began in the first half of the twentieth century as the black sheep of their rich families: Horace Liveright, Roger

W. Straus, Jr., Barney Rosset, to name only a few. One example tells the larger story: Bennett Cerf and Donald Klopfer founded Random House in 1927 and bought Alfred A. Knopf in 1960 and Pantheon the following year. Four years later, in 1965, they sold it to RCA and then RCA, in turn, sold it in 1980 to Si Newhouse's privately owned Advance Publications for between $65 million and $70 million in cash. Newhouse ruled the roost for eighteen years and then sold in 1998 to the private German multinational conglomerate Bertelsmann, which paid a reported $1 billion, making Bertelsmann a publishing Goliath. Fifteen years later, in 2013, Random House and the Penguin Group combined because of a deal between Bertelsmann and Pearson, the parent companies of their respective publishing houses, a response to the threat posed by Amazon. Other publishers followed suit, the French company Hachette buying Little, Brown, the German firm of Holtzbrinck absorbing Farrar, Straus & Giroux, Rupert Murdoch's News Corporation swallowing HarperCollins, and the global private equity and investment firm of KKR gobbling up Simon & Schuster, leaving today just five corporate empires dominating the American publishing landscape. Corporate raiders made out like bandits; authors and editors not so much.

To be sure, opportunism and market agility are among the requirements of a successful business. But fear hollows out the good kind of opportunism, and mainstream publishers grew wary of alienating readers and found themselves cleaving to the familiar, the safe bet, the tried-and-true. A certain predictability set in; and, as ever, smaller publishers — independents who had almost no money — were less encumbered and therefore nimbler and more willing to take on risk. Kris Kristoferson was right: freedom's just another word for nothing left to lose. Big publishing blew itself up, and much of its current predicament is the result of self-inflicted wounds, prompting the emergence of an arcadia of small publishing houses, many of which display all the qualities of imagination and taste and pluck which largely elude the established firms.

Today, thanks to a concerted campaign to discover and publish a wider array of voices, more representative of America's changing racial and ethnic demography than had been permitted in the past by a publishing elite hostage to its own class and racial and ethnic origins, more writers from every corner of the country and the world, ostensibly reflecting a greater range of human experience, are being published than ever before. But this politically inspired expansion has also prompted a politically inspired contraction. The politicization of American publishing — from both the left and the right — has become more pronounced in recent years. All the self-congratulation and the virtue-signaling that often accompanies the appearance of this or that new novelist cannot disguise the fact that the stories that are told in many of these new books, especially those peddled by the mainstream houses, no matter the ethnic or racial origin of their respective authors, seem mainly to be chapters in a single tale of trauma, survival, and resilience, testimonies intended to keep open the wound of victimhood whose suppurating nature is seen as a sign of moral authenticity.

A new orthodoxy has arisen. As David Rieff points out in his incisive and important book *Desire and Fate* (recently published by a small courageous house in London called Eris and distributed by Columbia University Press), we live today in a therapeutic culture in which the idea of trauma has become central. Rieff worries that "we are entering a Woke version of the Victorian Age, or post-Hays Code Hollywood, in which censorship will be the norm, not the exception" and suspects "that the increasing consensus that a writer or an artist's moral character, and political and increasingly racial and gender bona fides, should determine whether they are published or exhibited, celebrated or ignored, will grow stronger, not weaker in the decades to come." Rieff denounces the "ecstatic philistinism of identity politics" and locates its origins in the "old axiom of small-town White Protestant America — 'If you don't have something nice to say, don't say anything at all' — a trope that has now been "redeployed in the service of supposed emancipation and reparation." The use of "sensitivity readers" by publishers to assure them that nothing heretical or insensitive (heretics are always insensitive!) appears in their books, that characters and language that might offend are expunged from publication, is common, as is the proliferation of "trigger warnings." There is, Rieff concludes, "a new kind of politicized moral prudery sailing under the flag of anti-racism and inclusivity (not to mention under medicalized fetishization of trauma) to impose the claim that only morally defensible art is acceptable art."

Rieff's book is likely the most intellectually sophisticated and rigorous critique of "wokeness" that we will have, but by now the anxiety is hardly his alone. One hears it also in the book trade. "We all know the elephant in the room," the literary agent Andy Ross and former owner of the great Cody's Books in Berkeley told me. "It goes by the name of 'cultural appropriation.' It supposes that authentic fiction demands the writer can only write in the point of view of characters of the same sex, race, or ethnicity as the writer. It's become a tyranny. It's dangerous to speak out against it. When you do, you get accused of things like 'literary colonialism' or something like that. Everybody in publishing agrees, but nobody will do anything about it or even talk about it out loud. I'm glad I don't represent Arthur Golden, a Jewish guy who wrote a wonderful novel in 1997, a bestseller, *Memoirs of a Geisha*. It would never be published today." In our culture now, like seeks only like, and only like can speak with any authority about like. We know only what we ourselves are. We have permission to write only about ourselves and people like us. Fiction has been inundated with "auto-fiction." Authenticity is the supreme literary value, when in fact it is not an aesthetic value at all. Can there be a prescription more discouraging to the imagination than this?

This is not an entirely unprecedented debate in American letters. It is useful to recall, for example, the controversy that erupted in 1983 over *Famous All Over Town*, a novel of Chicano life, by one Danny Santiago. Hailed by the *New York Times* as "a classic of the Chicano urban experience" and by the *Dallas Times Herald* as the work of an author with "a voice rich with barrio talk and a comic touch" and by the street-wise Richard Price as "utterly seductive. . . funky, cocky, innocent, cagey and at times he said he was. He was unmasked by John Gregory Dunne as his former landlord and friend Daniel James, not Chicano at all, a Yale graduate and past member of the American Communist Party and middling Hollywood screenwriter whose career had tanked and who had been so frightened by being blacklisted that he resorted to using a pseudonym to get over his writer's block. "The idea of an Anglo presenting himself as a Chicano, I found troubling," Dunne confessed. He felt that "this particular kind of literary deception could, if discovered . . . have unpleasant extraliterary ramifications." James, however, insisted that as Danny Santiago he was "so much freer" to write and it was under that guise that he was able to publish the stories that would become his novel in *Redbook* and *Playboy* in 1971, including one called "The Somebody" that was chosen in Martha Foley's annual collection, *Best American Short Stories.*

The identity police were aroused. Philip Hererra, the editor of *Nuestro*, a champion of Latino writers who had published one of Santiago's stories, was outraged: "We were deceived. We were led to believe that Danny Santiago was a Mexican American. Clearly, he was not." Alvin Poussaint, Harvard's resident progressive psychiatrist, joined the chorus of denunciations, saying that "by implying it was written by a Mexican, it gave the book an authenticity it simply did not have." Others rose to James' defense, including many Latino writers. Thomas Sanchez, for one, author of both the bestselling *Zoot-Suit Murders* and the acclaimed *Rabbit Boss,* a novel that through an act of gifted literary ventriloquism gives voice to four generations of Washo Indians in the California Sierras, declared that "I don't care who writes a book — a man, a woman, a cat or a dog. They say you shouldn't judge a book by its cover. Well, you shouldn't judge it by the author's ethnic or cultural background."

Dunne, Herrera, and the others got it backwards. Surely it is a tribute to the scope of a writer's imagination if he can create a world *not* his own, if he can persuasively write not within difference but across difference. *Madame Bovary, c'est moi,* Flaubert thrillingly proclaimed, in defiance of the writer's confinement to his inherited circumstances. There is an old and honorable literary tradition of writing in somebody else's lane. Besides, are we not all traveling in humanity's lane?

More recently, in 2020, the publishing world was roiled by the controversy over Jeanine Cummins' novel *American Dirt*, a story about the calamity that befalls a Mexican mother and son who slip the noose of a drug cartel and seek refuge in the United States. Cummins, a white woman of Irish and Puerto Rican extraction, sold the book to Doubleday for a reported advance of seven figures, received early praise from Stephen King and John Grisham, and saw her book become an Oprah Book Club smash hit, selling more than four million copies in nearly forty languages. But Oprah, the supreme voice of conventionality, spoke too soon. To the author's astonishment and the distress of her publisher, *American Dirt* was excoriated by more than one hundred and forty writers who signed an open letter calling the book "exploitative, oversimplified, and ill-informed, too often erring on the side of trauma fetishization." These were not literary objections. Condemned for its alleged caricatures of Mexico, and despite Cummins' wistful and not altogether savory admission that she wished that someone "slightly browner than me" had been the author, she was unable to avoid becoming, as she put it, an "example of the white supremacy problem in publishing, as a part Puerto Rican woman from a working-class background." In reality, of course, it was she who had sought to tackle "the white supremacy" problem by writing a book that tried to transcend all such extra-literary considerations.

Among the commissars of publishing, Cummins took a beating. The battle over *American Dirt* was so bruising that she was unable to write for a year. (Her new novel, *Speak to Me of Home*, appeared last spring.) Ordinary readers didn't care about the disputations; they bought the book by the millions. Yet her public shaming had a chilling effect on many agents and authors. A curtain of fear descended, and you could feel the dread especially in the corridors of corporate publishers who dared not admit what had become common knowledge: that they were operating according to certain ideological and sociological constraints. Despite their market clout, they worried about provoking the wrath of the Red Guards of Woke. For all the chest-thumping triumphalism of the new dispensation, ballyhooing the enfranchisement of voices previously excluded from mainstream publishing, what was striking was the unacknowledged conformism of the stories now being championed.

Less noticed was the long retreat among mainstream publishers, with, as ever, notable exceptions, from the highwater mark of an earlier period to publish works of serious history and daring, even offensive fiction. Following the Second World War and the subsequent expansion of American colleges and universities as the Baby Boom generation reflected the country's growing middle class, publishers were quick to seize the opportunity to expand their publishing programs. The growing archipelago of institutions of higher education and public libraries helped underwrite this growth. In 1953, Jason Epstein founded Anchor quality paperbacks at Doubleday, while three years later Harper & Row started Harper Torchbooks, both imprints making classic works of history, literature, philosophy, and criticism popularly available to ordinary readers. Other publishers (Beacon, Meridian, Norton Library) followed. A taste for the serious was encouraged. In 1953, for example, Random House was happy to publish the recondite journals of the sixteenth-century Jesuit Matteo Ricci, one of the first Westerners to visit Japan. Today doing so would be considered commercial suicide and never mind the intellectual glory. Such a book would be consigned to the ghetto of the university presses, deemed (not altogether wrongly) to be of interest only to scholars and specialists. And so we must award plaudits to the university presses — many of them beleaguered by parent institutions that have increasingly lost faith in the intrinsic significance of core humanities curricula — who have taken up the slack of the trade houses' reluctance and have been publishing many important works of history with all the editorial scrupulousness and marketing zeal that such books require.

History as a category has suffered especially, and those publishers still committed to bringing out serious works of history complain bitterly. A case in point is the Penguin Press' recent publication of Ian Buruma's fine book *The Collaborators*, a forensic exhumation of three morally complicated lives in imperial Japan, Nazi Germany, and occupied Netherlands. The book was acclaimed in America's few remaining review publications — but the book bombed, selling only slightly more than 1,000 hardcover copies. The number was so disappointingly small that the publisher decided against bringing the book out in paperback. And this is not an exceptional circumstance in today's unforgiving market. A recent visit with a former longtime editor at Alfred A. Knopf with decades of experience editing many of the nation's most distinguished historians confirms the disobliging sales reality: readers are neither reading nor buying history in the numbers needed to make such publishing profitable. Buruma, of course, is a well-known writer, and at least his book made it into hardcover. What about all the gifted but less celebrated historians whom the trade houses ignore and can no longer imagine publishing in hard cover or soft? (Rest in peace, Ashbel Green.)

Perhaps this was to be expected. Americans have long suffered from a collective historical amnesia. Our politics are hobbled by our refusal to understand the manifold ways in which history, as was once famously said, weighs like a nightmare on the brain of the living. Americans have long cleaved to the conceit that history, insofar as it was deemed important at all, was more hindrance than help in our presumed unstoppable march to the munificent future. Optimistic, pragmatic, impatient, inventive, generous (when they are not other things), Americans have refused to be held hostage to the past, or even to be interested in it, believing America to have burst its bounds. The cost of such myopia is large. It enfeebles understanding, promotes false and ugly nostrums of all kinds, and licenses the infantilization of public debate. But the interest in facts has always taken a backseat in our culture to the easier and more seductive approach whose pleasures have tended to arouse a lasting echo of enthusiasm among a broad public, an approach best articulated by the reporter Maxwell Scott in that great mythmaker John Ford's film *The Man Who Shot Liberty Valance*: "When the legend becomes fact, print the legend." It is one of the more sinister American slogans.

The death of publishing, like the death of the novel, is an evergreen prediction. But the obituary is always premature. Neither the specter of AI nor the widespread and growing illiteracy of an alarming chunk of the public, nor the cowardice of all too many mainstream publishers, is enough to dim the passions of the word-addicted and the book-besotted. The current proliferation of small and independent publishers (I work at one of them) is remarkable proof of a thriving commitment to the written word, the serious written word, and even to the tactile pleasures to be had from the book as object. Kate Gale, the founder and intrepid head of Red Hen Press in Pasadena observes that "books run on thin margins; it's not the oil business. Yet writers like Percival Everett cup their hands over their keyboards to deliver stories and poems, and we who work in the independent press world, we press on. It was never about money, it was about story, the long game of reading a manuscript and saying as I did just yesterday this story about a creek and a girl has me. I am with this girl by the creek beaten down, getting back up again. As we do in this industry."

The list of these blessed and stalwart publishers continues to lengthen. The roll call includes Grove Atlantic, New Directions, City Lights, Tilted Axis, Beacon, Europa, Other Press, Faber and Faber, O/R, Two Lines Press, Melville House, Akashic, Verso, Milkweed Editions, Graywolf, Transit Books, Archipelago, PM Press, Ren Hen Press, Taschen, Copper Canyon, Zone, and, not least, Wiley & Sons, family-owned since 1807, an unrivalled record of independence in the American publishing industry, and W. W. Norton, not exactly a small press but the country's only employee-owned press. Many are regional in nature, devoted to this or that interest, to one literary, political, or cultural tendency or another. Some have owed their survival, in part, to the largess of federal institutions such as the National Endowment for the Arts, now under ruthless assault by the Trump administration; others, to private philanthropy. Many would find it hard to thrive without continued reliance on their nonprofit status. But these fragilities notwithstanding, they exist. There is a feistiness that refuses to fold. One is tempted to say that, despite all the challenges, we may be entering a renaissance of independent publishing, remarkably nimble and business savvy, intellectually curious and culturally indispensable; and the corporations be damned. This may well be enough to keep despair at bay.

HARIS VLAVIANOS

Niccolò Machiavelli (1469–1527)

To my son

I still remember Hedley Bull
his slow, regular footfall
in front of the podium;
the sudden way he would look up
and turn his handsome head to us
before asking in that droll Australian accent:
"Gentlemen, it all hinges on the meaning of the word *virtù*.
Bacon, Hobbes, Adams, Strauss, Skinner —
they each provide an interpretation.
What's yours?"
    I knew in a few months he would no longer be with us.
(Riddled with bone cancer
he continued teaching
with the assistance of daily morphine injections.)
I also knew
out of all the political philosophers we were studying
    that semester
this one was my favorite.
I raised my hand
he gave me the floor:
"Without *virtù*, even though a ruler may gain an empire
he will fail to attain *gloria*.
If I had to choose between Scipio Africanus and Agathocles
I'd opt for the first, no question."
Pleased, he smiled and continued:
"It's all too easy to create utopian communities;
it's a lot more difficult

to truly come to grips
with harsh political realities.
We have spent enough time on Plato and Augustine's
'What is as it ought to be.'
Let's turn to Thucydides
for he remains key."
Machiavelli survived that spring.
Next semester, Adam Roberts
(hired in Bull's place)
was not as charitable to the Florentine.
As he sets his sights on deconstructing
the "realist school" in lecture after lecture
I kept thinking about one of our final sessions with Bull:
"Could someone
who wrote such poems and plays
whose writing was so elegant
whose thought, so sharp and lucid
possessor of a sense of humor
truly lack all morality and ethics?
When we speak of him
why do we allow the scarecrow created by the Catholic Church
to carry the day?"

When he was very ill and homebound
I had gone to visit him one night
and he gave me a volume of
Machiavelli's *Letters*
which includes one addressed
to Francesco Vettori
his "benefactor" (10 December 1513)
written while he was living in exile
at his country retreat outside the city
(the Medicis had returned to Florence, you see).
After describing his daily work on the farm
he eagerly turns to the coming of evening
and his study

where he is writing
his "little work" *On Principalities*
(later to become *The Prince*)
at which point he observes:
"And because Dante
says it does not produce knowledge
when we hear but do not remember
I have tried to remember
what a great man once said to me."

Same here, *caro* Hedley.

Sofonisba Anguissola (c. 1532–1625)

To my daughter

Because she was a woman
no one
— neither the Vatican nor the Medicis, the Sforzas
and the respectable *condottieri* —
commissioned of her
the religious or historical paintings
that were the exclusive domain
of the male artist.
Perforce she turned to portraiture.

She, of course, exacted her vengeance
for in one of her self-portraits
the one housed today
in Poland's Łańcut Museum
she paints herself
painting the Virgin embracing the holy infant.
Despite her poise
her somewhat irritated expression
— as if having burst uninvited into her studio
we are interrupting her finishing touches —
throws into relief
the courage and determination
even Vasari acknowledged.

After an eventful life
she settled in Palermo with husband number three
painting portraits
for the next forty years.

Haris Vlavianos

She was now so famous
artists like Rubens and Van Dyck
visited her
to see "the brilliant woman"
in the flesh.

Van Dyck's painting
of the now elderly Sofonisba
(almost ninety-two at the time)
still survives.
She looks at the young painter
much like Michelangelo
must have once looked
upon her twenty-year-old self
at their first meeting:

"My dear Anthony
we artists strive
to immortalize
a few traces of life
before our unfurling shadows
veil it all in oblivion.
I wonder in the future
what will people think
when they see my work?
Perhaps that I was a woman
who spent her life fleeing her prison cell
and shaking off the dust
stifling her soul.
You, however, as a man
what do you know of dust?"

Desiderius Erasmus (1466?–1536)

Theologians lost their night's sleep
pondering portentous questions:
Why had God chosen to incarnate Christ
as a man, not a woman
or, for that matter, a donkey?
But how was a donkey-Christ to preach the Jewish law?
Or perform the miracle of Cana?
Thoroughly amused by this scholastic nonsense
Erasmus wrote *In Praise of Folly*
during his second sojourn in England
to entertain his friend Thomas More.
(Lacking the Dutchman's humor
the latter eventually lost his head
whereas Henry VIII likely had more than his fair share
for he was playing tennis
when the executioner brought down the ax
on More's "very short neck").

In one of Oxford's second-hand bookstores
(I must have spent over twenty hours a week on Turl Street)
I found one of Erasmus' travel letters
(to my knowledge
the only scholar with the audacity
to teach at both Oxford and Cambridge).
I could not find a single fault with it:

"English girls are divinely pretty and have a most admirable
custom:
When you go anywhere on a visit the girls kiss you.
They kiss you when you arrive.

Haris Vlavianos

They kiss you when you leave.
They kiss you when you return.
If you are lucky enough to get a taste of those soft and fragrant lips
you will long to spend your life in that blessed land."

While Erasmus was exchanging kisses with English girls
the teenaged Luther was conscientiously studying
The Summa Angelica by Angelo Carletti di Chivasso,
which twenty years later
(along with the latest bull of Pope Leon X)
he would toss into the fire
in Wittenberg's central square
exclaiming as he did so:
"the burning of sinful books
is an age-old custom
in Germany."

Undeniably true.
Four centuries later
this "age-old custom"
still held strong.
And books were not its only victims.

SECRETARIES OF THE INVISIBLE

YAHIA LABABIDI

"I am no more than a secretary of the invisible thing." Czesław Miłosz begins one of his poems with this evocative declaration of artistic vocation. In this spare statement, the poet abandons any pretense of authorship in the conventional sense and presents himself as a vessel, one who listens inwardly and transcribes what he cannot claim as his own. The image is metaphysical, drawn from a lineage of writers who serve something higher than craft or culture, something closer to sacred obligation. Among the few who recognized this rare calling and lived its demands with equal gravity was Thomas Merton, the monastic contemplative who saw writing as a form of listening and language as a possible bridge to the divine.

In "Secretaries," Miłosz evokes a quiet community scattered across the globe. These fellow scribes do not know one another, and perhaps never will.

> Secretaries, mutually unknown, we walk the earth
> Without much comprehension.

There is a tender humility here. These mysterious and diligent figures are possessed by a duty to record what has no fixed origin. They receive fragments, phrases that begin in the middle or trail off into uncertainty. They are faithful to what comes, though they may never understand what it means. Their labor is characterized by humble devotion.

This sense of transmission deepens in "*Ars Poetica?*" in which Miłosz wrestles more urgently with the demands of his calling:

> I have always aspired to a more spacious form
> that would be free from the claims of poetry or prose,
> and would let us understand each other without exposing
> the author or reader to sublime agonies.

Here the poet yearns for a language that does not distort reality for the sake of literary fashion. He dreams of a form capacious enough to accommodate the full weight of experience without exaggeration or disguise. The "sublime agonies" he speaks of are the wounds that authentic encounter inflicts: the cost of genuine transparency between souls, the pain of being truly seen and of truly seeing. This is a longing for a deeper sincerity, a mode of expression that neither conceals nor flaunts, but clarifies without inflicting such wounds. What Miłosz calls "a more spacious form" finds its echo in Merton's yearning for a contemplative language free from violence — both artists seek words that heal rather than wound, that open rather than close.

In "*Ars Poetica?*" Miłosz elaborates further on the burden of the secretary's task.

The purpose of poetry is to remind us
how difficult it is to remain just one person,
for our house is open, there are no keys in the doors,
and invisible guests come in and out at will.
What I'm saying here is not, I agree, poetry,
as poems should be written rarely and reluctantly,
under unbearable duress and only with the hope
that good spirits, not evil ones, choose us for their instrument.

To write poetry, in Miłosz's understanding, is a spiritual practice, a response to pressures that move beneath the surface of ordinary perception.

Thomas Merton would have understood this calling and its attendant burdens instinctively. In his journals and letters, one discerns the same search for unguarded language, a mode of speech not marred by pretense. As a poet Merton wrote to reveal what could only be discovered in solitude. For him, words were vessels of reverence. He believed the truest writing arises from stillness and must preserve something of that stillness if it is to be believed. In *No Man Is an Island*, Merton describes the paradoxical power of creative work as transformative and self-effacing: "Art enables us to find ourselves and lose ourselves at the same time."

In their remarkable correspondence across continents — one writing from a monastic cell in Kentucky, the other from intellectual exile in California — Miłosz and Merton recognized in each other this same fidelity to the unseen. Merton found in Miłosz's work the same refusal to domesticate mystery that characterized his own contemplative practice. Miłosz discovered in Merton's letters a kindred spirit who understood writing as a form of prayer. The spiritual terrain they shared was unmistakably intimate, marked by the same willingness to serve as conduits rather than creators.

When Miłosz writes in "Secretaries" "how it looks when completed / Is not up to us to inquire, we won't read it anyway," he articulates a rare trust in the work as something independent from the self. The poem, once written, belongs to a deeper order, one that resists the hunger for evaluation or finality. This surrender is faith by another name. It reflects a refusal to dominate what one has received, and a willingness to let it pass on into the world without being possessed or explained.

Such submission characterized Merton's spiritual life as well, who declared that "true contemplation is not a psychological trick but a theological grace. It can come to us only as a gift, and not as a result of our own clever techniques." His best writing holds space for bearing witness to that which exceeds the intellect. In passages such as this one from his journal *The Sign of Jonas* — "There is in all visible things an invisible fecundity, a dimmed light, a hidden wholeness. In the visible world around us, there is a glory that is greater than anything else that can be seen, but this glory is not visible except by faith and by the interior light of wisdom" — we witness the secretary at work, transcribing what arrives from the margins of perception. The language is precise yet porous, faithful to an experience that cannot be fully captured yet must be attempted.

Both men practiced an ethic of restraint that in our time appears quite radical. They did not chase acclaim, nor did they try to simplify their vision for popular understanding. Their fidelity was to the unseen, the unspeakable, the barely intuited. With his characteristic humility with regard to language and mystery, Merton put it this way in *Thoughts on Solitude*: "No writing on the solitary, meditative dimensions of life can say anything that has not already been said better by the wind in the pine trees." In a culture that mistakes noise for substance and demands constant visibility, their example offers a different possibility, that of writing as resistance to the tyranny of the seen and the immediate, as a way of preserving space for what cannot be commodified or consumed. And "Secretaries" and "*Ars Poetica?*" invite us to think of poetry as a form of ethical transmission, where the goal is beyond self-expression, a spiritual self-emptying that is an offering. They speak for those who serve in obscurity, who give without expectation of recognition, who understand their task as larger than their own literary ambitions.

Miłosz and Merton belong to a consecrated company. Through them, we are reminded that writing may still be a sacred act. When it is done without possession, without pride, without explanation, it becomes a form of listening. And in that act of listening, something of the invisible may enter the world. As Merton wrote, "The deepest level of communication is not communication, but communion. It is wordless. It is beyond words, and it is beyond speech, and it is beyond concept."

THE PSYCHOANALYST AND THE POET

CONSTANTIN WALDSCHMIDT

The following is, for the first time translated and brought to print, the written correspondence between Sigmund Freud and Rainer Maria Rilke. The record was only completed in late 2022, when the German Literature Archive (GLA) acquired Rilke's entire literary estate from his descendants. Letters between the two went unnoticed by scholarship; the GLA itself didn't seem aware at the time of acquisition that Freud was one of Rilke's correspondents. Over a century after they were written, the German literary review *Sinn und Form* corrected that astonishing oversight, and through their publication granted us the two writers' reflections on psychoanalysis and war.

Freud and Rilke had a strong (albeit indirect) relationship through their close friendships with Lou-Andreas Salomé. Salomé was a pupil of Sigmund Freud (she is often labeled the first female psychoanalyst), and a sometime lover of Rilke. The epistolary exchanges between Rilke and Salomé lasted until his death, and formed the contact surface between him and psychoanalysis, a subject which terrified and allured him. Analysis and poetry brawl throughout their letters for mastery of the soul. Rilke likened it to an exorcism, a ritual that would drive out the demons underneath both his hypochondria and his sensitivity to nature. Salomé agreed, at last warning him: "Never let yourself be analyzed. Your creativity will die."

This context infuses the conversation between Freud and Rilke with a sinister air. Rilke is vulnerable, even frightened by an animal sense of who has the power. The poet wants to keep his distance from the analyst, due not to mundane social anxiety, but to his fear of what that meeting might bring. Freud meanwhile strolls casually through topics sensitive to Rilke: the assault on Duino, and his own verdicts on human nature. Near the end of his letter, Rilke resigns: "the choice to see it through alone prevailed, insofar as I still retain the dregs of my solitude." By choosing loneliness over therapy, while revealing that loneliness is all that he has left, a paradox is simultaneously created and resolved. Declining company because you are alone is obviously a contradiction, but, by incarnating loneliness and joining himself to it, he collapses subject and object into one. Against the brutal invasions of his world by analysis and war, he replaces that world with solitude and rejects that which he could have lost. In doing so, Rilke places himself in an untamed expanse of will, at the origin of art, a poet to the bitter end.

Freud to Rilke, February 11th 1916

Prof. Dr. Freud

Wien, IX. Berggasse 19.

11.2.16

My dearest and most esteemed doctor,

It was somehow brought to my attention that you are back in Vienna, on military duties, and live at this mailing address. I had to suppress my urge to visit until you showed signs of life, that is, until I gathered that you had ordered your affairs. But my son Ernst (to whom you were kind enough to write, and even somewhat resembles you) is on leave from Isonzo for a few days. He had me ask when and where he could meet you. Naturally, I'd much rather have you at ours for a bite, but I don't know if you'll make it – Tuesday evening I'm holding a lecture somewhere, and either Thursday or Friday my wife travels to Hamburg with Ernst.

That is to say, a prompt response would be most kind.

Your most humble servant,

Freud

Rilke to Freud, February 17th 1916

Hopfners Park-Hôtel

Wien XIII. (Hietzing.)

on Feb. 17, 1916

My esteemed Professor Freud,

Have I missed your son? It's as I fear: your letter is dated the eleventh, but consider this — I first found it today, have been away on "business" since precisely the eleventh, and returned this morning. Could the timing be any worse? Or do you still have him in Vienna? In this case, can he come tomorrow evening at five–?, for I am too tired, too upset, too confused to come myself; indeed so oppressed by these incommensurable daily circumstances, I'm saddened to think that he'll even see me like this. This strange world and its demands are so preposterous, that they petrify me deep within. First were some fourteen days of basic training. Then came my assignment to the War Archives, where I squander the hours in intellectual despair, just as I had in physical despair. But the greatest terror is the rubble burying my heart, deeper by the day, and often I've thought that a talk with you would save me from this burial. Alas, the choice to see it through alone prevailed, insofar as I still retain the dregs of my solitude. If I can gradually collect myself, then I'll be sure to call on you and visit; I know this will be good.

In the meantime, convey my greetings to your ladies, and should your son Ernst already have departed, the most heartfelt regret at not having met. Should he still be in Vienna, I'd request a word by phone: but here [at home], for we may not receive calls in the Archive.

Yours truly and sincerely devoted,

R.M.Rilke

Freud to Rilke, February 18th 1916

Prof. Dr. Freud

Wien, IX. Berggasse 19.
18.2.16
Most esteemed,

The pattern has continued: on the very evening that your pneumatic letter arrived, my Ernst departed for Germany. But he returns in a week, and now knows where to find you.

If you do feel the urge to unburden yourself with a chat, don't hide yourself from us. I've struggled with this particular monstrosity for 1½ years. I armor my weak spots here and there, hoping to check it, so long as it leaves my four weakest alone – my three sons, and my son-in-law in the service. And even if you aren't as vivid, composed, or polished as during your first visit, we'll make it work.

The war confused me, but only at first. I soon developed a pessimistic revulsion and ever since have had general license to cast authoritative judgements on human nature, as I've always secretly wanted to do. I can be pessimistic without bitterness. It's most advisable.

Perhaps you've gone too far in separating your inner and outer lives. Now the dam is full to bursting. Perhaps — but I won't triumph presenting this image, I'd rather not compete against a poet. Yet, it's rather easy for me to empathize with your fate. If I were to be sentenced to spend half the day under one roof with psychiatrists!

Your beloved Duino is now under bombardment! Ernst tells me the enemy shoots wastefully, while we hold back.

In conclusion, let's rendezvous soon on a Monday, Friday, or Sunday! Tuesdays and Wednesdays are association days, Thursdays are game nights, and Saturdays are for lectures.

With warm regards on behalf of yours truly,

Freud

HIDDEN IN THE BOURGEOIS

MORTEN HØI JENSEN

The hero of *The Magic Mountain* — the perfectly ordinary, blond, blue-eyed Hans Castorp — is the typological bourgeois male. I spent seven years writing a book about the novel of which he serves as protagonist and in that time I wondered often what possessed me to devote so much energy to him and to it. At a certain point, I rather tragically resigned myself to the obvious answer that I have a deplorably bourgeois soul.

The Magic Mountain is one of the great novels about the bourgeois soul.

It challenges Joseph Schumpeter's idea that the bourgeois is a fundamentally unheroic narrative type. "The stock exchange is a poor substitute for the Holy Grail," Schumpeter wrote. Yet, rather ironically, the poet Howard Nemerov interprets Hans Castorp's quest for knowledge as precisely a quest for the Holy Grail. Thomas Mann would have approved of Nemerov's interpretation.

Hans Castorp, significantly, is from Hamburg, the merchant city of the middle classes, a city whose center is dominated by that most bourgeois of German buildings, the *Rathaus*, or Townhall. As the novel opens, he is about to join the ship-building firm Tunder and Wilms, and seems to everyone around him "an honest, unadulterated product of the local soil, superbly at home in it." And yet as we read on, we learn that the family doctor suspects Hans Castorp of being anemic and has prescribed him a daily glass of robust porter — intended to help build his blood, but which Hans Castorp enjoys for its soothing, dozing effects. We also learn that although he is a decent tennis-player and oarsman, Castorp prefers sitting on a terrace of the boathouse with a drink in hand, "listening to music and watching the boats as they drifted among the swans." Hans Castorp is not especially interested in exerting effort, in working, that supreme of bourgeois activity. Effort strains his nerves and exhausts him. He prefers it when time passes "easily, unencumbered by the leaden weight of toil…" When he first meets the shrewd, intellectually active Ludovico Settembrini, Castorp declares: "I only really feel healthy when I am doing nothing at all."

Hans Castorp resists our understanding, he is difficult to know — perhaps because he is insubstantial. (Though maybe not! Hard to say.) When asked by the director of the Berghof why he chose to become an engineer, Castorp claims he did so purely by chance, and that he could just as well have become a doctor or a clergyman. Similarly, when local citizens of Hamburg wonder if Hans Castorp will ever seek a career in politics, given his good family name, they cannot decide if he would stand as a conservative, like his grandfather, or as a progressive, as he has entered the fields of commerce and technology. "That was quite possible - but so was the opposite."

The narrator hypothesizes that Hans Castorp may be suffering from the nihilistic condition of his age, from the hollow silence with which the universe around him responds to the question of meaning. It is above all this question that Hans Castorp is confronted with during his seven years at the Berghof, where his latent sympathy with death is awakened and aroused by Clavdia Chauchat, who teasingly calls him "my little bourgeois."

And indeed, what could be more bourgeois — as Thomas Mann understands the term — than Hans Castorp's celebrated epiphany in the famous "Snow" subchapter, that "man is the master of contradictions." The coexistence of apparent opposites is characteristic of the bourgeois. Werner Sombart, in his *The Quintessence of Capitalism*, makes the Faustian claim that "two souls dwell in the breast of every complete bourgeois: the soul of the adventurer and the soul of the respectable middle-class man." A claim that sounds quite a bit like Thomas Mann's Tonio Kröger, who, in the eponymous novella, cries out: "As an artist I'm already enough of an adventurer in my inner life. So far as outward appearances are concerned one should dress decently, damn it, and behave like a respectable citizen..."

Thomas Mann offers the image of the writer as someone who keeps his office hours and dresses appropriately, whose writing is characterized not by the heat and flame of inspiration but by the cold comfort of thoroughness and industry. "There is much to be said for a wife and children," Thomas Mann wrote in his diary in 1919, "but given my nature, the decisive consideration for me is that it allows me to hide in the bourgeois realm without actually becoming bourgeois." As the French writer Bernard Groethuysen observed in 1927, "the bourgeois likes to keep his incognito."

It was Flaubert who originally formulated the contradictory character of the bourgeois when he observed, in a letter, that "one should live like a bourgeois and think like a demi-god." But it was Thomas Mann in whom this dialectic, the yes and the no of bourgeois culture, found its most prophetic repository. "I have become what I am," Thomas Buddenbrook, the good bourgeois, tells his brother, Christian, the failed artist, "because I did not want to become like you." Many years after writing those words, Mann described his enemy Adolf Hitler as "a brother, a rather unpleasant and mortifying brother," by which he meant that Hitler, like himself, was an artist, only he was an artist gone astray, a good-for-nothing who believed himself "reserved for something else — as yet quite indefinite, but something which, if it could be named, would be greeted with roars of laughter." Significantly, Mann titled his essay "A Brother," as though aware that he and Hitler represented two paths for Germany. *I have become what I am, because I did not want to become like you.* A few weeks after the war, Mann, ever the conscientious artist, confessed: "it is all within me, I have been through it all."

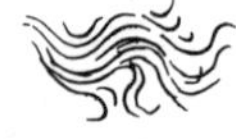

CELESTE MARCUS

"I Am Trying To Live A Life I Do Not Understand"

Frequently, in conversation with others or in an incessant inner monologue, I try to imagine what a world after *this*, after *this* political crisis, after *this* historical paroxysm, will look like. I love two countries — America and Israel — which have, let us say, transformed themselves. I am rich in crises, overwhelmed by hopelessness and heartache the causes of which are so enormous I cannot fully fathom their implications for the world or for my conception of myself. My loyalties torment me. After October 7 a certain cohort that has since fragmented spoke wistfully of "the day after," but even in those early weeks the phrase was an insult to human wisdom. The phrase itself has become a synecdoche in my mind for our outrageous lack of a proper understanding of what was occurring around us and what we have become.

I am trying to imagine an Israel-and-Palestine *and* an America in which the word "peace" means something substantial, a world in which that word has not been thinned to a pixelated, politicized flourish. But neither of these places — neither of my homes — are sufficiently familiar to me anymore, and so I do not trust my own intuitions about what will happen and what is possible in either context. I want ruminations on these futures to be rooted in reality, to be based in deep understandings of the peoples at stake. But it never feels that way. When I listen to or participate in discussions about a future worth living for, they feel grotesquely ignorant or fanciful. I think I know why that is. No one alive today was raised to understand the versions of our countries that exist now. This is not only because we were living "in a bubble," but also because genuine transformations have taken place. And we cannot responsibly possess what we do not know. It is difficult to conceive of ourselves as leaders (or even members) of the strange places we live in now, these mutations of the countries we used to think of as ours but which have become alien to us.

In my mind these ruminations are associated with a particular image of nullity. I am a painter and so I am familiar with the dread of staring at a blank canvas — and that is the sensation that comes over me when conversation turns to "the day after" and related themes. I recently spent an afternoon in my studio face to face with an easel on which there rested an unblemished canvas. The trouble was I did not have something particular I wanted to paint, I just wanted to be painting. I wanted to feel the brush sliding pleasantly along the slick primed surface. I wanted to make something intelligent and even beautiful. But that abstract yearning could not bear fruit. Beauty — the kind I am occasionally capable of when properly prepared, and the kind I most admire — is the result of having intimately understood an entrancing subject (entrancing at least to me) and communicating that intimate understanding through a medium over which I have a measure of control. Yearning to create some unknown beautiful thing is exactly like yearning to be in love without loving someone. What intimacy? What understanding? (A relevant Jewish piece of wisdom: in an essay excoriating a literary critic, the great Yiddish writer I.L.

Peretz scolded, "It is not enough to write in Yiddish. You have to have something to say.") Usually the memory of actively engaging with my bouts of creative sterility is disturbing enough to keep me from entering the studio without proper preparation.

The urge to paint has to come from within. I need to be captivated by some subject and driven to communicate its seductions, to externalize in paint what has occurred inside me. I have to arrive at the easel possessed by this inspiration. The assignment of meaning to a subject comes from me: I am forced to action because of an inner necessity. I am not referring to "self-expression," but rather to the effort to be loyal to my sense of an intuition or a perception. But in the realms of other loyalties, particularly collective and political allegiances, I act on values that I did not assign to myself but that were assigned to me. I used to move through the world armed with a profound sense of received meaning and conscious of the life choices that a serious life required of me. There was a time in my life when my sense of loyalty and honor was so concrete to me that I could rely on my inherited frameworks to give me both a worldview and a course of action. My life was plotted according to that heritage. This is no longer true. In so many essential ways the world I was born into does not any longer exist. The countries which I had been raised to love and serve have revealed characteristics so strange I cannot recognize them, so unattractive that I am no longer pulled toward them, though I still derive meaning from my loyalty to... them? To my idea of them? To a version of them for which I try to fight and in which I tell myself I still believe? If honor is a matter of loyalty, then honor will mean something new to me now.

The artist Chaim Soutine called the compulsion to paint something new "being hit by lightning" or "the lightning bolt." If it did not come, he would not paint; and not painting was, for him, a form of not living. Soutine experienced two of the most devastating horrors in human history and throughout both of them his primary context, his significant world, remained the canvas. The first of these crucibles was the first war. He spent much of World War I in the south of France weak with hunger (he had made no name for himself and so had no money for food), subsisting on the goodwill of Amedeo Modigliani, his closest friend, and the kind-hearted members of Modi's social circle. For everyone else the scarcity of resources was the stuff of war — for Soutine it was what kept him from his vocation.

Soutine's most famous period as a painter began just after the war was over, the same year that Modigliani died, in a small French village in the foothills of the Pyrenees miles from the Spanish border, called Céret. He was a long way away from his community, lonely, poor, and recently bereft of his closest friend (Modigliani was just thirty-five when he died), but he thought *only* of his work. This is not an exaggeration: his single-mindedness was fanatical. Each day was like his last: he painted with gusto for as long as he could sustain the energy. When his agent Léopold Zborowski made the long drive from Paris to Céret to visit him, he found Soutine holed up in a small, airless shack with all the windows sealed shut. Apparently he feared that his paintings — which were piled in a massive stack — would be damaged by the oxygen outdoors. The agent asked to see the completed works but Soutine refused. He said they were failures, unfit for view. Zborowski determined that he had better find his painter some food before continuing the argument, and when he came back he found that Soutine had set fire to the heap of canvases. It was with great difficulty and no small risk that Zborowski salvaged a number of them.

The mania with which Soutine worked during the Céret period he never matched again. He spent the rest of his career waiting for the next thunderbolt to strike. He would on occasion try to put himself in the way of inspiration, to invite the bolt. His most trusted mechanism when in such straits was to go for a drive, to shift location, to shake up his context. Soutine was intensely affected by his surroundings, and when he felt stultified rather than excited by the quality of the sunlight or the vertiginousness of the landscape in which he found himself, he would peripatetically seek out someplace else. In the years after he achieved success Zborowski secured Soutine a chauffeur for precisely this purpose, and that man – his name was Daneyrole – recalled that there was a particular tree situated in Vence in the south of France to which Soutine would instruct Daneyrole to drive. The tree's shape or placement, or the way the light hit it, could trigger a trance. The drive from Paris, where Soutine usually lived, and the tree to which he pilgrimaged took roughly ten hours. Such an intensity of commitment strikes ordinary people as excessive and bizarre, but the regular ten-hour slog was not the strangest or most unpleasant inconvenience Soutine endured in service to his passion.

In the mid-1920s Soutine was overcome by the need to paint a painting inspired by Rembrandt's *Woman Bathing in a Stream*. That canvas, which hangs in the National Gallery in London, depicts a woman hoisting a thin white dress to her knees while standing in what appears to be a lake licking the sides of a cave. Soutine had to paint from life — he could copy neither a painting nor a photograph nor could he paint from memory and imagination. If he wanted to paint a woman in a stream, he had to be standing in front of such a person. Soutine enlisted his patroness, a wealthy eccentric woman named Madeleine Castaing, and her husband in a mad search for an appropriate model. The group drove about the Castaing estate in Lèves until such a woman was identified, convinced to model, and dressed in appropriate garb. A lake was located. The woman was placed to Soutine's satisfaction and then... a thunderstorm came over the pair. But Soutine would not hear of stopping — he had to paint a whole picture from start to finish while the paint was still wet — and so he painted through the gales as the woman shrieked for permission to leave and he shouted back instructions to stand still.

During his episodes of creative commotion Soutine was in thrall to a mandate that no one else could fathom. What seems inconceivable to the rest of us was obvious and necessary to him. He was obeying the dictates of a value-framework which assigned worth and honor known only to him. This was not the result of reflection; Soutine was not consciously deducing a system of appropriate painterly behavior. He was heeding an edict that came from the interior, that was a part of who he was. It was not inherited. It was not subject to any nature but his own; it would exist for as long as he did. He could not separate himself from this orientation, and it could not be altered by outside forces. They were insulated from history — so long as Soutine's health, wealth, and safety permitted him to follow his own course.

The love of Soutine's life was a woman named Gerda Michaelis. She understood nothing of his painting and she was, for the entirety of their relationship, uninterested in discussing it with him. But she did grasp what it was to be borne forward by a force that compelled her to deep and irrational action. Her love for Soutine was like that. It was not as violent or idiosyncratic as his analogous aesthetic mania, but it was the effulgence of a similar maniacal configuration, and it did become the central force which conferred meaning on her life. Her obedience to her own romantic impulses was as much the result of her self-understanding as his obedience to his painterly dictates was evidence of a similarly visceral self-knowledge. Their loyalties, you might say, were entirely self-generated, which made them invulnerable to the world-transforming events which took place in the years in which they lived together. In fact, those events both occasioned their meeting and forced their separation.

Michaelis was born in 1910 into a Jewish family in Magdeburg, a German city on the Elbe. The racial laws that the Nazis enforced after their rise to power in 1932 stripped Michaelis' father of his livelihood and then the entire family was forcibly relocated from Magdeburg to Berlin — the Nazis had decided to address the housing crisis by seizing Jewish homes and collecting Jews in centralized locations. Gerda was not optimistic, stupid, or dedicated enough to the *Volk* to ignore the tidal pull towards what could only be a brutal end and so she decided to flee to

France. Michaelis returned to Germany only once, in 1935, to see her family. Her mother, father, and two sisters were killed shortly afterwards.

She met Soutine on an autumn evening in 1937. She had stumbled into her usual café, **Le Dome**, at Vavin, the white-hot center of Montparnasse and the meeting spot for a community of German refugees and other émigré artists. Immediately upon entering she noticed a man whom she had never seen before. He was seated at a table near three of her friends. "Medium build, pale complexion, with deep black hair and dark brown eyes, he could have been about forty… Everything about his physicality pleased me." On their first date he took her with him to a boxing match — one of his favorite pastimes — but he collapsed in the middle of it. In a prefiguration of the beneficent role that she was to play in his life, she took him home and nursed him the whole night through. When he awoke to find her preparing to leave for work, he told her not to go. He said that he would take care of her from then on, as she had taken care of him. *Garde*, he called her, for she was his guardian.

She moved in with him immediately, and she loved him forcefully and totally. They had three years together. Soutine's health deteriorated and on the strength of a doctor's advice he and Garde left Paris in the summer of 1939 for a visit in Civry-sur-Serein. While they were there, war with Germany broke out and Garde was suddenly a citizen of an enemy country. She could not leave the city freely, but Soutine's poor health necessitated trips to specialists in the capital and so he would leave her alone for long stretches while she laid low awaiting his return. This tormented status quo held for eight months till the pair snuck back into Paris. A full third of their relationship was consumed by the fear and helplessness which stalks all people with precarious legal status during wartime. And Soutine was a Jew, as was Garde. She spent those months agonizing over what could have happened to him in her absence, and what might happen to her before he had a chance to return. She would subsist on the food and meager funds that he left behind and so she was always at risk of running out of basic necessities. When they could no longer submit to these conditions, the pair fled overnight. Clutching what they could fit in bags light enough to carry, they walked for miles in silence holding their breath until the city thinned out. They reached the train station at one o'clock. When the train pulled into the outskirts of Lyon, Soutine took Garde in his arms and whispered, "You are saved." Two Jews fleeing *into* Paris in April 1940, laboring under the delusion that safety was a luxury that they still enjoyed.

Reality rapidly asserted itself. The morning after their return all German women were commanded to report to the bicycle stadium known as the Vel d'Hiv, from where they would be transported to an internment camp in the Pyrenees. On their last night together they repeated promises to find one another as soon as they could, to write, to wait until the war was over before resuming life as before. The next day they took a taxi together across Paris. He kissed her goodbye and she disappeared behind a mass of uniformed bodies. They never saw each other again.

The historical paroxysms which decimated her family, her home, and all the frameworks for happiness, success, and meaning that she had been bequeathed are hardly mentioned in the only remaining account of her life. Garde's memoir is a slim volume of reflections on the fleeting years she and Soutine lived together, written decades after his death, as if her whole life up to and since the time they spent in the world they created together was the only stretch of years that she recognized as "my life." The book begins "today, like yesterday, despite the time, his image is constantly present to me." This, though his final years were spent in hiding with another woman, a woman he met just weeks after Garde was rounded up along with all German nationals in Paris while France was still at war with Germany. Soutine remained for her a fixed ideal, a constant phantom companion.

Michaelis recounts her great love story in straightforward language, as if she wrote it to help her remember exactly what had happened. She does not recount an instant of hesitation. From the moment she saw him her fate was sealed. The only standard of existence for Gerda Michaelis was generated organically from her love and her dedication to Soutine. Her needs grew around his motion forward, much like his needs emerged from his ferocious commitment to painting. And both of these concerns, these ever-fixed marks, bore the two of them forward in a world in which the communities they both knew were decimated.

Soutine and Michaelis were blessed. Their primary sources of meaning came from within themselves. They were not blind to the evils around them, but in some essential way they were living outside of those evils and so their souls could not be snuffed out by social and political events until death forced extinguishment. Their souls, as Leon Wieseltier once wrote, exceeded their circumstances. In ordinary times, Soutine's and Michaelis' oblivious behavior might have been called clueless or insane. In fact, during his life and since his death Soutine was and often is referred to as a madman, and this characterization is due largely to the public way he lived utterly beholden to a system of values and actions that made little sense to others and that was in violation of the ones which governed the commonplace life around him. Even his admirers cannot enter into his stirringly idiosyncratic psyche and understand it. The same is true about Michaelis — though her *folie* is more familiar to us. We have seen mad love and there is a literature about it. But still she led a rationally incomprehensible life.

Is such monomania admirable? Is it admirable to think only of art or only of a beloved while your family (and many other people) are being rounded up and slaughtered? Is such a myopia, such an exclusive commitment, an aesthetic strength or an ethical weakness? Admirable or not, that model of existence certainly provided Soutine and Garde with an answer to a question that many now have to grapple with: how can one live after one's world has been mutilated or even obliterated?

We have all been born into contexts that offered us blueprints for how to live our lives and standards for how to measure our success or failure. We hold ourselves in contempt or with pride depending on the degree to which we rise or fall against those expectations. But we have also all been born into communities that have already been outgrown and sloughed off. Soutine and Michaelis witnessed the engine of industrialized decimation which altered their worlds and ours. To this day our ur-example of mass destruction is the war that forced them apart. The Holocaust did not only destroy people, it also destroyed the conditions, the ethos, that made possible the worldviews that made life comprehensible and meaningful to the victims and the survivors. But genocide is hardly necessary for such an obliteration. Technological development has whipped us all into ceaseless forward motion and we are helpless in its grip. Our constant velocity is violent even without the blood and the ash — though it does seem to catalyze much blood and ash. We are living in our own crucible of erasure and destruction. It too is wounding and pitiless.

The late Jonathan Lear's astonishing book *Radical Hope* valiantly treats a response to such an experience of obliteration. It is an interrogation of a philosophically perplexing pronouncement made by Plenty Coups, the last great chief of the Native American Crow Tribe. Just before his death, Plenty Coups told the first part of his life's story to a white man who pressed him to continue it up to the present day. The last great chief refused, and he offered the following as explanation: "When the buffalo went away the hearts of my people fell to the ground and they could not lift them up again. After this nothing happened." After this nothing happened. What could that possibly mean, Lear asks. And he proposes the possibility that after a certain way of life was destroyed it became impossible for "happenings" to continue in the sense that happenings had before the buffalo's departure — in other words, Plenty Coups was speaking literally. "Happening" in the sense that the Crow could understand the word no longer occurred. The Crow "conception of *what happiness is* could no longer be lived. The characteristic activities that used to constitute the good life ceased to be intelligible acts."

We might suppose that Garde experienced a similar loss of

meaning after Soutine's death — after a secret emergency surgery in Paris — in 1943, and that subsequent "happenings" were not possible or not vital in the way that they had been while the two were together. Garde was the kind of person who was especially vulnerable to the loss of a beloved. There are people who can continue living after such a loss. Most people find their partners in a community and choose their partners with the intention of creating a certain kind of family which belongs within a certain kind of communal context. Such people are less vulnerable to complete desolation and inconsolable grief after a beloved's death, though the prospect of the destruction of communal life would surely terrify them. Garde was not like this. She had no community, she had only him. Soutine perished, her heart fell to the ground, after this nothing happened.

Lear suggests that courageous people are especially vulnerable to the destruction of their community. As he puts it, "the very traits of character that make for a courageous person would place such a person in an especially disadvantaged position to make a courageous transition out of traditional forms of courage. The courageous Crow warrior willingly gave up his life... all his training and encouragement from early youth was directed toward producing such character." But, as Lear explains, after the buffalo went away the very acts that had previously accrued honor were suddenly rendered ridiculous. Lear emphasizes courage because his chosen case study is the Crow Tribe and for them — as for all warrior communities — courage was the highest virtue. Every element of their way of life was defined in relation to battle, and honor itself was derived in relation to that occupation. When battle was no longer possible, their rituals, their vernacular, their very family structure, ceased to be comprehensible even to themselves. As one Crow elder woman repeats throughout the book, "I am trying to live a life I do not understand."

This is why we are so starved for honorable models now. The frameworks that we have for conferring honor have themselves been degraded and disgraced. The leaders among us who pledged fealty to a country that has betrayed itself have themselves been delegitimated. Even if they are not guilty of ideological betrayal they are at least guilty of poor stewardship. Courage has absconded. What can we do when the world in which we derived honor by professing loyalty to our country changes so dramatically that the reasons for that profession no longer hold? What if the foundations of our patriotism, the premises about our country and its trajectory toward justice, have been ruptured, perhaps irreparably? What do we do when, say, a country that represented freedom, liberalism, equality, and generosity violently *and democratically* overturns those commitments? Who decides what America is? Who decides who Americans are?

The natural response to all of this horror, in the wake of the catastrophes that have destroyed our worlds, is to flip things, to invert the value systems that we inherited and to condemn the attributes and people and symbols we once admired with energy equal to the energy with which we once loved them. I am conscious of a powerful impulse to detest what I once loved. This detestation has the added benefit of allowing me to preserve the frameworks according to which I used to live, just in the negative. That way the energy I have exerted developing intimate knowledge of people and ideas can remain alive inside me — as it will anyway, since I am inseparable from it. The tactic of philosophical and emotional inversion allows me to take vengeance in my own heart and my own mind against the figures who made a fool of me by accepting my loyalty and my admiration and then traducing and abandoning the values that undergird them. A bloated self-hatred swollen to encompass my entire peoples, the peoples in whom I locate my essence, is a great temptation. Another sip of rage, please, another glass, the bottle, I can't help myself. We are pitiable.

Jonathan Lear suggests that when Plenty Coups was still young he intuited great tragedy ahead for his people and he offered the Crow a method for living beyond the time of the buffalo. He did this through a prophetic dream and its interpretation, one of the holy rituals of the tribe and one which fused together the tribe's spirit allies and its generations: it was customary for the young to have prophetic visitations in their dreams and then for the elders to interpret the dreams' meanings for the community — a collaborative prophetic exercise. This way the authority of the prophecy was affirmed by the old, the young, and the gods. Plenty Coups' dream was interpreted by the elders to mean that, though great tragedy and destruction would befall the Crow, there would be life for them on the other side of it if they did not resist the violence of the white man. This dream allowed Plenty Coups to invoke the authorities the Crow already revered in service to the transformation of Crow life. The integrity of the tribe was in that way intact. Meaning could survive. Faith in that possibility is what Lear called "radical hope."

I have no such hope. How could I? Plenty Coups saved the Crow from losing faith in their elders and in the spiritual authorities to which his community devoted itself. He provided them with a framework for preserving the structures that assigned honor, and updated them for an unrecognizable age. But the authorities I know how to trust, the ones who lead the countries and communities that I love, are now thoroughly debased. Even if I believed in prophecy I have no elders to interpret one, except those elders who are as alienated as I am. The only mentors left to me are the ones who share in my disgust. We are all equally lost. But disgust is not a policy. It is abundantly warranted, but we need something more to live: some force propelling us forward in service to an ideal.

When I come to the easel freighted with the image and the ambition of a painting, itching to begin the process of articulating through paint this vision which has taken possession of me, I do not pause for questions. I do not wonder if this is a worthy subject or if I am the proper person to paint it. The subject and I are one thing — it is an experience of absorption. I want to spend myself through painting, to exhaust myself the way Soutine used to do, to hold nothing back. I used to feel this way at the sight of my countries' flags — I was not distinguishable from the objects of my loyalty and each had total claim on me. (I believe in multiple loyalties as long as they are genuine.) I long for that feeling, for the oceanic thrill of being bound up in a movement that I believe has a right to all my heart and mind. I would have given so much, perhaps even everything, for those flags and all that they represent. But what do they still represent? What is my life worth without that loyalty, without those loyalties, now?

LEON WIESELTIER

Temporalities

Remembering Jonathan Lear

A vision of the future must never be only about the future. Otherwise we will commit the terrible mistake known as futurism, which is nothing more than an attempt to make a virtue out of velocity.

Whether in the form of impatience or dread, the future can deplete the life out of the present, and no less ravenously than the present can deplete the life out of the past.

It makes no sense to believe in a mode of time. To believe in the future is to believe in a cipher, or to perpetuate the illusion that the future will be one thing, this and not that, when in truth it will be everything, as all life is everything. And to believe in the past is also to believe in everything, because everything may be found in the past. The past does not all go together and neither will the future. (This is abundantly demonstrated by the historical origins of every innovation, by every "unprecedented" breakthrough. Chemists may look with contempt upon alchemists, but the science of chemistry was born in the superstition of alchemy, and for a while they coexisted in an incongruous explosion of the desire to know.) Until we make decisions about what we wish to retain and to cultivate from the past, until we make selections from among the survivals, until we impose some italics on the welter, the past is only a pile of events — an annals and not a history. It is only rich clay. But on what grounds can we make such selections? Only on ahistorical grounds, I would say; on philosophical grounds. And what certifies these philosophical grounds as criteria for our commitments is not that we find them in the past. The fact that certain values once existed and once animated a society does not establish their legitimacy. Their pastness teaches nothing about their correctness. Evil communities also had elders. Venerability verifies nothing, though their possible irrelevance to truth is no excuse for the wanton destruction of inherited beliefs. And contemporaneity, too, verifies nothing.

Conservatism — remember conservatism?— is no less selective about the past than progressivism, and no less committed to the future. The distinction between conservatism and progressivism lies in the philosophical criteria for choices among the many legacies.

We have no right to erase something old merely because it displeases us; the erasure of disagreeable survivals of the past — statues, etc. — will establish not justice, but only a chimera of innocence. The grand telos of all the history that came before us was not to affirm us. We are the past's stewards, not its tyrants; its stewards and its interpreters. There is no point in fighting its facticity, its finality. And what we gain from our stewardship of the remains of evil is knowledge, which is one of the conditions of responsibly established belief.

Iconoclasm has a sterling reputation for its independence of mind, but it is also a variety of vandalism. Where were the independent of mind in the iconoclastic mobs? Consider, for example, the paintings of the sixteenth-century iconoclastic riots in the Low Countries, particularly in Antwerp. They give the lie to the categorical loftiness of iconoclasm. They depict only power and hatred.

Spit, abhor, but don't demolish.

A mile away, as I write this, the East Wing of the White House is being transformed into a heap of dust. Not a catastrophe by any means, and nothing like the rubble that one encounters in other locations in this roughed-up world. At least the local debris is not the work of war. But this demolition is certainly a perfect emblem of the Trump regime's flippancy toward the past. Historical figures should be less casual about history, which normally should serve as a quarry for the inhibitions that are among their qualifications for office. An inhibition is often the expression of an appropriate reverence. An uninhibited man is an ahistorical man. There is something essentially disrespectful, essentially callous, about a rampaging backhoe, as there is about a rampaging president.

Our power over the past is so immense that often we prefer not to know that the responsibility for what endures is ours. Secular and religious doctrines of inevitability relieve us of the anxiety of stewardship, not least by providing us with alibis for obsolescence, as if certain things are simply doomed to disappear, destined by time or by science or by providence. But nothing is obsolete until we agree that it is obsolete. *We* make it so. We let it go.

The inheritance of the past and the reception of the past are two discrete moments. The former is passive, but the latter is, or must be, active. Without active reception, tradition expires. Culture advances when we revolt against the heir's passivity, when we refuse to certify raw contingencies and we rise above our apathy about the flow of things. Allowing valuable pieces of the past to slip through your fingers is worse than melodramatically discarding them.

Natural oblivion, the passing of memory with the passing of the years, is a permanent feature of human experience, and it may also be a blessing by leaving room for those who come after us, who would otherwise face an extremely discouraging sense of their own redundancy, the asphyxiating feeling that there is nothing left for them to say or to do. Yet there is also unnatural oblivion, which is what we wreak upon the past with our laziness and our indifference. Unnatural oblivion can also be the consequence of persecution and oppression. We not only neglect and forget our own patrimonies, other people sometimes attempt to erase them, to coerce oblivion, so that the development of certain cultures, particularly the cultures of oppressed peoples, must proceed not least by means of salvage. And we sometimes attempt to coerce oblivion on others.

Finding a responsible position among the generations is a matter of calibrating the feeling that we are not worthy of what we have been bequeathed with the feeling that what we have been bequeathed is not worthy of us.

Futurism is a fantasy of a new beginning, a new birth — but really there is only a single beginning and only a single birth. We can travel far from our origins, but we cannot abolish them. Yehuda Amichai wrote: "I search for new beginnings / and find only changes."

It makes no sense to be born again. A transformation owes its resonance, its softly tragic consciousness of an earlier privation, to the lingering awareness of what preceded it. Otherwise a second birth is just an escape hatch, a "do-over" (what children want when they are too young to grasp the constraints of meaningful activity and seek to be held unaccountable for a mistake or a failure and want it not to "count"), like a third birth and a fourth birth. Moral and spiritual progress can be measured only against a continuous substrate.

Marx's famous pronouncement that "the tradition of all dead

generations weighs like a nightmare on the brains of the living" was a little cheap — another outlandish bid for newness. All the dead generations will never be overthrown, nor should they be. A war on origins is a waste of spirit, and misuses the energies that are required for constructing our own place in the epic chain, for creating the material with which to stimulate our descendants in their own nightmares of being trapped by the past, that is, by us.

What we call the past is only the remainder of the past. However overwhelming the past may feel, the truth is that we inherit only relics. By the time the past reaches us, oblivion has already done its work; so much has been forgotten or destroyed. "The past" is what's left.

There are always grounds, big ones and small ones, for the complaint about entrapment in the past. Until theories of necessity are cobbled together, the circumstances into which we have been tossed will seem capricious. Most people live their lives conquered by accident. The absence of restlessness, which can be mistaken for wisdom, can also denote a premature surrender to the given. But what home ever sufficed for a living soul? Restlessness is the attribute of a significant existence, or more accurately, of an existence laudably anxious about significance.

My tradition teaches me that inherited customs are sacred, but all the customs that I inherited were invented. (They are sacred but they are not divine.) The problem with our derivativeness and our belatedness is not that we were robbed of the opportunity for self-creation, which is the adolescent Nietzschean-Rortyan objection. The problem is that we may not know what to do with what came before us, how to interpret it and to adapt it, how to hear it and how to see it.

And what about the dead hand of the present that weighs like a nightmare on the brains of the living? In the alienation sweepstakes, the past is a piker.

One of the sins of the traditionalists is to regard restlessness as a sin.

Whoever wishes to be born again really wishes to be blameless. And blamelessness is not in our cards.

Ex nihilo: that train left the station on the day you were born. "Self-fashioning" as it is propounded by the professors — who have the sabbaticals required for it — is a haughty doctrine; Emersonian arrogance without Emersonian humility. Who really wants to come from nowhere? And who is so vain to believe that he can suffice with his own resources for his identity and his improvement? A wish for a different beginning may be an expression of early pain — a wish, say, for different parents; a common wish, I suppose, since human beings are more biologically equipped to have children than they are psychologically equipped to raise them. But a wish for no parents? Self-fashioning is self-orphaning, and with the passage of one's years it becomes more and more clear that orphanhood is overrated as an experience of emancipation. Nor is racination the threat that certain freethinkers have said it is, in the way that language is not such a threat. Obstacles can sometimes be overcome. Our specificity certainly condemns us to limits, but it is not obvious that we can flourish without limits. Whether or not we stand on the shoulders of giants, we stand on shoulders.

In a tiny, low-ceilinged, plainly tiled room in a modest house in an obscure town in the countryside Spinoza conjured the entirety of the cosmos. On my first visit to Rijnsburg the disparity between the scale of his setting and the scale of his thinking made me spin. Limited or not?

Nothing is true because it is old, and much that is old is false. The history of science, for instance, is a history of mistakes, which is why contemporary scientists need not consult their ancient and medieval precursors. Old physics does not belong in the science of physics but in the history of physics. That is not so with old philosophy. We still study Aristotle, because the obscurity in which many questions of human meaning are shrouded, and the slim likelihood of arriving at perfect certainty about them, transforms ancient opinions about them into contemporary opinions. When we reject an Aristotelian theory of justice or truth, it is not in the way that we reject the Ptolemaic cosmos or the theory of phlogiston. Rational argument is transhistorical, which in our historicist culture, drunk as it is on developmental analysis, is an exhilerating respite.

The prestige of antiquity, of what came long ago, can be easily exaggerated, and culminate in a thoughtless piety — a counter-futurism, which longs for a cessation of movement, for stasis. For this reason, the querelle des anciens et des modernes of the seventeenth century seems beside the point. In its time, the exaltations of newness, the inebriating phenomenon called modernity, were becoming undeniable, provoking a panic about the tenacity of the past. The panic, and therefore quarrel, was unavoidable — but we have the privilege of considering it more calmly, because modernity, too, is now a piece of our past. Those modernes are our anciens! Time makes all precedence ironic. In that grand early modern disputation, both parties were right and both parties were wrong.

There is a similar tension in the Talmudic tradition. One Talmudic opinion declares that certified instruction, or binding independent rulings, the ancient authority known as *hora'ah*, ended in the sixth century, which implies that the earlier a rabbinical decision was made, the more confident we may be in its correctness. Priority takes priority. But another Talmudic opinion states that the law is to be determined according to the "later ones," the most recent experts, because the later you live the more you know. (Would that this were always so!) Belatedness, in this view, is an advantage.

For the purpose of living meaningfully, one is always right on time.

The recognition of one's genealogy, of one's place in the parade, should be a source of humility. But here is Nietzsche, moving steadily from brilliance to madness, denouncing humility and confusing it with timidity, and demagogically recommending self-origination, and bequeathing his culture not only the most challenging questions that have so far been asked about it but also a crass assertion of ontological arrogance. He once wondered how God can exist if he is not God. Nietzsche liked to call himself a psychologist, and sometimes he makes philosophical expressions seem like clinical expressions.

Heine once said of a French industrialist: "He is a self-made man, which relieves God of a terrible responsibility."

We have it backwards. The ancients are not old. They are young, because they came first. That is why we find their limitations not exasperating but enchanting, as with infants, and also why we marvel at the depths of their understandings when they are deep. But we are old. The later you come in the history of a culture, the older you are. And we will be judged by how much we have to show for it.

The price we pay for our late appearance in history is that our avowals lack the patina of wisdom. This may not be altogether a bad thing, since the promotion of an idea into wisdom often insulates it from skepticism and removes it from the requirements of critical examination. Sanctification is an efficient way of ending a discussion. Whereas a laboring mind is too busy for wisdom. And wisdom is easily degraded: consider only the wisdom racket of our own era, in which there is a Stoic on every corner. Wisdom may be reduced to a style, to the style of wisdom. Maybe the difference between truth and wisdom is merely that wisdom is truth that has aged. Did the contemporaries of Anaximander and Empedocles regard their opinions as wisdom, or as physical and metaphysical propositions for their consideration? (I omit the adepts, which anybody can attract.) I do not recall that Descartes and Hume and Kant and Hegel were regarded as too immortal for their contemporaries to challenge. The thinkers of one's own time must never be beatified as sages, since we are still in the midst of evaluating the merits of their ideas. Pedestals make people stupid. And wisdom, to count as wisdom, must manifest the additional quality of being true.

The problem for the wisdom-lovers among us is that all the wisdoms do not agree with each other, and sanctimony alone will not resolve the contradiction.

Conservatives often chastise us for having forgotten wisdom. If they mean that we are wasting ourselves with intellectual ephemera and simulacra, it is hard not to agree. But there is often a churchly sentimentality in their complaint. The important question is not, Do we have wisdom? The important question is, What do we believe, and why?

A wise man knows also the limits of wisdom. The worship of wisdom does not make one wise.

Unlike some wines and cheeses, truths do not get better with age. Unlike other wines and cheeses, truths do not get worse with age.

In his ravishing writing about his old manse — have any more beautiful pages ever been written by an American? — Hawthorne declares that we should be grateful for our ancestors and grateful for our distance from them. Of course there are cases when gratitude for our ancestors is impossible, because they were evil or otherwise wrong, but generally Hawthorne's prescription gets it right. There need be no ingratitude, no treason, in our distance from our ancestors. Indeed, one of the reasons that we admire them is for the distance that they put between themselves and their own ancestors, so that they could become themselves, the figures whom we admire. The distance between fathers and sons, however agonistically it is established, is a necessary test of the sons' capacity for freedom.

The perfect reproduction of oneself in one's child is a narcissist's fantasy. All heirs are deviationists.

The pathos of the traditionalists lies in their futile belief that the forward movement that has characterized their traditions on their long journey to the present, to the traditionalists themselves, should stop with them. Yet even within orthodoxies there was always movement. The forms that the traditionalists wish to freeze were themselves the products of churnings and revisions. Unlike tradition, traditionalism is often a formula for unhappiness. The unhappiness is often weaponized.

In traditional Judaism, authors are known to posterity not by their own names but by the names of their important works. This pious habit can have a slightly comic effect. It would be like referring to Kant as The Critique and to Hegel as The Phenomenology. (As in: Did the Phenomenology ever meet the Critique? Or: I have a friend who studied with a direct descendant of the Critique.) This personification of books is an astonishingly effective device for making books live. The author's name is scanted in favor of the author's work. And this, ironically, makes you feel closer and more personal.

The nostalgist is an editor, and with no pretense to impartiality: he omits the disagreeable parts of the past, the episodes that are unedifying or useless to his intellectual framework, which is why every nostalgic picture of the past is axiomatically incomplete. In this way nostalgia takes the critical edge off the encounter with the past: it softens the life lived in time and is a kind of early stage of self-forgiveness. It is a cure for vertigo and a cure for loneliness, if ghosts can do the trick. But nostalgia is not quite happy. It is laced with melancholy, because it is born in the sense of loss, of disorientation in one's own surroundings. Sadness always runs through its delight. Yet what delight! Surely the present in its various degrees of oppressiveness owes us such a passing recompense, a spate of rest. We can be hard-boiled and up-to-the-minute later. We must never become the sum of our carapaces. When Adam was discovering the first sweat on his brow and Eve was enduring her first labor pains, who could begrudge them a recollection of Eden?

One afternoon, when my son was two years old, I asked him how his day was going, and he replied: "I don't remember yet." I have pondered that remark for decades. Too soon for a past! Experience without memory! I was jealous.

The police captain: "Those were the good old days!" Nick Charles, serving drinks: "Don't kid yourself. *These* are the good old days!" In 1934.

Language confers upon us the illusion that the modes of time are distinct from one another, conceptually and even existentially separable phases, when in fact the past, the present, and the future are always spilling into each other like sauces on a plate. How porous can a border be and still be a border? Duration is, among other things, a condition of initial chaos. How we live, individually and collectively, depends on how we make order out of the ticking disorder.

A vision of the future cannot be inspired by the future, because the future is still a nullity and without substance. Of course we never experience it as such: since it arrives as early as tomorrow, it will look a lot like today. But not always; and there will come days in which the differences will exceed the similarities — days of genuine departure, of the emergence of something new out of the old. Where else could it emerge from? We tiresomely refer to these hours of mutability as "inflection points." Kinetically we adore them. Only inflect! But they are certainly not as common as we think, as we hectically inflect the recently inflected on our way to the next inflection; and sometimes we are forced, for stability's sake, to devise mental techniques to retard the rapids and mitigate the shock of the discontinuity, to preserve connections across the crucibles, to incorporate the breakthroughs into prior schemes and systems even when they will not fit. (Many years ago I had a

Syrian Marxist friend who used to amuse me when we argued, because every time I presented him with a logical contradiction or an empirical refutation of his views he would blithely respond: "Well, I just have to work that into the analysis.") But there are moments when we must concede, or lament, or rejoice, that things really are no longer what they were. The people who make these announcements regularly are called visionaries. The problem is that the visionary mode — like the prophetic mode — is notoriously facile. In contemporary America, who is not a visionary? Here all it takes to qualify as a visionary is a t-shirt and the latest iteration of a jargon. (Unless you are a visionary, you won't get the financing.) We are drowning in the clichés of our dime-a-dozen visionaries. An entire population suffers from vision migraines.

Tocqueville's most profound contribution to historical understanding may have been not his dazzling intuitions about America but his careful descriptions of how much of prerevolutionary France persisted into post-revolutionary France. In the age of revolution the incompleteness of revolution was a revolutionary idea. He wrote the greatest book ever written against the tabula rasa.

Our fashion in visionaries accounts also for the inundation of our culture by science fiction, which is the literary form that futurism takes. From Jules Verne on, radical depictions of the future have occasionally inspired a more helpful and sophisticated grasp of what may be possible: innovation is always the product of an expanded imagination. The problem with these prophecies is that too often they loosen not only the imagination but also the mind. The imagination involved in those visions is chiefly technological: the master plot of science fiction is the behavior of familiar human beings in unfamiliar technological circumstances. It is only lately that the imbecilic geniuses of Silicon Valley have had the effrontery to also promote the technologization of the human being – that "post-humanity" has become an ideal. Replicants are too human for these futurists. (Phillip K. Dick, the most accomplished futurist imagination of our time, never surrendered his humaneness and what he liked to call "the authentic human being.") The insolence of the Kurzweils and the Andreesens and the rest of the Prometheans with offshore accounts knows no bounds. Billions and billions in the cause of de-humanization! I have been reading the unintentionally risible theological speculations of Peter Thiel — on the legend of "a zombie Nero resurrected in a parody of Christ," for example, and its source in the Book of Revelations: "Saint John identified 666 as the number of the beast, and Nero's Hebrew name, Neron Kaisar, has a gematric value of 666." And so on, in this pseudo-esoteric vein. Thiel's deep original thinking is a parody of hermetic tripe, a witless exchange of engineering arcana for chiliastic arcana, according to which what most direly imperils us now is the Antichrist. In this way thinking outside the box culminates in the least original and most poisonius thinking of all. "One question ripe for literary treatment," Thiel reflects, "is how the Antichrist will take over the world." His literary standard is low, since he treats comic books as metaphysical sources. (In one of these scriptures Christlike Luffy defeats Kaidou and Big Mom. Praise the Lord!) It will come as no surprise that the *quasi figura Antichristi* of our day is for Thiel the critic of artificial intelligence - or more generally, "in the twenty-first century the Antichrist is a Luddite who wants to stop all science," as if the technical (and economic) connivings of Thiel and Altman and the others are coterminous with science itself. (Needless to say, Carl Schmitt has a cameo.) We are paying heavily for one undergraduate's infatuation with René Girard's vaporizings about the redemptive power of violent unreason.

It is no wonder, amid this outburst of science fiction and its antihumanist sensibility, that another genre of film and fiction is also thriving. The genry of the moment is horror. In our culture now it is everywhere. It responds to one variety of antihumanism with another variety of antihumanism, the genre of horror is consecrated to giving the darkness the last word. It, too, is visionary, except that its vision of the future is of a time in which uncontrollable sadistic forces have not been eradicated because they are ineradicable. What did the *Saw* and *Hostel* and *Chainsaw* franchises advertise if not the eternal recurrence of human depravity? Which, as a fact of history, is of course indubitable. But there is no courage in horror, no fearless confrontation with what must be faced, no high-minded reckoning with the worst that we need to know about ourselves. It is merely a commercial formula that exploits the fragility of our dignity, and the emotional infirmity of those who find pleasure in fear. Horror is to Thanatos what porn is to Eros. There is nothing especially tough-minded about the presentation of torture as entertainment. It is only a program for learning not to feel. Everybody was so frantically searching for the feminist lessons in that repulsive Demi Moore movie about a woman's viscera that they neglected to note its virulent hatred of the human, its nihilism disguised as a bracing interpretation of body dysmorphia. (5,500 gallons of phony blood!) And the Gothic blockbusters of the nineteenth century — which like Dracula will never die, but continue to seduce filmmakers who prefer the demagoguery of special effects, Guillermo del Toro most recently — these allegedly transgressive classics teach the perdurability of the past at its most despairing: that there is nothing anachronistic about all those medieval castles and capes because the descent into the irrational and the insane is a perennial norm. Neither reason nor religion will keep the demons down. Transylvania forever! Pessimism with popcorn. We are at the same time so advanced and so atavistic. I guess atavism is the flip side of advancement. Or is it the other way around? For every gleaming gadget, a lopped-off limb. For every app, a fang.

There was a time — all of human history until approximately now — when the existence of the future could be taken for granted, all the histrionics of apocalypse notwithstanding. But now we must pause over the houses slipping into the sea and the fires in the rain forests and the ice caps as they vanish to reflect that this platitude — this quotidian assurance about the lastingness of the world, upon which all human activity was premised — may have been a momentous blunder. Futurity is no longer what it used to be. We must begin to picture what it will be like to live in the absence of any confidence about the year after this one and then the day after this one and then the moment after this one. What will it be like to carry on without the sense of an unbounded and unendangered future? Only the condemned have known that feeling. The sensation of ordinary mortality is certainly nothing like it. After all, the steadiness of the dying, or so I imagine, the equilibrium of the soul on the brink of the body's extinction, is premised on the conviction that the world will not die with them. What will it be like to die without the certainty that the world will live on? What will it be like to be the last one to die? Bill Gates now declares that we need not worry about the end of the line "for the foreseeable future," but what exactly is the foreseeable future? I am not yet prepared to exhale and open a bottle. Futurism (and its cult of the machine) may turn out to have been the indulgence of a shallow and greedy species that could not be bothered to look after the vast portion of nature that was not itself.

"The end of the line": I suppose that the phrase comes from the railroads. Anybody who has ever been to the end of a line, to the final buffer where the tracks ignominiously stop, will agree that it is a peculiarly melancholy place. Whereas the sight of tracks running into infinity is peculiarly heartening.

There is something funny about the fashion in infinity pools. Another game that the rich play with limits.

Why should boundlessness be heartening? Why should we aspire to what we cannot be? (Americans evade the difficulty of such questions by hiding behind "the aspirational.") To want to be what one can never be is damaging and dangerous, to oneself and to others. Surely it is the work of a lifetime to become no more than what one can be. In that enterprise we are in no danger of early or easy success. If you think hard about infinity, you will recognize that it is terrifying — but perhaps not for its silence, as Pascal remarked. The silence may be the best part of it.

The name that finite creatures have often given to what they are not is God. Some religious philosophers have been so militant about the conception of God as everything that we are not, as the strict and perfect antithesis of what we are, that they unwittingly lend support to the modern criticism that theology is no more than an exercise in human projection, except in the form of a negation. (This negation also explains how the idea of infinity can occur to a finite mind, which centuries ago was regarded as a miracle that proved the existence of the deity.) I do not see how a God worthy of the name, or the Name, can have anything in common with human attributes, or how infinity can also be finite, which is why the Christian idea of the Incarnation is philosophically offensive to me; but it is not hard to understand why finite creatures would need to find something of themselves in infinity – a link, a sign, a wink, a loophole — a back door to pagan satisfaction, the body of Christ.

Unless you already believe that Jesus was the Son of God, the effect of a beautiful representation of Christ — say, Zurbaran's huge corpus floating in a field of the purest black, in Chicago — is to encourage not heavenly religion but earthly desire. Listen to Buxtehude's lachrymose seven-cantata cycle, *Membra Jesu Nostri patientis sanctissima,* or *The Most Holy Limbs of Our Suffering Jesus,* each cantata a penitential celebration of a different part of his body, and you will hear the sound of monotheism gently vanishing.

The most daunting challenge of all is to believe in a God who provides little or no satisfaction.

In the very few instances in my life when I seemed to have been lifted to some sort of brush with infinity — by the third movement of Beethoven's fifteenth string quartet, for example, the "Lydian" movement, on a rainy night in a small room in an old stone manor at Oxford, a rickety gramophone on the trunk next to my monk's bed — it was a relief to come away from the uncanniness without an obligation of worship. It was real, but it was only an experience.

Is there a less reliable authority for cosmic conclusions? Epiphany, delirium, ecstasy, apotheosis: I wish I were visited by more of these heightened moments, but not because they are intellectually trustworthy. There are many reasons to want to vibrate, but a climactic illumination, the vouchsafing of an irreversible clarity, is not one of them. I am, alas, spiritually overprotective, with a phobic attitude toward illusion, which can interfere with pleasures of the imagination, and with experiences of abandon, and this almost neurotic skepticism has condemned me to a relatively unadventurous mundanity; but still I would rather be starved than swindled.

A brush with the unlimited, maybe; but contact, never. Or not yet. No, never.

The doors of perception? Don't let them hit you on your way out.

The plot thickens with the introduction of the infinitesimal — a thing not infinitely large but infinitely small. The origins of the concept are to be found in mathematics, where I am never to be found. My understanding is that it refers to a numerical value that is as close to zero as it can be without being zero. Or it could refer to a minute point somewhere far down an infinite line. Yet the dissociation of infinity from size permits a marvelous thought — that there is no end to littleness, or: the grandeur of humility. It is big to be small. (The self-abnegation of a point: an ethical allegory from poorly understood mathematics.)

"There will be no other end of the world, / There will be no other end of the world." Czeslaw Miłosz wrote those lines in one of his scorching poems about the Warsaw Ghetto, which he composed from the other side of the ghetto walls. Just think: a second end of the world! It sounds unbearable. But really it may be the most comforting thought of all. To live after the end — which, unless the entire planet burns up, somebody always will — is to benevolently recontextualize the idea of an ending, to fight back successfully against the most frightening aspect of extinction, which is its finality. Panic owes its power to its literalness, but a with panic disarms that literalness. The future may be good or bad, but so far it has never not arrived.

We go through our lives attempting to create permanent things — commitments and institutions — but the permanence to which we aspire for our creations is premised on the open-endedness of life, on the banality of time. What if time is no longer banal? My parents, and all the other survivors of the modern world's protracted kingdoms of killing, lived for years without being able to rely on the open-endedness of life, while around them so much of the world stayed open-ended — which, for them, between 1939 and 1945, was one of its worst cruelties.

The end of the world is more coherent than the end of a people. It is at least a shared human fate.

In 1948, a time when Jewish history was simultaneously flush with sorrow and joy in an impossible disequilibration of feeling, the Jewish thinker and scholar Simon Rawidowicz wrote a mordant and gentle essay called "Israel: The Ever-Dying People." It was a critique of Jewish morbidity, in which he observed this about the chronic Jewish "fear of the end": "A nation dying for thousands of years means a living nation. Our incessant dying means uninterrupted living, rising, standing up, beginning anew." And also this great release from the prison of grief: "But if we are the last – let us be the last as our fathers and forefathers were the last, let us prepare the ground for the last Jews who will come after us, and for the last Jews who will rise after them." That prayer belongs in the prayerbook.

But what about calamities that are in some way without precedent, and cannot be tucked into prior patterns, into a salving familiarity which can lessen the temptation to hopelessness? I am thinking of the political nausea that occurs with the first appearance of post-liberalism in liberal societies. It is the sickening moment that we are living presently. The Trump era in America and the

Netanyahu era in Israel are groundbreaking calamities in the histories of these countries, first iterations of national nightmares, and while they do not come out of nowhere they are an incontrovertibly new chapter, and so the customary consolation of historical irony will avail us nothing. About these developments there is as yet no way to knowing or weary. The first time is a heartbreak all its community.

Never, ever write the story of your own as a narrative of angels. Otherwise the discovery that you are not perfect strangers to evil will shipwreck you.

Is every heartbreak like the first one?

We are mongrels of temporality: all the tenses exist in us at every moment, and our task is to attend to the proportions in the mix. Is the past colonizing the present? Is the future? Guard the frontiers! But we are never unmixed.

This is the case also about previous epochs. In his defense of "the painting of modern life," and more generally of the legitimacy of modernity, Baudelaire wrote that "by 'modernity' I mean the ephemeral, the fugitive, the contingent" — He was concerned that the speed of the new urban life, its pandemonium of people and incident, its noisy vulgarities, would disqualify it from the classical ambitions of art. And so he sagely pointed out that "every old master has had his own modernity," because everybody has lived in their time, which was the latest time, and no time is incapable of transmutations into beauty. The poet - who was writing here as an art critic — was not privileging modernity; he was insisting that it be treated with the same philosophical and cultural privilege that other eras enjoyed — that the transience of a streetcar is no less real and interesting than the transience of a blossom, and no less inviting to art. Baudelaire's whole sentence reads: "By 'modernity' I mean the ephemeral, the fugitive, the contingent, the half of art whose other half is the eternal and the immutable." Never unmixed.

So, the temporal and the eternal share in all things, or all things share in them – a partnership of opposites. But the alliance is not always legible. It is easier for me to find the eternal in Brueghel's pictures of tiny people shitting on the ice than to find the temporal in Poussin's ideality composed pastorals. (In his *The Rape of the Sabines*, a true masterpiece of pictorial design, the *sub specie aeternitatis* mood has, for me, always offended against the terror that is portrayed. What on earth is an orderly breakdown of order?)

And for those who do not believe in the eternal or the absolute? Even for them, reality is not just a landfill of data. As long as there is form, we are not forever shut up inside our empirical preoccupations and conditions. Form has the power to alter our experience of a thing, of any thing, and to broach a beyond. How distant a beyond? Not necessarily as far as the heavens: no metaphysics are necessary for a faith in form, though a measure of abstraction is. The godless are not excluded from this realm of numinousness. And form is utterly neutral, devoid of prejudices or prerequisites: it will put up with, or shape, or disfigure, or transfigure, any material.

There is nothing more difficult than to live significantly in the present. Most people accomplish this by, well, cheating: they borrow from the past and from the future, from memory and from hope, until the present is overrun by the other modes and comes to consist chiefly in commemorations and in dreams, in hindsight and in anticipation. To be sure, the influences of the past and the future upon the present are impossible to annul; as I say, in the matter of temporality we are forever mixed. But can we control their intrusions? Can we calibrate our own temporality? This gave birth to the riveting notion of a pure present, an Eternal Present — to the view that the present is spiritually primary because it is the only mode of time in which we may experience the transcendence that we seek. In one sense, of course, this observation is trivial. When else is transcendence supposed to take place? In this sense, the ideal of living solely in the present, though it may be a fiction, is a magnificent attempt to protect transcendence from the relentless interferences of time — to insulate the soul's shot at fulfillment from the distractions of memory and desire. One prooftext out of many: in the second part of *Faust*, Goethe has his hero declare that "the spirit looks neither ahead nor behind. Only the present is our happiness."

Whether or not it is easy to seize the day, it is not easy to seize the instant. Modern philosophers — Husserl, Heidegger, Wittgenstein, Bergson, Bachelard, and others — have gone to pains to isolate the instant from the flux and attempt a characterization of it. The project proved to be rather Sisyphean. In 1932, Bachelard, inspired by an amateur play by a university colleague who was a historian and a winemaker, suggested that, as opposed to Bergson's search for time itself, "the only way we ourselves can feel time is by multiplying conscious instants." An instant is "the compressed center around which we would posit an evanescent duration." But is evanescent duration the answer or the question? Four years earlier Heidegger edited and published the lectures that his teacher Husserl delivered in the 1910s on "the phenomenology of internal time-consciousness." This may be the most impossible book I have ever read. A sentence randomly chosen from the discussion of "longitudinal intentionality": "If we now let the flux flow away, we then have the flux-continuum as running-off, which allows the continuity to be retentionally modified, and thereby every new continuity of phases momentarily existing all at once is retention with reference to the total continuity of what is all-at-once in the preceding phase." I do not adduce such a passage to make fun of it. In his admirable search for a close account of the lived experience of the fleeting moment, the philosopher was heroically undeterred by the difficulty of trying to capture in language what probably cannot be captured in language, even in the compound-coinages of a style of philosophy unfazed by turgidity. Husserl was braver than Heraclitus, who believed that he could make do with the metaphor of the river. Yet the more one considers these attempts to clarify the smallest and most immediate units of lived time, the more plausibly one may conclude that a life lived completely in the present would be incoherent without the shadows and the foreshadows of the past and the future. The coherence of a temporal life may require a mess of temporal intrusions. What, after all, can we do with an instant?

There are perfunctory versions of the ideal of pure instantaneity. Animals live completely in the present. So do voluptuaries (Casanova's memoirs are eight volumes of pure presents), and so do the beaded forever-young Baba Ram Dassians on the coasts and in the mountains. Yet they experience nothing like an eternal present: they live merely in a series, moment to moment, climax upon climax, high after high, sensation followed by sensation, over and over, robotically, by rote, in a frantic and unconnected collection of what Americans call "peak experiences." But peaks are nothing without valleys. There are peak people and valley people. An existence of endless stimulation — the peak people — requires a deformation of time based on its complete atomization: be here now, and then now, and then now, and then now. Never mind that *there* may be more attractive than *here*. But the passage from here to there takes time — dumb extended duration of an unatomized and unmagical kind, provisional and continuous. Be there and then there and then there and then there, until the achievement of arrival will be yours. A series of theres is often deeper and more sustaining than a series of heres. The fantasy of a pure present expresses a kind of temporal provincialism; it is the connections between the instants out of which a life is made. (For the animals with whom I have gratefully lived, by contrast, I detected no distinction between ordinary experience and peak experience, except for sleep. Lucky pugs!)

Another name for a pure present: immanent exile. What else could follow it?

Nothing valuable can be accomplished without repetition, but repetition deadens more than it quickens. The only solution I know for this problem is the musical form of theme and variations.

The colonization of the present by the past — there is so much past! — is a more common phenomenon than its colonization by the future, but there is an increasingly troublesome instance of the latter: messianism, or more precisely, political messianism. No matter how traditional they seem, messianists are people who derive the meaning of their lives not from the past but from the future — or rather from a particular construction of the future in which it will reproduce a particular construction of the past. Restorations are conspiracies between the future and the past. In their own minds the restorationists are already living in the future because they have already been living in the past, usually an ancient past that ended badly, and this hallucination of time travel accounts for their obnoxious tone of spiritual superiority. (All redeemers are obnoxious. They come with love but without respect.) They have come from their future to drag the rest of us into it. They are high on historical rupture. They mourn destruction and are ready to destroy. Guns sometimes follow.

Another reason for preferring the present, a completely worldly reason, was given by Pierre Hadot. "Ordinarily our life is always incomplete, because we project all our hopes, all our aspirations, all our attention, into the future, telling ourselves that we will be happy when we have attained this or that goal. We are scared as long as the goal is not attained, but if we attain it, already it no longer interests us and we continue to run after something else. We do not live, we hope to live, we are waiting to live." Hadot, as is well known, argued that the Stoics and the Epicureans had devised the solution to this conundrum: "to live not in the future but as though there were no future, as though we only had this day, only this moment, to live." This is a little precious. We must add, compassionately, that hoping to live, and living in hope, is not the worst fate that can be imagined. Having lived but living no more, or having no grounds for hoping to live, is much worse. As for waiting, it is an art, a lost art; it is not a grudging way of meeting an inconvenient or frustrating delay, but a mature way of grappling with the stubbornness of time and the work requirements of truth and goodness and beauty.

To recommend impatience is to play with fire.

Hadot goes beyond his customary proselytization for Stoicism and its illusion of personal immunity. He suggests that an intensity of focus upon the present confers a different advantage. "To live in the present moment is to live as though one were seeing the world both for the last and for the first time. To work at seeing the world as though one were seeing it for the first time is to get rid of the conventional and routine vision we have of things, to discover a brute, naïve version of reality, to take note of the splendor of the world, which habitually escapes us." How splendid this is. Since we are so accustomed to confusion in the present, it is encouraging to be reminded of its power to clarify. The purpose of Hadot's putative ban on the past and the future is to prevent them from blurring a precise apprehension of what actually now exists. For lucidity's sake they sometimes need to get out of the way.

To see clearly: a stupendously immodest goal. It is the secular mysticism, the sharpening of perception as a spiritual elevation, that one finds in many modern poets and painters — the thrilling notion that seeing clearly is not only a practical matter but also, when the focus rises above our everyday eyes, and we succeed in a degree of detachment from our commonplace cognitive practices, an attainment of transcendence, even if it remains terrestrial. Seeing clearly is a life's work. I am reminded of the passage in Rilke's 'Ninth Elegy' when he suspends his swooning and wonders whether the most that we can do in the way of an accurate grasp of reality is to delineate it properly, to say "house, bridge, fountain, gate, jug, fruit tree, window" — "such saying as the things themselves never hoped so intensely to be." Nouns and nothing more, but each of them with the force of a revelation. Behind this dream of comprehensive clarity, of complete optical definition, was the poet's revelatory encounter with Cezanne's apples, which, like Zurbaran's lemons and Chardin's cherries and Morandi's bottles, challenge ordinary perception with their distinctness and their vividness and their concreteness — with their overwhelming but immanent presence.

Will someone who seeks a better view of heaven be satisfied with a better view of earth? Can apples do the work of angels?

The plot thickens. A jug figures prominently — two jugs, actually — in another twentieth-century attempt to seize the instant. This one occurred not in philosophy but in psychology, and this endeavor arrived at the opposite conclusion: that clarity about an object is to be found not in the delineation of its boundaries but in the blurring of its boundaries. Marion Milner was a British psychoanalyst and a strangely riveting writer about lived experience, born in 1897, a colleague of D. W. Winnicott and a friend of Adrian Stokes, who in 1950 published an exciting book called *On Not Being Able to Paint*. The story begins, as it often does for the analytical Milner, with a subtle observation of a small incident:

> I woke one morning and saw two jugs on the table; without any mental struggle I saw the edges in relation to each other and how gaily they seemed almost to ripple now that they were freed from this grimly practical business of enclosing an object and keeping it in its place. This was surely what painters meant about the play of edges: certainly they did play, and I tried a five-minute sketch of the jugs.

Her sketch is reproduced in her book: two jugs overlapping, two solid objects with open borders. This imprecision gladdened Milner, and provoked her to a war against outline, against "the need to make objects keep themselves to themselves within a rigid boundary," against "the fear of losing all sense of separating boundaries." Her actual experience of the jugs was tentative and unclear and transitory, very much akin to the "transitional objects" that Winnicott interposed between the "inner reality" and the "outer reality" that the baby and then the child had to negotiate. Milner, in the realm of the visual arts, argued what Winnicott did in the realm of child psychology: against hypostatization, against too much fixity. When Rilke said *jug*, in other words, he had it backwards. He was distorting the object by means of excessive definition. In his search for a lasting crystalline reality, he made the object overly distinct. In this way he sought to idealize it, to make poetry out of it, but by idealizing it, by seeking to complete what revealed itself best in its incompleteness, he withdrew it from the world of natural perception. There is no instant, no present, in which you see the jug, unless you have the stamina for mysticism. Winnicott wrote wisely about "the strain inherent in objective perception," which is to say that objectivity involves both a gain and a loss, because it represents an elaborate treatment of perceptual experience; it may grant truth but not immediacy. It might even be a stranger to experience.

I look again at Cezanne's apples, first with Rilke's eyes and then with Milner's eyes. It's a wash. Sometimes they have edges but not outlines, sometimes they have outlines in place of edges, and sometimes the shadows make the inquiry moot. How much of a shape must one see to know it? Not the entirety of it, to judge by the evidence of some of Cezanne's incomplete still-lifes. Sometimes it is more powerful to suggest a shape than to document it. (One of the most precious aspects of Milner's writing is her loss of interest in wholeness.)

Freedom may lie in the difference between an edge and a border, though both can be emboldening.

As they were together contemplating one of Cezanne's depictions of Mont Sainte-Victoire, Rilke remarked to Count Harry Kessler: "Not since Moses has anyone seen a mountain so greatly." Was he thinking of Sinai or Nebo? Not every peak is the same.

Presence occurs only in the present. This is not as pretentious as it sounds. A presence that has departed and a presence that has not arrived are poor nourishments, though we snack on them constantly.

Why would mortal creatures expend themselves with a longing for the end? It will come, it will come.

A short drive from Alamogordo, the cursed town in New Mexico where the first nuclear weapon was created, is one of the strangest and most spiritually addling places in the world. It is White Sands National Park, almost three hundred square miles of blindingly white gypsum sand. Truly one feels translated to another reality. With the rare exception of the skeleton of a dead tree — nothing can grow in that glistening ground — the white desert stretches featurelessly and without interruption in all directions as far as the eye can see. I never comprehended the obliterative power of white until I walked those dunes. The infinite was there, and so was the infinitesimal. I was surrounded by sublimity and I was lost.

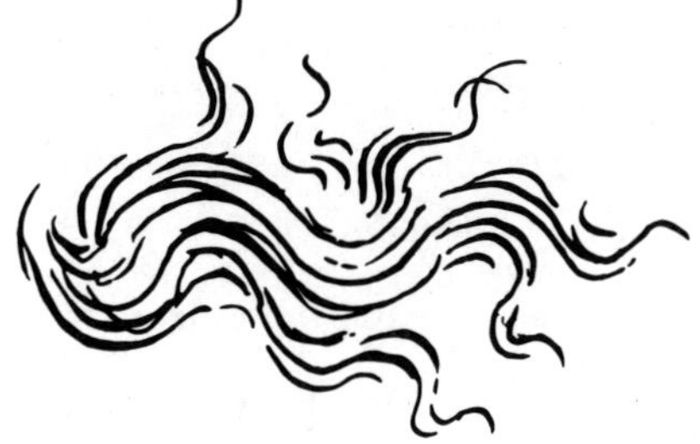

CONTRIBUTORS

WILLIAM BAUDE is the Harry Kalven Jr. Professor of Law at the University of Chicago Law School and the director of its Constitutional Law Institute.

ABBAS MILANI is the Hamid and Christina Moghadam Director of the Iranian Studies program at Stanford University and the author of many books on Iran.

SUSIE LINFIELD is a professor in the department of journalism at New York University and the author of *The Lion's Den: Zionism and the Left from Hannah Arendt to Noam Chomsky*.

JAMES WOLCOTT is the author of *Critical Mass: Four Decades of Essays, Reviews, Hand Grenades and Hurrahs*.

HAMZE AWAWDE is an activist and writer from the West Bank.

SHEILA O'MALLEY is a film critic who writes regularly for *Liberties*, *Roger Ebert*, and the Criterion Collection.

JULIA KIESERMAN is a doctoral student at New York University. She writes about security and privacy issues.

AGNES CALLARD is a professor of philosophy at the University of Chicago and the author most recently of *Open Socrates: The Case for a Philosophical Life*.

ROSANNA WARREN'S most recent collection of poetry is *Hindsight*.

MELANIE W. SISSON is a fellow at the Center for Security, Strategy, and Technology at the Brookings Institution.

EVAN PARKS is the Director of Education for The Bronfman Fellowship.

ANDREW BUTTERFIELD is President of Andrew Butterfield Fine Arts and has written widely on Renaissance sculpture and painting.

AMIR GILBOA was an Israeli poet who was born in Ukraine in 1917 and died in Petah Tikva in 1984. "In Darkness" was written in 1952.

MARK EDMUNDSON is a professor of English at the University of Virginia His most recent book is *Song of Ourselves: Walt Whitman and the Fight for Democracy*.

STEVE WASSERMAN is the publisher of Heyday Books and the author of *Tell Me Something, Tell Me Anything, Even If It's a Lie: A Memoir in Essays*.

HARIS VLAVIANOS' forthcoming collection of poetry, *Renaissance*, will be published by World Poetry Press.

YAHIA LABABIDI is an Egyptian-American writer and poet.

CONSTANIN WALDSCHMIDT is a writer and translator based in Washington, DC.

MORTEN HØI Jensen is Liberties' European Liaison and the author most recently of *The Master of Contradictions: Thomas Mann and the Making of "The Magic Mountain."*

CELESTE MARCUS is the executive editor of *Liberties* and the author of *Chaim Soutine: Genius, Obsession, and A Dramatic Life in Art*.

LEON WIESELTIER is the editor of *Liberties*.

The passage Stefan Zweig on the back flap was translated by **WILL STONE**.

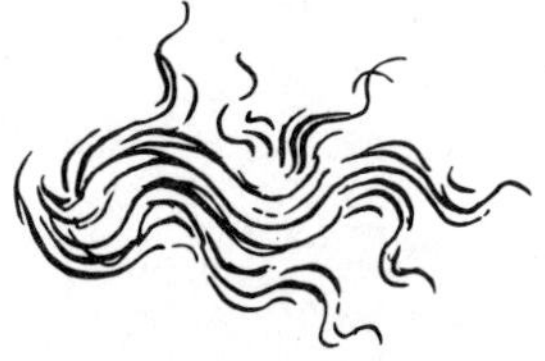

The insignia that appears in the pages of *Liberties* is derived from details in Botticelli's drawings for Dante's *Divine Comedy*, which were executed between 1480 and 1495.

SUBSCRIPTIONS

There's Nothing Artificial about Our Intelligence

Surprise your intellectually curious friend with a gift that keeps on giving — a subscription to *Liberties*.

Scan this QR code or go to libertiesjournal.com/subscribe to make a present of groundbreaking essays, criticism, and commentary. *Liberties* brings together leading thinkers exploring ideas that matter for our culture and our politics.

Subscriber benefits include choices of in-print, all digital access, new monthly online content, invitations to in-person salons and other events, and weekly emails of the latest in the global world of *Liberties*.

Professional discounts available for active military; faculty, students, and education administrators; government employees; and those working in the not-for-profit sector.

JOIN IN OUR WORK

Help ensure the future of Liberties

Liberties: A Journal of Culture & Politics features essays from award-winning writers, significant scholars, the next generation's rising talents, and poets from around the world. There's a reason why cultural warriors, political leaders, opinion makers, and engaged citizens from across the political and cultural spectrum read and cherish *Liberties*. Through this quarterly in-print publication, new weekly online content, podcasts, vodcasts, and in-person events, *Liberties* champions liberal democracy and the humanities.

As a matter of principle, *Liberties* does not accept advertising or other funding sources that might influence our independence.

We look to our readers and those individuals and institutions that believe in our mission for contributions — large and small — to support this not-for-profit publication.

If you are interested in making a donation to *Liberties*, please contact Bill Reichblum, publisher by email, `bill@libertiesjournal.com`, or by phone, `202-891-7159`.

`libertiesjournal.com`.

Printed in Canada.

Liberties: A Journal of Culture and Politics is distributed to booksellers in the United States by Publishers Group West; in Canada by Publishers Group Canada; and internationally by Ingram Publisher Services International. It is available by annual subscription and by individual purchase from bookstores and online booksellers.